This book reviews contemporary campaigns
for community participation and empowerment with
examples from Europe, the USA, Australia, South and Southeast
Asia, Latin America and Africa. It critically assesses developments
in the 'mixed economy of welfare' in terms of their relevance for
self-help and community participation. It also considers the concept
of empowerment and its relation to public policy and developments
within social movements. The case studies demonstrate the
continuing struggle of communities to take more control over
the key issues they confront, including poverty and the impact
of international economic restructuring.

COMMUNITY EMPOWERMENT

A Reader in Participation and Development

Edited by
Gary Craig and Marjorie Mayo

ZED BOOKS
London & New Jersey

Community Empowerment was first published in 1995 by
Zed Books Ltd, 7 Cynthia Street, London N1 9JF, UK, and
165 First Avenue, Atlantic Highlands, New Jersey 07716, USA

Copyright © Individual contributors, 1995
Editorial copyright © Gary Craig, Marjorie Mayo, 1995

Cover designed by Andrew Corbett
Typeset in Monotype Garamond by Lucy Morton, London SE12
Printed and bound in the United Kingdom
by Biddles Ltd, Guildford and King's Lynn

A catalogue record for this book is available from the British Library
US CIP data is available from the Library of Congress

ISBN 1 85649 337 7 Hb
ISBN 1 85649 338 5 Pb

Contents

Acknowledgements

This book had its origins in the 25th anniversary issue of *Community Development Journal*. The editors owe a debt of thanks to the editorial advisory board of the *CDJ* and to Nina Curtis of Oxford University Press, for their encouragement to develop this present book, and to Robert Molteno of Zed Books for facilitating its realization. We would like also to thank Marilyn Taylor, Peter Oakley and David Marsden for specific ideas and contacts and for continuing support. Authors, without exception, met a tough timetable at a time when other pressures on their energy (such as the emergence of newly democratic states!) were growing: we hope the finished product meets their expectations. Many thanks also to Sue Coles and Gillian MacFarlane for their skills and patience, providing essential technical support.

Gary Craig offers his love and thanks to his co-editor, Marj Mayo, who, as always, has been a thoughtful and supportive colleague. Marjorie Mayo offers her love and thanks to Gary Craig: as always, working with Gary has been both stimulating and supportive. The book is dedicated to Gill, Dan, Scarlet and Clyde, and to Olive, who died in the week that the book was completed.

'When I give food to the poor, they call me a saint. When I ask why the poor have no food, they call me a communist.'

Dom Helder Camara

Community Participation and Empowerment: The Human Face of Structural Adjustment or Tools for Democratic Transformation?

Marjorie Mayo and Gary Craig

'Community participation' and 'empowerment' have become more vital and yet more overtly problematic than ever in the current global context. In the face of deepening poverty resulting from international recession and restructuring, international agencies and national and local states have demonstrated increasing interest in strategies to promote community participation as a means of enhancing the development process. And there has been increasing emphasis upon the importance of alternative, grassroots approaches to development, starting from the empowerment of local communities.

This introduction sets out to identify and unravel some of the different, often contradictory, ways in which the terms 'community participation' and 'empowerment' have been used, together with the reasons why these terms have come to enjoy widespread, albeit divergent, popularity. This initial analysis lays out the framework for the subsequent discussions of these central themes from the particular perspectives of contributors to this book. This, in turn, sets the scene for the discussion of a number of key questions and issues which run through the following chapters. These questions and themes, whilst realistic about inherent tensions and limitations, relate to the positive potential of strategies to promote community participation and empowerment within the framework of wider strategies to promote economic, political, social and cultural transformation. Whilst there are important differences between the chapters, differences reflecting some of the major themes for further debate, they do nevertheless share some common features, based upon the contribution of community participation and empowerment to strategies that promote sustainable, people-centred development, equal opportunities and social justice.

The shared perspective that underpins this book stands in contrast with the more varied and sometimes internally competing perspectives and

agendas of organizations which have been discovering community participation and empowerment with such interest in the contemporary global
context. Typically, international agencies such as the World Bank have seen
community participation as a means for ensuring that Third World development projects reach the poorest in the most efficient and cost-effective
way, sharing costs as well as benefits, through the promotion of self-help
(Paul 1987). As the Human Development Report (UNDP 1993)
commented, in face of current challenges for development, 'The best
route is to unleash people's entrepreneurial spirit – to take risks, to compete,
to innovate, to determine the direction and pace of development. It is
fitting, therefore, that this year's Human Development Report has people's
participation as its special focus. People's participation is becoming the
central issue of our time' (p. 1). And although there has been such a strong
focus upon participation in the context of development strategies in the
Third World, community participation has also been seen as central to
cost-effective strategies for regeneration in urban, industrialized contexts
(*Community Development Journal* 1993).

But this institutional support for community participation in terms of
cost-saving, project efficiency and self-help has also included some recognition of community participation in relation to the importance of
strategies for empowerment. These potentially more radical agendas and
strategies to promote empowerment, however, have been more particularly associated with the voluntary, or non-governmental, organization
(NGO) sectors, and with community organizations and people's movements (Clarke 1991). Quoting the Brundtland Commission's conclusion
that one of the main prerequisites of sustainable development is 'securing
effective citizen's participation', Clarke has argued (p. 56) that this sums
up the central tenet of progressive NGOs, with effective participation as
the key to the poor's struggle for equity, human rights and democracy.
But the voluntary/NGO sectors are not alone in this apparent commitment to empowerment; the World Bank, for instance, has also included
'empowerment' as one of the main objectives of community participation
(if not necessarily the objective which has been most dominant) (Paul
1987). Similarly, the Human Development Report defines participation in
terms of people having constant 'access to decision-making and power',
as well as in terms of economic participation (UNDP 1993: 21).
Empowering the poor has become an almost universal slogan (Thomas
1992).

Has there, then, effectively been global conversion to this recognition
of the vital importance of community participation and empowerment in
developing responses to increasing poverty and underdevelopment, both
in the North and in the South? In fact, as Conroy's chapter and others in
this volume point out, the consensus has not in reality been quite so
overwhelming – citing, for example, the experience of parts of the Euro-

pean Union. Yet overall, the concepts at least have enjoyed increasing interest and support. Why, then, have divergent institutions and organizations, with such widely differing aims, come to such apparent agreement on this? And why has the voluntary/NGO sector, which has been, at least in part, historically identified with community participation and empowerment, itself acquired such widespread interest and seemingly enthusiastic support in official quarters, moving 'closer to centre stage' internationally, with a higher profile and a wider range of supporters than ever (Clarke 1991)? Or does this apparent consensus, the current orthodoxy, actually conceal very divergent interests and meanings?

This volume starts from the position that if these themes are to be tackled critically, as well as positively, then a number of underlying threads in the current global context need to be identified, and key concepts defined and analysed. Crucially, community participation and empowerment have been increasingly widely advocated, both in the North and in the South, in the context of increasing poverty, polarization and social exclusion. As Donnison has argued, 'we live in frightening times.' (1993: 293). In the wealthy countries of the West, economic recession and restructuring have resulted in growing numbers of people being excluded, 'many of them into long-term unemployment or in low-paid insecure jobs'. In Chapter 6, Pauline Conroy focuses upon some of the dilemmas around citizen participation in the European context, where a hidden, disenfranchised class of these excluded non-citizens has emerged. In Third World contexts, the results of recession and restructuring are lethal on an even wider and deeper scale. Famine represents an extreme form of a far wider phenomenon of endemic hunger. By the end of the 1980s there were estimates that between some 20 and 30 per cent of the world's population lived in households which were too poor to obtain the food necessary to maintain sufficient energy levels.

Free market/neo-liberal strategies, which were increasingly advocated from the late 1970s to promote economic development, were supposed to 'trickle down' to benefit the poor and the poorest. But the reality was that the structural adjustment programmes being advocated by the World Bank and IMF, intended to encourage Third World countries to promote market-led development, were failing most particularly to benefit the poorest – an aspect recognized even by the World Bank itself (Lipton 1991). On the contrary, in fact, these programmes, involving cutbacks in governments' spending as part of the shift towards more market-oriented economies, were leading to increasing poverty, whilst simultaneously pressurizing governments to reduce the social welfare programmes which could have gone towards meeting these increasing economic and social needs. Children in the poorest countries have been amongst the most vulnerable, in terms of their health (with the rate of decline of mortality now slowing down and the prevalence of diseases increasing – linked to changes in nutritional standards) and in terms of their educational attendance and attainments (UNICEF 1989).

Free-market, neo-liberal, New Right strategies to 'roll back the state', both in Third World and in urban, industrialized contexts, aimed specifically to reduce state spending on social welfare and to promote alternative solutions based upon the private market, as well as upon the voluntary/ NGO sectors and community-based self-help. This has been a worldwide trend, with specific support from international organizations such as the World Bank and the IMF; although the trend has taken different forms in different contexts, with widely differing outcomes, depending upon local circumstances, including the strength of countervailing political pressures and struggles (Mishra 1990; Glennerster and Midgely 1991).

According to this perspective, community participation, in so far as this should be promoted, should be related to overall goals of cost-sharing/ cost reduction for the public sector (that is, shifting costs from public sector budgets by persuading communities to make increased contributions through voluntary effort and/or self-help/voluntary unpaid labour) and through increased project/programme efficiency. Alongside this, it is argued, programmes and development/regeneration projects should be more effectively designed, targeted and delivered in more sustainable ways. In this context, programmes and projects should be delivered in ways which do not involve continuing subsidies and costs reduced through cost-sharing, including community inputs on a self-help basis. And through targeting initiatives towards the poor and the poorest, adjustment also acquires a 'human face'. Similar arguments have been applied, both to Third World rural development programmes and to urban renewal schemes and social-service provision for 'community care' in the North. Community participation in this context is thus part of a wider strategy to promote savings, to target services only towards those who have been identified as being most desperately in need of them, and to shift the burden of resource provision away from the public sector towards communities, including communities in greatest need themselves (Craig 1993; Mayo 1994). This emphasis upon reducing public spending as far as possible (through promoting self-help and through targeting) has been a recurring theme in debates about shifting the boundaries of the 'mixed economy of welfare'. In Chapter 9, Marilyn Taylor sets out these debates in the UK context, together with some vital questions about ways of developing positive responses to the Mixed Economy of Welfare; how, for example, to 'release people's energies without exploiting and exhausting them'. In Chapter 12, Helen Meekosha and Martin Mowbray raise comparable issues in the Australian context, where governments from the 1980s have also seen 'community' in terms of cutting back the welfare state and privatizing social problems and provision.

But, as has already been suggested, community participation has also been taken up as a slogan by widely differing types of organizations in terms of promoting community empowerment. This raises the further question of what meanings have underpinned these varying uses of the term 'empowerment'. Is the World Bank using the term 'empowerment' in the same ways as progressive NGOs, for instance, or as popular/ peoples' movements for liberation and transformation in Brazil, Nicaragua, Bangladesh, or South Africa (as Frances O'Gorman, Hazel Plunkett, Muhammad Anisur Rahman and Viviene Taylor consider in critical ways in Chapters 17, 16, 3 and 14 respectively)?

Functionalist sociologists such as Parsons conceptualized power in society as a variable sum. According to this perspective, the total amount of power in society is not fixed but variable; power resides with members of society as a whole, and power can increase in society as a whole, as that society pursues collective goals (just as economic development, according to this perspective, can benefit society as a whole). The logic of such a position is that the 'empowerment' of the powerless could be achieved within the existing social order without any significant negative effects upon the power of the powerful. The powerless could be empowered, and they could then share in the fruits of development, alongside those who had already achieved power. Once empowered, poor people who had previously been relatively powerless could become agents of their own development. With the gift of knowledge, the powerless could gain the tools for self-reliance. This is the sense in which Schumacher, for instance, has conceptualized empowerment (Thomas 1992).

Alternatively, however, if power is conceptualized in zero-sum terms, 'empowerment' becomes more problematic. If there is a fixed amount of power in society, then increasing the power of one group or groups implies, by definition, decreasing the power of other groups. Such a concept of power involves relationships between those who have more of it and those who have less; Weber's definition of power involved the ability of one or more individuals/groups to realize their will, even against the resistance of others (whether this involves the use of force or the threat of force, or whether the powerless acquiesce in any case because they accept the legitimacy of the authority of the powerful). According to such a perspective, the 'empowerment' of the powerless would involve gains which would, of necessity, have to be achieved from the powerful (although such gains could, of course, be negotiated as part of wider strategies for social reform).

The Marxist perspective on power raises yet wider issues. According to this perspective, political power in capitalist society cannot ultimately be separated from economic power, the power associated with capitalist interests, such as transnational corporations operating on a global scale. Thus the 'empowerment' of the relatively powerless has inherently limited possibilities under capitalism. The poor and the relatively powerless may

become 'empowered' to participate more effectively in particular development projects and programmes. They may increase their ability to bargain
over jobs and services within urban renewal projects, for example. But,
however valuable, or even vital, this may be in terms of particular gains
and specific projects in certain places, these are all confined by the
constraints of the wider requirements of profitability and viability within
the increasingly global market. Gill Gordon (in Chapter 15) illustrates this
in relation to community participation, empowerment and sexual health in
Africa, showing how, even in this apparently most private sphere of
sexuality, the scope for community-based health initiatives is circumscribed
by the wider context of recession and structural adjustment programmes.
Vital gains have been achieved through community-based health programmes; but ultimately, as Gordon concludes, participatory and holistic
community development approaches to sexual health need to be adequately
resourced and backed by wider changes in the socio-economic context,
including a reduction in debt burdens and fairer trade terms.

Marxists have also been concerned, however, with the power of ideas:
in particular with the process of setting ideological agendas and the concept
of hegemony which Gramsci developed to analyse the ways in which
existing frameworks of economic and political power come to be seen as
both legitimate and effectively non-contestable within capitalist society.
Understanding and challenging this hegemony, then, becomes central to
the development of alternative struggles for economic, political and social
transformation. Freire's approach to adult education (discussed both by
Plunkett and by Rahman) in terms of dialogue – to enable the oppressed
to become active and reflective about their reality in order to struggle to
transform this reality (the process of 'conscientization') – can be related
to such a perspective. 'Empowerment' in this sense is about collective,
community (and ultimately class) conscientization – to understand reality
critically in order to use the (currently limited) power which even the
relatively powerless possess to challenge the powerful, and ultimately to
transform that reality through conscious political struggles.

Just as the terms 'community participation' and 'empowerment' have
been problematic, concealing differing meanings based upon different
perspectives beneath their apparently widespread espousal, so has the
associated notion of the voluntary/NGO sector itself been problematic.
As has already been suggested, voluntary organizations/NGOs have been
seen to have moved centre stage, embodying the hope of dealing with the
global development crisis, alongside the peace, environment, women's and
human-rights movements (Korten 1990). Progressive NGOs have been
characterized as providing alternative approaches to the failures of the
development industry and of paternalistic top-down state initiatives and
services – alternatives based upon the participation and empowerment of
the poor and the poorest, women as well as men, working from the

grassroots, in small-scale, innovative, committed, cost-effective and environmentally sustainable ways. The voluntary/NGO sector has been identified as a third sector, having potential in terms of an alternative strategy for 'counterdevelopment' (critically evaluated by Benno Galjart in Chapter 2) or even as a new alternative model for community development itself, based upon NGOs' assumed commitment to development based upon community empowerment.

As Galjart and, subsequently, Karina Constantino-David (in Chapter 13) reflect, with particular reference to experiences in Latin America and the Philippines, and as Rahman considers and evaluates more generally, there are a number of issues to be identified here. The voluntary/NGO sector comprises a range of widely differing types of organization and movement, from international NGOs based in the North, through government-sponsored agencies, to voluntary bodies which increasingly concentrate upon providing services to the public sector on a contract basis in the 'mixed economy of welfare', to popular development agencies and to grassroots community organizations. These differing types of voluntary organization/NGO have been focused upon relief and the provision of welfare services and/or advocacy, networking and campaigning, whether or not particular combinations of these activities form part of more strategic approaches to development, community participation and empowerment at local and regional levels and beyond.

As a number of authors point out, in the current context voluntary organizations/NGOs are being pulled in different directions. On the one hand, there have been efforts to convince NGOs that they need to move from being relief and welfare agencies, or even the supporters of local development projects, to the next stage of developing a more strategic approach (these stages broadly relate to 'the three generations' of NGOs identified by Korten [1990]). NGOs, it has been argued, need to press and negotiate with national and local government structures, working in partnership with them and with the private sector to move towards this more strategic approach. And international NGOs, it has been further stated, need to develop networks, and to campaign internationally, to lobby Northern governments for the changes that are necessary for international justice (Clarke 1991).

Meanwhile, NGOs are also being pulled in the direction of closer incorporation into official structures, and into operating in more market-driven ways, as a direct result of their engagement with the contracting-out processes (Gutch 1992; Mayo 1994). In order to survive in the contract culture, voluntary organizations, both in the North and in the South, are forced to behave in a commercially viable fashion, a competitive process which risks driving the smaller, less commercial and more community-based organizations out of the market, leaving the survivors less and less clearly distinguishable from their private-sector counterparts. Advocacy and campaigning may be particularly threatened, as the voluntary/ community sector becomes increasingly involved in public-sector contracts to provide services; in the contract culture the focus has to be upon those services which are clearly specified in the contract, rather than upon broader 'watchdog'-type functions, let alone the advocacy and campaigning functions which historically have been central to genuine community participation. This shift of focus is the potential logic, after all, of the 'mixed economy of welfare' (which emerges as a key theme in the chapters that address experiences in the UK and the USA as well as Third World contexts). This parallels Rahman's view that NGO 'functionaries' can all too often act in ways which are accountable only to foreign donors, dictated by World Bank free-market strategies – ways which are ultimately poverty-augmenting rather than participative, let alone transformational.

Given this variety of meanings and focuses, and these competing pressures and tendencies, it becomes increasingly problematic to see the voluntary/NGO sector as one sector at all, let alone to argue that it represents some single alternative development model, neither left nor right but radical; and different chapters duly address a number of the issues arising. The variety of the voluntary/NGO sectors and the conflicting pressures they face are analysed, for example, by Constantino-David. Other chapters address some of the dilemmas arising from the potential incorporation of voluntary/NGO efforts, and the potential for self-help and community-participation initiatives to be abused, inasmuch as they can substitute for effective and appropriate public-sector provision. Discussion here includes experiences in East Germany (Prue Chamberlayne in Chapter 8), the UK (Marilyn Taylor), and Australia (Meekosha and Mowbray); it also specifically includes the experiences of older women (Jenny Onyx and Pam Benton in Chapter 5).

Several chapters also reflect upon the possible tensions and conflicts of interest that can arise, as well as the potential for cooperation and partnership, between community-based initiatives and community activists on the one hand, and the role of professionals on the other (whether these professionals are employed through the state/local government and/or through voluntary organizations/NGOs – as explored by Rahman). These issues emerge in the discussion by Colin Barnes and Geof Mercer (in Chapter 4) of disabled people's struggles for participation and empowerment in both industrialized and developing countries. Similar tensions emerge in Viviene Taylor's discussion of the role of professionals in NGOs in South Africa.

This, in turn, raises the wider issue of the role of the state, whether locally, regionally or nationally and beyond. Whatever the disappointments with the role of the state in the past, even some of the more passionately committed advocates of voluntary/NGO action and community participation have argued for the importance of greater dialogue between the public and the voluntary/NGO sectors. Clarke (1991), for instance, sets out the case for relating more closely to the state, whether to campaign against it and/or to transform it, to agitate for reform, or to find ways of working together to develop strategies for community development. Korten (1990) has similarly argued that government support and resource provision is key, if the voluntary/community sector is to move into third- and fourth-generation strategies 'aimed at redefining policies, transforming institutions, and helping people define, internalise and actualise a people-centred development vision' (p. 186). This point deserves emphasis precisely because both of these authors represent views which are particularly committed to the importance of the role of the voluntary/NGO/community sector; yet both also emphasize that this necessitates positive support and resourcing from the public sector, working in partnership with people's organizations and movements.

The role of the state/local state in planning and implementing wider, more strategic approaches to development – linking local, regional and sectional projects and programmes – emerges as a major theme in a number of chapters. As S.M. Miller, Martin Rein and Peggy Levitt argue in Chapter 10 in relation to the USA, 'one formidable need is a way of transforming local issues into a cohesive national agenda and integrating effectively the many forms of organising into the electoral process.' Several chapters also demonstrate that, without engaging with the state and with political processes at different levels, localized community actions risk remaining marginalized, if occasionally incorporated. The importance of developing strategies to link local projects and movements into wider strategies and movements for change at both national and international levels is clearly defined. Peadar Shanahan and John Ward, for example, in Chapter 7 raise the question of how to think globally whilst acting locally, in the context of community adult education for local economic development.

There is a particular set of issues connected with formal political processes and relations with progressive political parties/movements of the left. As Chapters 16, 13, 11 and 14 – on Nicaragua, the Philippines, Chicago (under the progressive coalition of Mayor Washington) and South Africa in the post-apartheid context, respectively – illustrate, for example, there are inherent tensions as well as strengths involved in developing alliances between community-based organizations and peoples' movements and parties of the left. One of the recurrent tensions which the Philippines experience illustrates is between the immediate, highly localized and issue-specific focus of some community organizations and the emphasis of progressive political organizations on the importance of challenging the wider structural causes of these local problems. Striking the appropriate balance between these two approaches is typically problematic, though essential, for the development of effective long-term strategies for community development as a tool for transformation.

These potential tensions between community-based organizations and movements, on the one hand, and progressive political parties, on the other, tend to become heightened when progressive parties participate directly in state power. A key issue emerging here is how to forge effective alliances without submerging the community organizations and people's movements' own identities. The chapters on the Nicaraguan and South African experiences both imply that progressive political parties need to recognize this fact and respect the separate identity and integrity of people's organizations and movements, including their continuing right to criticize governments, even governments formed by their own allies that they have struggled to put in power in the first place. Insufficient recognition of the need of people's organizations' for separate space and autonomy in practice also emerges as a major point of criticism in Chapter 8, on experiences in East Germany.

This issue is ultimately critical in relation to the longer-term goals of transformation. If community participation and empowerment are to contribute to such longer-term goals, then strategies do need to be formulated within the framework of alternative critical economic, social and political perspectives. None of the chapters provides experiences to support the view that such longer-term change could be achieved by people's organizations and movements on their own, without engaging with wider political processes. But this need to relate to alternative economic, social and political perspectives has become even more inherently problematic in the contemporary international context. As Rahman argues, the end of the Cold War took 'the pressure off global and national vested interests to make any serious pretence towards socio-economic development to promote the well-being of the broad masses'. This reduction in the pressure for alternative approaches and perspectives became particularly marked in the post-1989 global scenario, following the collapse of socialist governments in East and Central Europe. It was argued in a number of quarters that this demonstrated that there were no longer alternatives to market-led solutions – even that history as we knew it, in terms of competition between different perspectives and ideologies, had come to an end. But the logic of these chapters is precisely the opposite: that it is precisely these free-market approaches to development that have been at the root of increasing poverty and social exclusion in both the North and the South, and that the associated strategies of structural adjustment have been exacerbating the problems of unmet needs within the poorest communities. In the case of South Africa, with the particular legacy of the apartheid state, these unmet needs and the related competition for extremely scarce resources have been associated with conflict and violence on an appalling scale.

Korten has characterized the interlocking crises left from the 1980s in terms of poverty, environmental stress and communal violence, which together 'pose a threat to human civilization that is now more real and more important in its implications than the threat of nuclear war' (1990: 1). In response to these growing threats, the case for the importance of developing alternative strategies to challenge this supposedly global victory for free-market approaches has correspondingly been growing. And in developing such alternative strategies, the importance of democratic approaches to planning, drawing upon the experiences of community participation and movements to promote empowerment, is more vitally important than ever.

References

Clarke, J. (1991), *Democratising Development: The Role of Voluntary Organisations*, Earthscan, London.

Community Development Journal (1993), in association with OECD, Special Issue, 'Community Development and Urban Regeneration', vol. 28, no. 4, October.

Craig, G. (1993), *The Community Care Reforms and Local Government Change*, University of Humberside, Hull.

Donnison, D. (1993), 'The Challenge of Urban Regeneration for Community Development', *Community Development Journal*, vol. 28, no. 4, pp. 293–8.

Glennerster, H., and J. Midgely, eds (1991), *The Radical Right and the Welfare State*, Harvester Wheatsheaf, Brighton.

Gutch, R. (1992), *Contracting Out: Lessons from the US*, National Council for Voluntary Organizations, London.

Korten, D. (1990), *Getting to the 21st Century*, Kumarian Press, Connecticut, USA.

Lipton, M. (1991), *The Poor and the Poorest*, World Bank Discussion Papers, 25, Washington DC.

Mayo, M. (1994), *Communities and Caring: The Mixed Economy of Welfare*, Macmillan, London.

Mishra, R. (1990), *The Welfare State in Capitalist Society*, Harvester Wheatsheaf, Brighton.

Paul, S. (1987), *Community Participation in Development Projects*, World Bank Discussion Paper, New York.

Thomas, A. (1992), 'Non-governmental Organisations and the Limits to Empowerment', in M. Wuyts, M. Mackintosh and T. Hewitt, eds, *Development Policy and Public Action*, Oxford University Press, Oxford.

UNDP (1993), *Human Development Report 1993*, Oxford University Press, Oxford.

UNICEF (1989), *The State of the World's Children*, Oxford University Press, Oxford.

2

Counter-development:
Possibilities and Constraints

Benno Galjart

Introduction

Historically, development doesn't usually start from below. Where economic development takes place at all, the poor are generally the last population category to be affected because they lack the resources, land, skills, knowledge, or even labour time, to avail themselves of the opportunities which incorporation into a wider economic system provides. In the 1960s and 1970s, when disappointment at the failure of the trickle-down effect was widespread, some development social scientists recommended an alternative, non-Western development practice (Nerfin 1977). Some were influenced by dependency theories, which held that less-developed countries had to 'delink' from the industrialized West, economically and politically; those failing to do so would be 'underdeveloped' further. Other authors did so because their political preference was for a socialist economic order which was presumed to bring both rapid growth and equitable income distribution.

The idea on which the concept of 'counter-development' (Galjart 1981) was based was different. Could a group of poor people, aware of the outcome of 'normal' development, consciously agree on collective action which would challenge that process? If 'normal' development implied investment decisions taken by capital owners who then employed largely unskilled labourers for wages which left the latter no better off, could this process be avoided without major institutional change in the economy? Could poor people, taking advantage of economies of scale, start and manage an economic enterprise in which they would be both owners (making choices between consumption and investment) and labourers, where the enterprise operated in the market, but also overcame the conflict between capital and labour and met certain key social objectives?

In the beginning, the group would be assisted by some change agent, who could provide the necessary technical training and credit. As I shall argue, change agents, in relation to counter-development approaches, have been particularly associated with non-governmental organizations (NGOs) and their focus upon a 'third way'/NGO development approach. Eventually, however, the enterprise should be able to continue on its own. 'Counter-development' also implied the willingness of economically successful groups to apply profits as credit to similar initiatives elsewhere, instead of making their own enterprise more capital-intensive. In this way some sort of 'oil-stain effect' could be realized. The term *counter*-development supposed that cooperative economic units were possible which functioned much like religious communes in an economic sense, but whose internal solidarity did not rest on religious or ideological values but on the conviction that they provided, over time, some security to their members. Counter-*development*, however, was still a form of development within the global market economy, and hence implied economic growth, increasing incomes, specialization of labour and enterprises, production for (market) exchange, the use of machines, of inanimate sources of energy, and, more generally, of external scientific knowledge. Likewise, it implied a democratic decision-making.

These ideas were based partly on theoretical convictions, that society-wide structural change, with all its implications for redistribution and conflict, was not likely, at least in the short run, and partly on practical experience. At the societal level, various development goals seemed contradictory with respect to the mechanisms and policies which each of them implied, and hence could not all be achieved at the same time (Galjart 1978; Tiryakian 1991). These contradictions – for instance between aggregate growth and greater income equality, or between the power of states to shape development and the political participation of citizens – remained, whatever the dominant mode of production. In socialist countries, for instance, the institutions which went with centralized economic planning (thus allowing for non-market prices and wages) did not accord with a democratic political system. But at the level of a relatively small group it was perhaps possible to reconcile contradictory development goals, to combine aggregate growth with consensual, non-market rules for the distribution of benefits, to make good use of individuals' outstanding managerial skills without stifling member participation. Contemporary studies of self-managed enterprises (Vanek 1975) and of the Mondragon conglomerate (Thomas and Logan 1982) suggested that self-management enabled the participants to make their own rules with regard to wages, wage differentials, savings and investments. Also, the cooperative approach was said to make extremely rapid economic growth possible.

Since 1975, Thomas and I had been advising a Dutch–Colombian income-generating development project. Its aim was to form groups of poor people, train them so as to produce, collectively, some good or service, and provide them with enough credit to purchase necessary equipment and to start producing. Since it was impossible to designate one of the members of such a group as the owner, these enterprises had to be self-managed. Each year we examined how the team carrying out the project had fared (Galjart 1982). Although moulding cohesive groups, finding a feasible product and providing enough training to start production took much more time and was more labour-intensive than we had anticipated, it was not impossible. After eight years our Colombian counterpart, the Servicio Nacional de Aprendizaje, broke off the project, alleging that it cost too much in terms of funds and effort; but this decision was not based on a thorough comparison with its other development activities. Other, possibly sobering views, such as the argument that over time probably the best way to reduce absolute, as opposed to relative, poverty is the promotion of rapid 'normal' economic growth (Fields 1988), were not known to me. The findings of sociological studies take a long time to become established, and a still longer period to find acceptance.

More than a decade later, can we determine to what extent this vision of counter-development has been realistic? Did 'counter-development' actually occur and what can be learnt from the experiments that have taken place?

NGOs and Empowerment

To a much larger extent than government agencies, it has been NGOs which have addressed themselves to poor people, in rural as well as urban areas. NGOs have come to play a very particular role and to be associated with notions of counter-development, both in relation to cooperative development and to empowerment more generally. They have helped the poor organize and initiate joint income-generating activities. One could consider these projects as experiments in counter-development, and we shall return to them. First, however, we should recall that NGOs have also assisted grassroots organizations to acquire countervailing power. In macro-sociological terms, the idea was that such local organizations would form alliances with each other and with political parties, thus eventually constituting a power bloc at the national level. The poor, in short, were attributed the role of the Marxist proletariat. However, since the formation of such alliances necessarily takes time, in practice NGOs assisted grassroots organizations to approach local or regional authorities with claims for access to some government service or public good, as the first step towards empowerment.

When poor people acquire access to resources or services, redistribution occurs. The expansion of welfare certainly *is* a development goal. The question is whether, and to what extent, political pressure to promote redistribution hinders the realization of *other* development goals. As Hyden (1983: 49ff) has argued in relation to Africa, the overpoliticization of social and economic life has hindered economic growth. He held that a certain measure of depoliticization (less political pressure by interest groups, and fewer claims) was necessary. With respect to Latin America, Hirschman (1981: 98ff) came to a similar conclusion: that, far too early, an ideological shift occurred, from a stress on growth and industrialization to demands for reform and redistribution. Others have found that the more outspoken the redistributive intentions of some Latin American governments, the less likely it was that they obtained the results they desired, and the more likely was economic stagnation. In general, the lesson of the 1970s and early 1980s was that it is important to keep prices right within national economies (Lal 1985). This is, of course, a partial view based on a particular perspective, and it is not necessarily the poor who, at the national level, succeed in getting their demands met. In many less-developed societies, 'rents' are sought and obtained by interest groups other than the poor. For this reason, amongst others, Evers and Schiel (1988) speak of strategic groups, collectivities which, in terms of income, are successful in enhancing and benefiting from their developmental role.

Apart from the possible consequences for market prices and the efficient allocation of resources in market terms, another issue is involved: to wit, whether in practice governments actually react to political pressure from below, with repression in the short run and with corporatist controls in the longer run. A recent Dutch evaluative study on the effects of NGO activities in six developing countries concluded that there was no evidence that the distribution of resources or of income *at the national level* had been affected by NGO-supported empowerment (Impactstudie Medefinancieringsprogramma 1991: 35). Howes and Sattar (1992), reporting on two development approaches pursued by a large Bangladesh NGO, BRAC, observe that the approach which emphasized consciousness-raising and empowerment was discontinued after some years for lack of practical success. An evaluative comparison of the results of these two approaches in a number of Bangladeshi villages (Streefland *et al.* 1986: 132ff) showed that, in the village where the emphasis had been on conscientization, the economic position of the poor had not improved.

However, some of the case studies carried out under the aegis of the Dutch Impactstudie did provide examples of grassroots organizations acquiring access to resources or services at the local level. Evidently, at a disaggregate level the 'room' for a certain amount of redistribution can be larger – as well as smaller – than at regional or national level, because the power and importance of interest groups differ from one place to the next, and because politicians have differing interests. Conceding such a claim does not imply nationwide redistribution. Also, cases vary as to the degree of distributional injustice involved; a market price which does not cover production costs differs from the dispossession by a government or private interests of a group's traditional user rights over areas of forest or land without adequate compensation (Hall 1992). Paradoxically, however, NGOs and their advocates appear to believe that the aggregation of claims at the national level always leads to *more* redistribution rather than less. They continue to exhort each other to form alliances (Said Khan and Basin 1986).

Income- and Employment-Generating Activities

What I understood by 'counter-development' resembles what have come to be called the 'income- and employment-generating activities' promoted by NGOs. For various reasons, in the early 1990s NGOs have become popular with official donors like the World Bank. First, in many less-developed countries (LDCs) the results of state-planned and state-led development activities have been disappointing. States, it has been argued, have taken on too many tasks without much success, indeed often facilitating economic exploitation by political power-holders. Secondly, NGOs appear to have become less radical or revolutionary. Since the promotion of income-generating activities had to be based on specialization of labour and market exchange, it implied some acceptance of the prevailing economic order. Successful projects effectively incorporated groups of poor people into that order, contradicting NGO efforts to imply that the economic order was unjust and had to be changed (Rosa Medellin 1979; Khan and Basin 1986; Wils 1990). More often than not, however, their 'target groups' expected it would bring immediate economic improvements, regardless of whether this would lead to longer-term structural change.

The present popularity of NGOs is not based on a systematic evaluation of project results but on the wide, though uncritical, acceptance of certain ideas and practices. Contrary to governmental bureaucracies, NGOs appear to be staffed with dedicated field personnel expected to remain for long periods of time in close contact with the local population, to establish relations of trust, as Goméz (1992) argues they do, and become acquainted with local knowledge. Because of this, and perhaps because NGO field staff in general are trained in social science rather than in some technological speciality, they encourage local participation in decision-making, even when they have prior ideas with regard to the best investment opportunities. Up to a point, NGOs can be regarded as theorists who put their development hypotheses to the test.

What are these ideas, and how realistic are they? In the remainder of this chapter I intend to discuss three central NGO ideas and practices. They are related to the selection of target groups; choice of income-generating activities; and popular participation in decision-making.

NGOs often regard it as their goal to oppose the uneven character of economic growth: they select a target group among the relatively disadvantaged, and thereafter see to it that the economic benefits of the group's investment are spread as evenly as possible. In other words, NGOs are loath to see the economic growth which they help to bring about create further inequality. In practice, however, selection of a target group often comes down to addressing the entire population of a poor village, rather than explicitly excluding the richer peasants or the village leadership. Exclusion, when it occurs at all, is often a by-product of the proposed activity. Some will be unable to contribute, others may not be interested. Experience has shown that it is very difficult to reach the poorest, and that initiatives and leadership will often come from people with higher status (Kronenburg 1986: 164; Verhagen 1987: 107ff).

The choice of remunerative economic activities is not an easy one. What essentially occurs is that poor people are asked to act as entrepreneurs. Since they are going to receive help such as training or financial subsidies, they may easily underestimate the difficulties implied by completely new activities. The literature reflects the importance of competent leadership (Robinson 1992), the time taken to develop competence (van Niekerk 1994), or the drawbacks the lack of management or bookkeeping skills entails. In writing about Peruvian NGO experiences, Eguiguren (1984) notes that when the NGO definitively withdraws and has to transfer the project, the larger the difference between the initial situation and the development goals set by the project, the greater the risk of failure as the NGO withdraws.

The idea of organizing exchange between groups involved in such projects appears attractive. Such exchange symbolizes the self-reliance of the poor and was an implicit ingredient of counter-development. It eliminates intermediaries, whose assumed enormous profits can then be divided between producers and consumers. However, this idea appeared to imply disregard for the real functions of markets, where buyers weigh prices against quality. The result was a neglect, on the part of the producers as well as of the supporting agency, of the demands of the market. The hope that feelings of solidarity encourage consumers to accept low-quality goods at relatively high prices is vain (Galjart 1985), as is, at either the macro- or the micro-level, the idea that a certain degree of 'delinking' furthers the development of an economic system. NGOs need to have a realistic understanding of market forces.

Understandably, NGOs want to promote economic activity to bring benefits to as many people as possible and prevent further inequality. However, both objectives may generate a too-optimistic assessment of the economies of scale that can be realized. To some extent NGOs, like socialist governments, appear to have had a predilection for collective production. In countries where the government had created collective agricultural enterprises, as in Peru and Mexico, NGOs were inclined to maintain them even when participants favoured partition of fields.

Paradoxically, the ideological preference for non-market-regulated distribution of economic benefits appears to imply neglect of, or even scorn for, the one group – the family – that has consistently managed to keep its internal rules of contributions and rewards separate from the market, even in capitalist societies. Families are regarded as if they were individuals. In an urban setting, where families normally are no longer units of production, this bias is not very important; but in rural areas, production groups compete with families for the solidarity of the mutual member. Often, the family wins.

The most important reason for NGOs' present popularity is that they have forcefully defended the idea that participation in decision-making is necessary for all development efforts, an ingredient now accorded magic qualities. The World Bank has recently installed an internal learning group to ensure that its entire staff not only becomes familiar with the pros and cons of participation, but practices it (Bhatnagar and Williams 1992: 1ff). What is at issue is that even poor people have agency, that is, are knowledgeable about their situation and can influence it. Not even coercive, let alone remunerative or normative, power is so absolute as to leave the least powerful persons entirely without agency. Thus, people supposed to benefit from some planned development project and therefore believed to accept it wholesale, may very well 'deconstruct' it, adopting only those parts which suit them (Olivier de Sardan 1988), or setting themselves alternative goals (Vries 1992). The danger that people will not do what they are supposed to do is greater, the more discretion they have. In many kinds of development projects this discretion is rather large.

It is therefore better than meeting with deconstruction or even obstruction, as a result of which the project fails, to allow for this agency beforehand, and to make sure that future beneficiaries agree with the plans. This can only be realized through a drawn-out process of consultation. An additional advantage is that people may become more willing to contribute to the realization of the plan out of their own resources, and afterwards more reluctant to see the project fail. A third consequence (and sometimes disadvantage) of participation is that some kind of tacit selection takes place of those with whom people are willing to cooperate; exclusion becomes the business of the target group rather than the NGO. The result may be that people with a higher social status have a larger say in what is to be done. Finally, participation in the sense of joint planning also implies that the NGO has to take local technical knowledge seriously.

Although NGOs have been very successful as advocates of participation, the concept remains vague. First, it does not mean that NGOs, or other change agents, do the bidding of the target group. Rather, it means that both parties, while seeking consensus, have a power of veto over the other's suggestions. Whatever plan – and thus investment – is finally agreed upon, it will almost always combine local with extra-local knowledge and practices.

Very little, in fact, has been written on this process of deliberation and negotiation. Full consensus reached by a large group is rare; for that reason different cultures have elaborated varying procedures for groups to reach conclusions. The institutionalized 'Western' way – that is, voting after having decided on the varying voting rights of the participants – is not necessarily a locally accepted procedure, even among members of a formal association. Verhagen's earlier comparative study (1984) of the participation of small farmers in planning development projects in Sri Lankan and Thai villages found that in the latter the conclusions reached in meetings did not reflect consensus, but rather an unwillingness publically to contradict certain powerful people. To know what they really thought, preliminary conversations with the individual farmers were necessary. What appears to be at issue here is that NGOs assume, often implicitly, that relatively traditional, relatively poor rural communities are homogeneous. In such a setting people are not only assumed to have the same interests but also to be willing to share burdens and benefits, rights and duties, equally (van der Drift 1992: 261ff). However, differences in gender, age, knowledge, kinship, let alone in wealth, often imply differences in social status, which may be incompatible with a one-person, one-vote rule.

NGOs can hardly force a project on those who do not agree with it; such people simply stop participating. In the planning stage this is not really evident, but it may become so at a later stage, when an association has been formed, money has been invested and work has to be done. The term 'participation' suggests, as it were, one continuous process; what is not taken into account is that the costs and benefits of participation greatly differ from one stage to the next. Taking part in meetings costs time, but the reward is not only that the participant learns about the intentions and, possibly, the funds of which the NGO personnel disposes, but also that s/he may exert some influence on the final outcome. In the next stages, however, monetary contributions and considerably more time and energy may have to be requested from participants, whereas the economic benefits of the joint undertaking may take years to materialize. In some cases – for instance, planting a village forest – what is asked from the participants is a once-only effort; in other cases – such as the joint production of lettuces in a collectively owned greenhouse – the contribution is continuous. The cost-benefit estimate which each prospective participant makes not only differs per stage, but may also contain uncosted items, such as doing the village headman a favour. As in practically all instances some form of cooperation is involved, participants make also a second – a self–other comparison (Blalock and Wilken 1979) – in which the individual *ratios* of costs and benefits are compared. Not equality, but equity is the norm.

The individual rewards of the joint effort should thus be proportional to the individual contributions. Put negatively, the implication is that people don't want to become the dupes of 'easy riders'. In both kinds of comparison, material as well as immaterial costs and benefits are taken into consideration – something which is also common in our Western culture. In many cases it is not the self–self comparison, but the self–other comparison which creates the most severe strains within the cooperative group, especially in collective agricultural production, in which it is extremely difficult to assess the value of one another's contributions. Elsewhere (Galjart 1992), a sociological analysis of participatory development projects in terms of 'pooling' helps make one aware of the possible pitfalls here.

Organizing groups of poor people and devising with them some income-generating – or time-saving (Verhagen 1987) – activity is a labour-intensive and therefore expensive process. To a large extent, NGOs depend on foreign funding. Although donors continuously demand that all expenses are accounted for, the literature contains few evaluations of project costs and benefits. The Dutch evaluative study concluded that NGOs were insufficiently cost-conscious (Impactstudie Medefinancieringsprogramma 1991: 30). Van Niekerk's study (1994) of NGO projects in Andean Bolivia and Peru calculated that, per beneficiary, the yearly benefits of projects varied between 57 and 75 per cent of the yearly costs of promotion. Robinson (1992: 30) found in an evaluative study of sixteen British-funded NGO projects that only in a minority of cases did benefits substantially outweigh the costs of intervention. What is really at issue is not the largesse with public money of which government agencies are sometimes accused. The promotion of development activities among the poor is extremely labour-intensive in any case. Paradoxically, the lion's share of the costs consists of the salaries and transport of NGO personnel, themselves members of a middle class. Although it is true that a pound can only be spent once, it is far from clear with what other development efforts NGO activities should be compared. The official international donor circuit has recently come in for a devastating critique (Hancock 1991). On the other hand, in the poorest Less Developed Countries (LDCs), billions of aid money have left very little trace. Even when governments or international agencies are donors, they have little influence on political decisions in recipient countries and thus on the final outcome of development efforts. NGOs can hardly do worse. And quite apart from the effects income-generating activities may have on target groups, NGOs appear to provide an excellent training ground for future officials. In the redemocratizing Latin American countries, NGO staff are recruited into both political and bureaucratic systems.

Evaluation studies (cf. Impactstudie Medefinancieringsprogramma 1991: 42; Robinson 1992: 30) found it difficult, even at the local level, to assess whether improvements effected by NGO projects are likely to be maintained when financial assistance is discontinued. At the macro-level the impact of this kind of NGO project is nil, economic growth depending much more on national processes and policies. Factors like inter-ethnic strife, the possibility of illegally growing some drug, or economic stagnation caused by an authoritarian government which has lost its legitimacy are more influential on national trends of change. And NGOs are not a substitute for government.

What, then, is their use? What effect do they have? Although NGO personnel might indignantly reject this conclusion, NGOs do what, in the early 1960s, development theory expected of intellectuals in LDCs: to wit, to modernize the folk culture of the poor. They do that not only by jointly planning change, but also by setting an example of concern, seriousness and diligent work that would fit Weber's Protestant ethic. Hirschman's (1988) suggestion that even relatively unsuccessful collective grassroots development efforts create a sort of social energy in the participants that may re-emerge in a later initiative points in the same direction. As long as development cannot be planned, and as long as research has not shown that governments do much better at promoting development than NGOs, there is room for the latter. But like all other actors on the scene, they should remain modest in their aims.

As to the ideas behind the concept of counter-development, most of these were too optimistic. Poor local groups may realize that they are left behind or are losing out, but they are unlikely to undertake collective economic action to reverse such a trend. Individuals may jump; but for groups, development generally implies taking small steps forward. Not only is it illusory to think that Schumpeterian entrepreneurs will suddenly arise among the poor. To expect a group of poor people to refrain to a large extent from relying on markets, and hierarchy, as organizing principles, relying only on trust, is to burden them with additional difficulties (Thompson *et al.* 1991).

References

Bhatnagar, B., and A.C. Williams, eds (1992), *Participatory Development and the World Bank*, World Bank (WB Discussion Papers no. 183), Washington DC.

Blalock, H.M., and R.H. Wilken (1979), *Intergroup Processes: A Micromacro Perspective*, Free Press, New York.

Edwards, M., and D. Hulme, eds (1992), *Making a Difference. NGOs and Development in a Changing World*, Earthscan Publications, London.

Eguiguren, F. (1984), 'Los programas de promoción y el problema de la "transferencia"', in F. Eguiguren *et al.*, *Experiencias de promoción del desarrollo y organización popular*, Desco, Lima, pp. 45–64.

Evers, H.D., and T. Schiel (1988), *Strategische Gruppen. Vergleichende Studien zu Staat, Bürokratie und Klassenbildung in der Dritten Welt*, Dietrich Reimer Verlag, Berlin.

Fields, G.S. (1988), 'Income Distribution and Economic Growth', in G. Ranis and T. Paul Schultz, eds, *The State of Development Economics*, Basil Blackwell, Oxford, pp. 459–85.

Galjart, B.F. (1976), *Peasant Mobilization and Solidarity*, Van Gorcum, Assen.

────── (1978),'Mythes en misverstanden rondom ontwikkeling', *Mens en Maatschappij*, vol. 53, no. 1, pp.53–62.

────── (1981), 'Counterdevelopment: A Position Paper', *Community Development Journal*, vol. 16, no. 2, pp. 88–97.

────── (1982), 'Dissection of an Alternative Development Project', in B.F. Galjart and D. Buijs, eds, *Participation of the Poor in Development*, Institute of Cultural and Social Studies (Leiden Development Studies no. 2), Leiden, pp. 253–72.

────── (1985), 'A Sociological Case-study of a Mexican Experiment in Participation and Self-management', in L. Boer *et al.*, eds, *Poverty and Interventions: Cases from Developing Countries*, Institute of Cultural and Social Studies (Leiden Development Studies no. 6), Leiden, pp. 133–52.

────── (1992), 'Cooperation as Pooling. A Rational Choice Perspective', *Sociologia Ruralis*, vol. 32, no. 4, pp. 389–407.

Gomez, S. (1992), *Dilemas de los ONGs Rurales en el Contexto Democratico*, Flacso (Estudios Sociales no. 41), Santiago.

Hall, A. (1992), 'From Victims to Victors: NGOs and Empowerment at Itaperica', in M. Edwards and D. Hulme, eds, *Making a Difference. NGOs and Development in a Changing World*, Earthscan, London, pp. 148–59.

Hancock, G. (1991), *Lords of Poverty. The Freewheeling Lifestyles, Power, Prestige and Corruption of the Multibillion Dollar Aid Business*, Mandarin, London.

Hirschman, A.O. (1981), *Essays in Trespassing. Economics to Politics and Beyond*, Cambridge University Press, Cambridge.

────── (1988), 'The Principle of Conservation and Mutation of Social Energy', in S. Annis and P. Hakim, eds, *Direct to the Poor. Grassroots Development in Latin America*, Lynne Riener Publishers, Boulder, Colo., pp. 7–14.

Hyden, G. (1983), *No Shortcuts to Progress. African Development Management in Perspective*, Heinemann, London.

Howes, M., and M.G. Sattar (1992), 'Bigger and Better? Scaling-up Strategies Pursued by BRAC 1972–1991', in M. Edwards and D. Hulme, eds, *Making a Difference. NGOs and Development in a Changing World*, Earthscan, London, pp. 99–110.

Impactstudie Medefinancieringsprogramma (1991), *Eindrapport Stuurgroep*, The Hague.

Kronenburg, J.B.M. (1986), *Empowerment of the Poor. A Comparative Analysis of Two Development Endeavours in Kenya*, Royal Tropical Institute, Amsterdam.

Lal, D. (1985), *The Poverty of 'Development Economics'*, Harvard University Press, Cambridge, Mass.

Nerfin, M., ed. (1977), *Another Development. Approaches and Strategies*, Dag Hammarskjöld Foundation, Uppsala.

Olivier de Sardan, J.P. (1988), 'Peasant Logics and Development Project Logics', *Sociologia Ruralis*, vol. 28, no. 2/3, pp. 216–26.

Robinson, M. (1992), 'NGOs and Rural Poverty Alleviation: Implications for Scaling-up', in M. Edwards and D. Hulme, eds, *Making a Difference. NGOs and Development in a Changing World*, Earthscan, London, pp. 28–39.

Rosa Medellin, M. de la (1979), *Promocion popular y lucha de clases (analisis de un caso)*, Servicios Educativos Populares, A.C., Netzahualcóyotl.

Said Khan, N., and K. Bhasin (1986), 'Role of Asian People's Organisations', *Ifda Dossier*, no. 53, pp. 9–21, and no. 54, pp. 3–17.

Streefland, P. *et al.* (1986), *Different Ways to Support the Rural Poor: Effects of Two Development Approaches in Bangladesh*, Royal Tropical Institute, Amsterdam.

Thomas, H., and C. Logan (1982), *Mondragon. An Economic Analysis*, Allen & Unwin, London.

Thompson, G., *et al.* (1991), *Markets, Hierarchies and Networks. The Coordination of Social Life*, Sage, London.

Tiryakian, E.A. (1991), 'Modernisation: Exhumetur in Pace (Rethinking Macrosociology in the 1990s)', *International Sociology*, vol. 6, no. 2, pp. 165–80.

van der Drift, R. (1992), *Arbeid en Alcohol. De dynamiek van de rijstverbouw en het gezag van de oudste bij de Balanta Brassa in Guinee Bissau*, Centre of Non-Western Studies, Leiden.

Vanek, J. (1975), *Self-Management. Economic Liberation of Man*, Penguin Books, Harmondsworth.

van Niekerk, N. (1994), *Desarrollo Rural en Los Andes. Un estudio sobre los programas de desarrollo de Organizaciones no Gubernamentales*, Institute of Cultural and Social Studies (Leiden Development Studies no. 13), Leiden.

Verhagen, K. (1984), *Cooperation for Survival. An Analysis of an Experiment in Participatory Research and Planning with Small Farmers in Sri Lanka and Thailand*, Royal Tropical Institute, Amsterdam.

——— (1987), *Self-Help Promotion: A Challenge to the NGO Community*, Foris Publications, Dordrecht.

Vries, P. de (1992), *Unruly Clients. A Study of How Bureaucrats Try and Fail to Transform Gatekeepers, Communists and Preachers into Ideal Beneficiaries*, dissertation, Agricultural University, Wageningen.

Wils, F. (1990), *Income and Employment Generating Activities of NGDOs: An Overview*, ISS (Working Paper Series no. 88), The Hague.

3

Participatory Development:
Toward Liberation or Co-optation?

Muhammad Anisur Rahman

Introduction

Over the last two decades, collective action by underprivileged people to improve their socio-economic life has been growing, noticeably in countries of the South. Some community organizations have been formed spontaneously, in the sense of having been created by the people themselves, but the greater number of organizations have been stimulated and assisted by external interventions.

The activities of such grassroots organizations vary widely. Some are purely economic, mobilizing internal resources of the people supplemented by resource and knowledge support from outside to undertake income-generating activities (including the development of infrastructure to support these activities). Such activities involve various forms and degrees of mutual cooperation among people who participate, in order to promote their economic position faster than would be possible on an individual basis. Some organizations engage in activities of a 'pressure-group' nature, to resist exploitation or oppression by other interest groups, assert economic, social and human rights (including women's rights), or demand services from public agencies. Some add social and cultural activities by way of programmes in areas such as health, family planning, education and culture. Others aim at the promotion of holistic life by way of activities that integrate spiritual advancement with economic and social development. Popular mobilizations to promote ecologically aware economic and social life are also growing, for example, to promote organic agriculture, integrated farming, social forestry. Finally, many grassroots mobilizations involve the promotion of the collective intellectual capacity of the people: a movement known as 'participatory (action) research' has spread, which seeks to stimulate and assist disadvantaged people to undertake their own collective investigations into their living conditions and environment. From this, they can develop their own systematic thinking – their own 'science'

– from which they can derive strength to negotiate with other quarters of society.

In this chapter we reflect, first, upon the theoretical and philosophical conceptions underlying such work and observe the increasing shift of development thinking in this direction. Then, we discuss the political economy of the subject. Finally, some reflections toward deepening the quality of grassroots work are presented.

Theoretical and Philosophical Conceptions

The theoretical and philosophical conceptions behind such popular mobilizations also have a varied nature. In the early stages, such movements were outside the paradigm of both conventional development theory and revolutionary theories of social change. But some theoretical conceptions of such work had a 'radical' stance, in the sense of advocating a major shift in the power balance between the 'elites' and the 'people' towards the people, presenting a vision of people's 'liberation'. The Freirian concept of 'conscientization', calling for raising the self-reflected awareness of the people rather than educating or indoctrinating them, for giving them the power to assert their 'voice' and for stimulating their self-driven collective action to transform their reality, influenced the philosophical vision of many grassroots programmes. Early proponents of participatory research drew some inspiration also from the Marxist vision of self-emancipation of the oppressed classes (Rahman 1985). Many practitioners as well as theoreticians involved with such grassroots work also articulated a view of development which is seen as the release of people's creativity (Rahman 1990). This was opposed to the conventional notion of development which saw economic growth as a measure of progress in the economy's ability to satisfy the consumption needs of the society, or as progress toward satisfaction of such needs, in particular the basic (consumption) needs of underprivileged people.

Such radical theoretical or philosophical conceptions of popular grassroots mobilizations have, however, lacked a political theory for macro-level social transformation, without which the micro-level assertion of popular power and release of people's creativity remain heavily circumscribed. Meanwhile, the failure of conventional development efforts led by state agencies to combat mass poverty has led civil development agencies (CDAs, popularly called 'NGOs', but a positive term may be preferred) to launch programmes funded mostly by foreign donors to promote people's collective initiatives to improve their economic and social status. This has progressively grown into a new worldwide culture of development action termed 'popular participation in development' or simply 'participatory development' (PD).

Participatory development is increasingly being adopted as a more secure way of taking development to the people. With the growing popu-larity of PD, more radical thinking and action toward 'empowerment' and 'liberation' of the people is becoming marginalized. Some previously radical grassroots interventions are even being co-opted by 'development' agencies. However, as a result of growing foreign donor support, grassroots work by CDAs to promote popular participation in development through the collective economic and social cooperation of popular groups has expanded significantly in a number of countries. Today this particular variety of grassroots work, rather than work of a 'radical' (liberation) character, looks like becoming the dominant trend.

The notion of popular participation in development is increasingly being endorsed by development scholars. International development cooperation agencies, including most UN agencies, are affirming popular participation as a necessary element of a strategy for poverty alleviation (UNDP 1993). Among regional forums, the 1990 Arusha Conference on Popular Partici-pation in the Recovery and Development Process in Africa issued the *African Charter on Popular Participation*, a strong call for popular participation in development. A cooler, analytical plea to make PD the central develop-ment strategy has recently come from SAARC's Independent South Asian Commission on Poverty Alleviation (1992). This Commission has argued that participatory development will not only alleviate poverty but also maximize the rate of economic growth. This analysis rests on the growing evidence cited by the Commission that the low-income producers of South Asian countries, once mobilized for cooperative development effort, are showing high marginal saving rates, low capital–output ratio, sharing and caring characteristics that reduce the cost of meeting their basic needs, and values of 'simplicity and frugality'. These values were exhibited by the early entrepreneurs of the Industrial Revolution of the West, but are no longer practised by the elite and elusive would-be entrepreneurs of countries of the South today.

The Political Economy of Participatory Development

However, such growing endorsement notwithstanding, participatory development is far from being adopted in practice anywhere in a way which leads to major structural reforms and the transfer of resources away from those vested interests that control dominant social and political structures towards underprivileged people. Dominant lobbies in Southern countries are accepting PD as at best a poverty alleviation strategy, to be implemented sporadically at the micro-level, and then only by mobilizing the resources of poverty groups themselves, supplemented by donor support, rather than redirecting the mainstream of development resources to promote PD on a national scale. Mainstream development efforts supported by the great bulk of foreign development assistance remains very much non-participatory, and *poverty-augmenting* rather than *poverty-alleviating*.

Most countries are following the 'structural adjustment programme' (SAP) approaches of the World Bank as a condition for the Bank's assistance. SAP is not concerned with PD, nor for that matter with poverty alleviation, except as a hypothetical long-run 'trickle-down' effect of economic growth. The SAP approach does not regard agrarian reform as necessary in most countries even for industrial development of the conventional variety, not to speak of the need to give the control of agrarian assets to direct producers as secure bases from which they could take participatory initiatives. Nor does it address the question of 'urban bias', which contributes to the premature growth of high consumption cultures, and locates people in contexts where life is more atomized, inhibiting the development of communal solidarity and mutual share and care as the cultural basis of PD.

The presumption of efficient resource allocation under SAP rests solely on the supposed virtue of the 'free market', which both in theory and in practice naturally favours the conspicuous consumption urges of the affluent of the society in question rather than the basic needs of the underprivileged. In reality, in the majority of the countries following the SAP approach, the expected acceleration of private investment as the main driving force of growth has not happened, and with a few exceptions the overall growth performance of the countries in the South has actually been worse in the 1980s compared to the previous decade and a half (Sobhan 1992). As regards public sector development efforts, they consist, in practice, largely of bureaucratic and technocratic approaches to the implementation of projects and programmes in a culture of unbridled corruption, which benefit those directly involved with the processing and implementation of these projects and programmes much more than the people at the grassroots. And in turn, these differential benefits strengthen the financial and social power of those same powerful interests, which enables them further to appropriate social resources to augment their private fortunes.

The process of transforming resources from the wider society to the affluent is further heightened through the banking sector. The evidence is strong today that with group liability and appropriate institutional support, low-income direct producers are excellent borrowers. The regular banking institutions nevertheless continue to channel society's savings into affluent and socially powerful hands although these have a low repayment record. Meanwhile, credit to the assetless and asset-poor are provided, if at all, by special programmes funded by limited donor grants more as humanitarian initiatives than as a part of a national development strategy. Taken together, such mainstream development strategies, controlled as they are by these vested interests, can only be expected to increase the 'flow of poverty', in the context of which participatory development as a marginal activity supported by limited donor finance may play the role at best of a 'safety net' to keep social discontent in check.

Even at the local level where PD initiatives are growing, there are few instances of PD work involving the bulk of low-income groups in any single locality (for example, village). Many CDAs have spread their work over significant areas of space, covering, for example, thousands of villages. But many amongst them work with only a small proportion of the low-income households in each specific locality. One wonders whether, in fact, interventions to promote PD are *surviving* in this way by not seriously challenging the *status quo* in any locality and instead spreading themselves thin over a wider geographical space. Even the celebrated Grameen Bank of Bangladesh, which is a credit-to-the-poor rather than a PD programme, working today in some 33,000 out of the country's 68,000 villages, has been unable to eliminate poverty from one single village. Notwithstanding the work of this programme and of hundreds of CDAs all over the country for nearly two decades, there has been no appreciable dent in the country's poverty situation (Task Force 1991).

Indeed, poverty in most countries is a macro-phenomenon and needs to be tackled with a macro-development strategy. This strategy, moreover, has to be balanced against the requirements of economic growth: without sustained growth at a high enough rate, poverty on a national scale cannot be alleviated. This means that a society has to find a strategy of economic growth which has poverty alleviation built into it, rather than pursue a growth strategy which augments poverty and then look for special poverty alleviation programmes as a palliative or 'safety net'. The Independent South Asian Commission on Poverty Alleviation has suggested the main-streaming of PD as just such a national strategy for growth-cum-poverty alleviation, concluding that, for this region, there is no conflict between these two objectives.

It seems important to ask this kind of question for other regions and countries, where growth is yet to pick up, notwithstanding structural adjustment programmes supported by significant flows of foreign develop-ment assistance. Is there, for these countries, really a conflict between growth and poverty alleviation so that one has to consider SAP-type approaches as a macro-development strategy for growth and consider PD mainly as a 'safety net' to keep poverty within socially tolerable limits? Can affluent classes of these societies be expected to deliver growth by thrifty hard-working entrepreneurship rather than wasting social surplus and foreign development resources in conspicuous consumption? Or does the hope of growth itself lie in mobilizing the collective initiatives of the poor-but-hardworking direct producers and bringing back to them the surplus that is currently being taken away from them, encouraging them to save and reinvest at high rates, and assisting them with the knowledge that modern science and technology has to offer? The hope for poverty alleviation on the scale at which poverty exists lies in a positive answer to this question, and not in a poverty-augmenting macro-development strategy merely tempered with sporadic poverty alleviation programmes, whether of the PD type or otherwise.

This, of course, is easier said than done. Part of the crisis of development today lies in the erosion of institutions and structures with a genuine social concern and real or potential influence. The end of the Cold War, with the collapse of experiments with socialism, has contributed in a major way to this crisis. Today, radical thinking and alternative sources of power are in disarray. This has taken the pressure off global and national vested interests to make any serious pretence toward socio-economic development to promote the well-being of the broad masses. International support for such efforts and SAP-type free-for-all policies, which would essentially serve the interests of those who have already amassed wealth and social power, are being glorified, instead, in the name of economic freedom and market guidance for resource allocation. Neither poverty alleviation nor even economic growth appear to be objectives in their own right today: they remain mainly as elements in monitoring the effects of economic freedom, in part as academic curiosities, and perhaps also to obtain advance warning of popular discontent.

In this state of affairs, a social perspective on grassroots work to promote participatory development seems to be getting lost or marginalized. Much of the recent growth of CDAs doing such work – indeed, their 'mushrooming' in several countries – may even be understood as an employment-generation phenomenon, with educated job-seekers in those countries responding to the growing supply of donor finances for such work. In several countries, this is also creating a new professional elite – the 'NGO' functionaries – with salaries and privileges matching or surpassing those of senior government functionaries. And why not, if they perform their functions with sophisticated professional expertise and bring genuine benefits where government agency functionaries have failed to deliver development at the grassroots?

Deepening the Quality of Grassroots Work

One might still wish that a 'radical' spirit be kept alive in grassroots work as far as possible; radical not necessarily in the sense of any particular ideology but in the sense of supporting values of social activism. A vision of the elements of such change is needed to influence the 'manifesto' of some existing or would-be political or social forces toward eventual transformation.

One starting point might be that no CDA working to promote participatory development should simply label the recipients of their programmes as 'poor' or call its programme a 'poverty alleviation' programme. This is because the idea of poverty alleviation looks at the question of poverty in terms of meeting a social *liability* rather than nourishing a social *asset*; it looks at people as objects of sympathy and invites some sacrifice from the rest of the society to mitigate their suffering rather than invoking the cooperation of that society towards releasing people's creativity for development. At the same time, those called 'poor' tend to develop a low self-image by internalizing this social identity, and so develop a mentality of dependence on others. Notwithstanding their poverty, these people are in fact sustaining the life of the broader society by their hard work and creativity, and it is very important that they take this positive self-image. This is one important step towards mobilizing themselves for self-development as creative beings (producers).

A corollary of a creative self-identity is a spirit of *self-reliance*. Human creativity is an organic quality embodied in one's own mental and labour power and processes and is inhibited by dependence (in which one's autonomy of thinking and action are surrendered). There are CDAs working at the grassroots to promote people's self-reliance, and there are impressive records of success, where CDAs have physically withdrawn after working in particular localities to create autonomous people's organizations (for example, in Sri Lanka and Thailand: see Tilakaratna 1985 and 1989). But this cannot be said of the great bulk of grassroots work, which seems to create the permanent dependence of people's organizations on guidance and support from the CDAs in question.

Grassroots work cannot spread fast enough without external resources and an ever-expanding supply of field workers. But, if the resource base of CDAs rests primarily on foreign donor funding, then national self-determination also becomes compromised. Such dependence of popular initiatives on continuous CDA support also invites various kinds of distortions in CDA work, giving them power over the people that can be abused. The principle of people's self-reliance is, in fact, professed by most CDAs; but in reality, there is much to improve in this regard.

As a rule, CDAs can provide various types of assistance to grassroots groups in their programmes, and primarily for the benefit of the members of these groups. This makes these groups relatively privileged compared to other people of similar socio-economic status in the same locality, whose relative poverty and hence misery may in fact increase as a result. As part of a strategy of creating a mere 'safety net', such a policy of dividing the 'poor' may be a sound one, making it more difficult for the poor to challenge wider power structures. A positive and more inspiring strategy would be to invite the groups who are being helped to assist other groups in the locality in turn, using the experience, skills and even rise in incomes which they would be gaining by being assisted by the CDAs in the first instance.

In many grassroots movements, people's groups and organizations are indeed providing such assistance to their fellow folk, spontaneously, to various degrees. The concept of using the primary groups as 'pioneers' to play 'spearhead' roles in spreading PD initiatives in their respective neighbourhoods could be ingrained in PD work as one of its essential and challenging elements, so that those thus assisted by CDAs become real partners in the task of facilitating people's mobilization more generally. There is no reason, in fact, why any CDA needs to feel obligated to assist any group of people at the grassroots with its scarce resources if that group is not willing to assist others in turn.

If one conceives genuine partnerships between CDAs and grassroots groups in their programmes, one might also like to see the related establishment of structures and modes of formal accountability of the CDAs to their grassroots partners. Currently most CDAs are accountable only to their foreign donors, without any accountability to structures within the society (except for formal registrational purposes to national governments, which are, in any case, ill-equipped to assess grassroots work belonging to an 'alternative paradigm'). This may not be such a serious matter for small-scale work. But large-scale grassroots mobilization of people by agencies who are accountable mainly to foreign donors (and following mandates given by donor funding), raises questions of social, cultural and political sensitivity. In several countries this has stood in the way of CDAs doing grassroots work, from receiving fuller support from within their own society.

CDAs can, if they wish, easily establish their own structures of accountability to popular forces within their society. There are, in fact, instances where no dichotomy of structures exists between a CDA and the popular organizations it helps to create. Social activists and professionals working with the people can belong to, and be accountable to, the same organization to which the popular organizations also belong and are accountable (for example, the Organization of Rural Associations for Progress in Zimbabwe, and the 'Six-S' movement in West Africa; see Rahman 1991). This is one way in which social activists may make themselves accountable to the people in whose lives they intervene, that is, by becoming 'organic intellectuals' in the people's movements.

CDAs which prefer to keep their own organizations structurally independent of people's organizations could also improve the credibility of their claims to be working to promote people's empowerment, as most CDAs profess, if they worked toward the creation of autonomous people's organizations which were strong enough to call the CDAs themselves into question. In fact, in several countries today, taken together, popular organizations potentially constitute a sizeable popular force were they to be linked across respective CDA programmes. Such a forum of people's bodies could represent the interests and voices of the underprivileged at a national level vis-à-vis other social structures, including the CDA structures (which are already linked among themselves in several countries to represent a national voice for CDAs). If CDAs could transcend their respective 'empire' mentalities to work toward the development of such independent popular and large-scale structures, challenging national as well as CDA policies with the combined strength of their constituent organizations, then grassroots work by CDAs would be contributing more significantly to the promotion of people's empowerment, self-reliance and a deeper participatory development.

The theoretical case for participatory development is strengthening, due to the failure of conventional development strategies; and the PD movement is growing quantitatively as well as receiving increasing endorsement from the development cooperation system and in development thinking. But the main thrust of development effort dictated by the World Bank's structural adjustment programmes and supported by the great bulk of external development assistance remains non-participatory: in fact, it is expected to be of a poverty-augmenting character. In this context, small-scale PD efforts seem to be serving the purpose mainly of providing a 'safety net' and do not promise fundamental movement toward people's liberation. Perhaps the liberation spirit may be kept alive, for now, only by deepening the quality of PD work and consciously reflecting the values of social activism, building towards a more genuinely participatory approach to transformation.

References

Rahman, Muhammad Anisur (1985), 'The Theory and Practice of Participatory Action Research', in Orlando Fals-Borda, ed., *The Challenge of Social Change*, Sage Studies in International Sociology 32, Sage Publications, Calif.

——— (1990), 'People's Self-development', *Community Development Journal*, vol. 24, no. 4, October, pp. 307–14.

——— (1991), 'Glimpses of the Other Africa', in Orlando Fals-Borda and M.A. Rahman, eds, *Action and Knowledge, Breaking the Monopoly with Participatory Action Research*, Apex Press.

Sobhan, Rehman (1992), *Structural Adjustment Policies in the Third World: Design and Experience*, University Press, Dhaka.

Task Force on Bangladesh Development Strategies for the 1990s (1991), *Report*, vol. 1, chapter on Poverty Alleviation.

Tilakaratna, Susanta (1985), *The Animator in Participatory Rural Development: Experiences from Sri Lanka,* World Employment Programme, Research Working Paper No. 37, ILO, Geneva.

——— (1989), *Retrieval of Roots of Self-reliant Development: Some Experiences from Thailand*, World Employment Programme, Research Working Paper No. 49, ILO, Geneva.

UNDP (1993), *Human Development Report 1993*, Oxford University Press, Oxford.

4

Disability: Emancipation, Community Participation and Disabled People

Colin Barnes and Geof Mercer

Introduction

Disabled people are 'oppressed and marginalised in every country in the world' (Coleridge 1993: 4). Prejudice, ignorance and institutional discrimination are rife. Although disabled people's struggle against oppression has a long history, over the last twenty-five years it has proved especially effective in highlighting the full extent of 'disabling' attitudes, practices and environments.

Campaigns for equality and social justice have facilitated a remarkable expansion of community-based self-help organizations. The mobilization of disabled people and their allies gathered momentum around the world with the formation of Disabled Peoples' International (DPI). Moreover, despite recent setbacks by right-of-centre and extremist governments, the movement has acquired a trans-global voice which can no longer be ignored.

Changing Perceptions of Disability

The low status of people with intellectual, physical and sensory impairments is not unique to contemporary societies. However, material and ideological changes which came with industrialization from the eighteenth century altered the form of social oppression, notably by undermining traditional patterns of economic and community life. For disabled people, the new economic and social order presented major obstacles to 'normal' social interaction. One consequence was the increased regulation of disabled people and their incarceration into a range of segregated institutions. Non-disabled 'normality' became the necessary prerequisite for community participation (Oliver 1990).

The relative position of disabled people has changed little through the present century. They endure levels of economic and social deprivation rarely encountered by other sections of the population. Exclusionary practices in the labour market lead to poverty and reliance on the charity of others. The resulting feelings of dependency and 'lack of worth' are deeply embedded. The everyday experience of disabled people is aptly summed up as a 'negative reality' (Finkelstein 1993).

Disability is regarded as a 'personal tragedy' for those 'afflicted'. In practical terms, disabled people are treated as 'passive victims'. This outlook permeates government social policy, upheld by the mistaken assumption that people with impairments are 'helpless' and unable to make decisions about their own lifestyle (Wood 1991). This sense of dependency has been promoted, directly and indirectly, by the 'medical model' of disability. The medical task is dominated by the search for cures and treatments to restore the body to health. When this is not possible, it provides the rationale for building packages of mainly institution-based, 'special needs' services.

Parallel social policy measures involve ranking disabled people for benefits and services according to their functional capacity and assumed dependency. At the same time, the role of professionals in the health and social-welfare sectors as the primary gatekeepers in service provision confirms the public's interpretation of disability as a medical problem. Disabled people have widely charged that their 'treatment' by professionals is inappropriate, degrading and divisive (Finkelstein 1993).

Rejection of this 'victim-blaming' approach is associated with a growing endorsement by disabled people of an alternative 'social model'. This defines 'impairment' as 'individual limitation', and 'disability' as 'socially imposed restriction' (Oliver 1983). Hence, 'disability' becomes the focus of attention, referring to the complex system of social constraints imposed on people with impairments by a highly discriminatory society: to be a disabled person means to be discriminated against because of one's impairment (Barnes 1991).

Most importantly, the interaction of 'disability' with gender, race, ethnicity and sexuality highlight specific forms of oppression by individuals and institutions (Conference of Indian Organizations 1987; Lonsdale 1990; Killin 1993; Stuart 1993). In addition to the immediate harmful consequences of the medicalization of 'disability', disabled people are excluded from involvement in a wide range of social and leisure activities. Studies of different cultural contexts have demonstrated how disablist imagery and language are widespread, sustained by deep-seated fears and prejudices (Barnes 1992; Hevey 1992).

Initially, political campaigns focused on improving state benefits and special services; more recently, concern has been with securing greater independence and eradicating disabling social attitudes and environments. Yet the 'social barriers' model of disability has gained ground in a partial and uncertain way (Finkelstein 1991).

Some aspects of medicalization have been diminished, but the 'beneficial' effects of changing medical knowledge on disabled people are not clear-cut. Major developments in medical technology, including pre-natal genetic screening, with associated pressure on women to have abortions rather than give birth to children with impairments, buttress the notion that disabled people are 'worthless' (Morris 1991: ch. 2).

A further damaging consequence is that attention is diverted from the social and economic causes of impairment. It is often overlooked that malnutrition produces one in five impairments in the world today. Further significant causes include industrial accidents, environmental pollution, stress and exhaustion, physical abuse, war and violence (Abberley 1987).

Disabled People's Movements in North America and Britain

The struggle against discrimination, dependency and segregation – in such areas as employment, education and the built environment – had an impact from the late 1960s (De Jong 1979; Pagel 1988; Driedger 1989). The key elements in this process were initiatives taken by disabled people. Perhaps the best-known early attempt to challenge their subordinate status was the growth of the independent living movement (ILM) in the United States. The ILM championed the view that independence is not measured by tasks that disabled people can perform, but rather by personal and economic decisions that they can make (Zola 1982). Ideals espoused by the ILM resonated with the intrinsic individualism and self-reliance of American culture (De Jong 1979 and 1983). Obstacles to disabled people's individual and collective empowerment were seen as hostile physical and social environments, and the operation of medical and rehabilitation services.

A central objective of the American ILM was to create alternative provision, directed and run by disabled people themselves. The first Centre for Independent Living (CIL) was established in Berkeley, California in 1972 by disabled students. Core services comprised peer counselling, the provision of information on organizing personal assistance schemes, accessible housing, welfare benefits and advocacy. Visible evidence of the impact of the Berkeley CIL is that the surrounding area became 'so accessible that disabled people are just part of the everyday community '(BCODP 1992: 19). It inspired the setting-up of over five hundred CILs throughout America. These are of varying scope, some operating more as information and community centres, but all are committed to the vision of disabled people taking effective control of their own lives. At its peak, the Berkeley CIL controlled a budget of $3.2 million and employed over two hundred staff. But, as with other community projects, funding was drastically reduced during the 1980s as part of the Reagan administrations' welfare expenditure cuts.

In Britain, CILs developed in a slightly different form due largely to the country's excessively paternalistic state-sponsored welfare system. They were designed to counter discriminatory attitudes and practices by providing a 'clearing house' for advice, services and support. One of the first and most influential became operational in Derbyshire in 1984/5. In contrast to the American approach, it emphasized the importance of building partnerships with local service providers, underlined by its change of name to the 'Derbyshire Centre for Integrated Living' (DCIL). The DCIL focused its attention on generating services, resources and support that linked with seven basic needs: information, peer counselling, housing, technical aids, personal assistance, transport and access (Davis 1983).

By the late 1980s, the DCIL employed thirty-five staff and had a budget of £500,000. However, it too suffered from welfare cutbacks, with Thatcherite reductions in local-government spending resulting in a halving of its budget over a three-year period. Nevertheless, DCIL has achieved a considerable reputation as a resource centre operated by, and for, disabled people. Its peer counselling service has served as a model for other UK schemes (BCODP 1992: 19–20).

The Canadian experience of Independent Living Centres (ILCs) demonstrates further ways of implementing the basic tenets of the independent living philosophy. Qualifying criteria for Centres are that they must be consumer controlled; cater for individuals regardless of their impairment; be community based; and promote the integration and participation of disabled people (CAILC 1990). ILCs act as general resource centres as well as monitoring existing programmes and identifying unmet needs and areas for development (Enns 1988).

In order to become a member of the Canadian Association of Independent Living Centres (CAILC), the centre must develop programmes in at least four areas deemed central to achieving an independent lifestyle: information and referral; peer support; individual advocacy; and service development capacity. ILCs may provide additional services such as 'attendant care schemes' and transport. For example, Calgary ILC set up a computerized data bank, listing services available to disabled people including a registry for services, 'care' attendants and employment. Winnipeg ILC has developed sophisticated programmes for indirect assistance, peer advocacy and training schemes so that disabled individuals can become their own advocates (CAILC 1990).

The growing strength of the disabled peoples' movement is further illustrated by campaigns mounted in industrialized societies for equality and basic citizenship rights. In the United States, organizations such as the American Coalition of Citizens with Disabilities campaigned for, and monitored, federal legislation affecting disabled people. It also organized a nationwide civil disobedience campaign to press for the enforcement of the Rehabilitation Act which outlawed unfair discrimination against dis-

abled people (De Jong 1979). Subsequent action helped bring about the
Americans with Disabilities Act, 1990 – the most comprehensive anti-
discrimination policy yet introduced (West 1991).

Comparable campaigns are evident in other parts of the developed
world. Australia, Canada, France and New Zealand all now have wide-
ranging anti-discrimination policies. Some countries, however, still refuse
to budge. For example, the British Government now acknowledges the
existence of widespread discrimination against disabled people – due mainly
to the efforts of the British Council of Organizations of Disabled People
(BCODP), the national umbrella for organizations controlled and run by
disabled people – but is still opposed to effective anti-discrimination
legislation.

These examples of 'independent living' in both Europe and North
America illustrate the vitality of the disabled peoples' movement at the
local level. Nevertheless, further progress has been threatened by the
changed political and economic climate since the 1980s, with many governments adopting policies of retrenchment of welfare-state services and
expenditure. Although not specifically targeted, any reduction in (already
inadequate) services for disabled people is especially severe given the
backcloth of considerable unmet need.

Professionals and officials in health and social welfare agencies also
continue to resist the meaningful participation of disabled people in identifying their own needs and deciding on relevant service provision. Much
work is needed to overturn entrenched 'disabling' attitudes and practices,
especially in the case of people with learning difficulties (Walmsley 1991).

Disabled People in the Developing World

It is widely accepted that the majority of disabled people live in developing
countries, although precise statistics are in dispute because of the variety
of methods employed in defining impairment and disability, and in data
collection (UN 1990). Early surveys suggested that about 10 per cent of
the world's population – around 400 million – had an impairment. More
recent calculations suggest this figure is too high. Helander (1993) has
estimated that the global average for the prevalence of 'moderate' and
'severe' impairment is 5.2 per cent. However, the proportion (rather than
the number) of disabled people is higher in the North (7.7 per cent)
compared with the South (4.5 per cent).

The combination of very high numbers of disabled people and low
economic development and poverty means that the problems facing individuals and their organizations are often very different to those evident in
the developed world. In poorer societies, where many people face a daily
struggle for basic necessities of life, disabled people are among the most
destitute, relying heavily on begging and charity. In such circumstances,

there are few opportunities for disabled people (or their organizations) to become service providers. According to the Zimbabwean activist Joshua Malinga:

> While people in the rich world are talking about Independent Living and improved services we are talking about survival. (quoted in Baird 1992: 7)

This has stimulated the exploration of alternative forms of self-help. The complaint has been that Western-type services are insufficient and inappropriate to meet the specific needs of those living in developing countries. Most especially, the traditional institution-based support has been criticized as too urban-based, separated from community organizations, and overreliant on highly trained professionals. Even so, only about 2 per cent of disabled people in urban areas currently receive institution-based services, with provision for rural dwellers almost nonexistent. The provision of institution-based services would consume 'more than the total health and education budgets of most developing countries if serious attempts were made to meet the needs of all disabled persons' (O'Toole 1993: 199). Hence the significance attached to generating alternative models of service delivery which demonstrate greater efficiency and effectiveness.

Community-led initiatives have thus become increasingly favoured. At the international level, the 1980 Brandt Commission Report emphasized the importance of egalitarian reforms and increased participation by those living in the poorer 'South' to stimulate economic and wider social development, whilst the World Health Organization promoted the adoption of primary health care (Macdonald 1993). The same reasoning led to increased support for community-based rehabilitation (CBR) to improve the quality of life of disabled people (Coleridge 1993; O'Toole 1993).

CBR highlights community involvement and self-reliance, and emphasizes the utilization of local resources, skills and enthusiasm. Considerable significance is attached to the recruitment, training and role of the 'local supervisor' who, by a 'cascade' process, engages the wider community in the project. By this means, people participate in training disabled people, promoting positive attitudes and removing barriers to their participation in the local environment. In theory, CBR is the antithesis of bureaucratic, top-down models of community-based service delivery synonymous with Western-type provision. There is an emphasis on participation, equity and collaboration between different service sectors. The intention is to move away from a situation of little, if any, consumer involvement, towards a 'new partnership' with disabled people.

CBR's implementation has given rise to many innovative schemes where it has tapped the potential for community-based self-help groups existing in developing societies (Coleridge 1993). For example, Zimbabwe's Zimcare programme introduced a novel outreach programme to help disabled people in their own communities, including the production of a teaching package for parents of children with learning difficulties. In Kenya, the 'Family Support Service' built up contacts with disabled people and their families using a local self-help network (O'Toole 1993).

One of the most widely referenced examples of community action is the Projimo Project in Mexico (Werner, in DPI 1992). It grew out of an initiative to establish 'village health bases' from the late 1960s, evolving into a project where assistance was provided by and for disabled people. Teams of disabled and non-disabled villagers organized and trained other health workers, with professional help only accepted temporarily. The priority has been to encourage local skills and confidence – and 'owner-ship'. As Projimo has flourished, so it has become more politicized. The early rejection of the medical model of rehabilitation has extended into broader 'liberation' struggles and campaigns for social justice, with disabled people acting in unison with other oppressed groups (Werner, in DPI 1992: 64).

That implementation of CBR must be tailored to local conditions and needs is well illustrated by a case study of CBR in India. In 1988, Action on Disability and Development (India) persuaded three development organizations operating in rural areas to integrate social action on dis-ability into their programmes.

> The principle for each was the same: stimulate the formation of disability 'sanghams' (associations) in each village which would assume responsibility for the needs of disabled people in that village. The members of these sanghams would be disabled people themselves. (Coleridge, 1993: 161)

In practice, contrasting interpretations of the basic theme of giving control to disabled people were applied. These ranged from direct action and non-violent mass struggle, to service provision and training more 'orthodox' cadres of trained staff to work with disabled people's associa-tions. In all cases, it took time to convince disabled people, other villagers and practitioners of the merits of dispensing with the traditional, paternal-istic approach. Nevertheless, taking action for themselves has been shown to be a generally positive experience for the disabled village people included in the projects (Coleridge 1993: 161–7).

Nevertheless, community-based projects are not an easy or cheap option. Many have foundered because of lack of time, resources and internal conflicts. There is often a gap between the rhetoric and practice of community participation. Whereas, initially, CBR was contrasted with institution-based services, the 'mainstream' institutions and orthodox pro-fessional roles have often proved resistant to community-based initiatives. It is also unclear whether 'CBR can develop beyond a relatively small-scale, home-based teaching model into a nationwide community care programme' (O'Toole 1993: 204). Additionally, there has sometimes been an under-, or inappropriate, utilization of local resources, whether people, knowledge or skills. Often, traditional community-based responses have been overlooked or undermined.

Miles's (1990) review of how disabled Afghans have coped is instructive. He notes how people trained in Western rehabilitative medicine rejected traditional resources as useless and sometimes harmful. The years of conflict severely disrupted what few formal services there were, and disabled Afghans increasingly found inspiration in traditional, informal, community-based resources and remedies. These not only proved effective but had the added advantage of being culturally more acceptable and more 'ecologically friendly'.

Nevertheless, in a politically uncertain world, the progress of disabled people remains insecure. For example, when the Sandinistas came to power in Nicaragua in 1979, emancipation of disabled people was high on the political agenda. Disabled citizens were given civil rights in law, and the newly created 'Organization for Revolutionary Disabled' promoted a range of self-help projects. One was a cooperative manufacturing lightweight, sturdy wheelchairs selling at a third of the price of imported ones, and much needed by local disabled people. But the election of a centre–right coalition government under Violeta Chamorro, though herself a disabled person, stifled these developments. Crucial financial support was withdrawn and disabled people have resumed their earlier struggle for political recognition (DPI 1992).

In Zimbabwe, disabled activists have expressed disenchantment at the lack of gains for disabled people after the end of the armed struggle for political independence. It was only after much local pressure, and with international aid, that the government built a huge rehabilitation centre called RUWA, especially for disabled ex-combatants. However, this proved extremely unpopular with those placed in the centre, and after they protested about their conditions it was closed down. According to Joshua Malinga,

> Our problems were not solved by the war of liberation because ours is a different war altogether ... We want to be involved in the development process and not treated as charity cases ... We must keep working and using our organizations as vehicles of self-help, self-expression and self-representation. (*New Internationalist* 1992: 13)

But the rejection of the resources of charity organizations is not easy in countries where funding is difficult to obtain and governments are heavily in debt.

Moreover, the spectre of the worst sort of victimization of disabled people by governments in some developing countries has been raised by China's recent draft plan to prohibit those with selected impairments from marrying, while pregnant women with an 'abnormal foetus' will be 'advised' to have an abortion, and in some cases be sterilized (*Disability Now* 1994: 1).

Disabled People's International

There are few countries where organizations for specific groups of disabled people have a long history, with the number and range of such organizations only growing on a worldwide basis from the 1950s. This trend spurred attempts to form parallel international organizations. Early initiatives comprised 'uni-disability' groups, such as the 'World Federation of the Deaf'. Yet truly international organizations proved difficult to establish, not least because of the lack of resources for disabled peoples' activities in developing countries. However, around the world, disaffection grew among disabled people at the way in which 'their' organizations were largely dominated by non-disabled professionals.

The catalyst for change was the World Congress of Rehabilitation International, held in Winnipeg, Canada in 1980 (Driedger 1989). During its proceedings, a motion that disabled people should have 50 per cent representation on its executive board was rejected. In response, disabled people among the delegates set up what became the Disabled Peoples' International (DPI). Its potential role in promoting the interests of disabled people on the international stage was quickly recognized. In 1981, over four hundred delegates from fifty-three countries attended DPI's first World Congress in Singapore (DPI 1982).

In 1992, the third World Congress took place in Vancouver. It coincided with the organization of Independence 92 at the end of the United Nations (UN) Decade of Disabled People. Together, these constituted 'the largest meeting of disabled people ever held, and included all disabled groups' (DPI 1992: 3). DPI now includes members from over one hundred countries, with the emphasis on encouraging national 'umbrella' organizations. Whereas the first congress in 1980 in Winnipeg 'launched a new social movement onto the world stage, the events of April 1992 in Vancouver demonstrated that this movement has come of age' (DPI 1992: 3).

DPI has now assumed a key leadership role in the disabled peoples' movement. It acts as an advocate of disabled people, lobbying governments and international organizations, having been granted consultative status with the UN, UNESCO and the ILO. The World Programme of Action Concerning Disabled Persons was ratified as the UN's official policy statement in 1982. This was enthusiastically described by disabled activists as a 'declaration for emancipation' (Driedger 1989: 97). It called for full participation by disabled people in society, although DPI's high expectations have been frustrated because its implementation was left to individual governments. In this and other campaigns, DPI actively discourages international organizations from adopting 'medical models' of disability.

DPI has been charged with liberating disabled people worldwide, concentrating its activities in developing countries where disabled people often lack any form of support or care. This decision was prompted by damning statistics which indicated, for example, that less than 2 per cent of disabled people in developing countries had access to any kind of services (DPI 1992). In working to counter such problems, DPI has had an input to several WHO projects, including the CBR programme mentioned earlier.

Of course, involvement in the consultation process is but a means to achieving disabled peoples' policy ends. Much needs to be accomplished internationally to increase resources for combating disability, monitoring human-rights abuses and instituting action against offending member states. For example, whilst the UN declared 1982 the International Year of Disabled People, and made 1983–92 the Decade of Disabled Persons, by 1987 few governments had taken positive steps towards improving the condition of disabled people. The DPI has had to pressurize governments continuously, taking its case to the UN Human Rights Sub-Commission. Its final report on 'Human Rights and Disability' (UN 1991) expressed broad agreement with the complaint that disabled people had not achieved comparability in the effective exercise of their human rights.

DPI has won considerable praise for developing a global membership and raising the consciousness of disability issues among international organizations. It has campaigned hard for disabled-people-led initiatives, and has invested considerably in a leadership-training programme. DPI stands for cross-disability initiatives, and encourages partnerships and action between organizations of disabled people worldwide. But, as with many other international organizations, it has its own internal tensions and conflicts.

At issue is DPI's capacity to develop and maintain mutually beneficial links between disabled people in different countries. Forging alliances between disabled people and their organizations in the North and the South opens up possibilities, but is also fraught with difficulties. Tentative steps have been taken by DPI to develop common ground with other 'liberation' movements. The initiative for taking action on a wider agenda of social justice and peace opportunities has, as yet, mainly rested with disabled people in individual countries.

Most conspicuously, in Lebanon, a country devastated by war since 1975, disabled people launched the first peaceful protest against the fighting. This proved a dramatic event in the emerging consciousness of local disabled people.

> It was the first time in Lebanon, in the Arab world perhaps, where disabled people took the lead in championing a social cause. (Kabbara, quoted in *New Internationalist* 1992: 12)

A further challenge for DPI is how to meet the demands of particular groups within the disabled population. One issue increasingly occupying DPI has been the problems experienced by disabled women.

The disabled woman is still the worst victim of ignorance, poverty and disease and is placed at the lowest rung of the social ladder. (Shah, quoted in DPI 1992: 18)

Disabled women have few opportunities for acquiring status through the traditional roles of wife and mother, while labouring in the home and fields is similarly restricted (Driedger and D'Aubin 1986). For DPI itself, the problem is how to recognize the diversity of the disabled peoples' movement whilst stimulating collective action at both national and grassroots levels. DPI stands for the improvement of disabled peoples' social conditions and human rights: its success will be judged by its impact in advancing the interests of disabled people, particularly in the developing world.

An Uncertain Future?

Most disabled people, relative to others in their respective societies, experience discrimination, social and economic disadvantages, and lack of control in their daily lives. Notwithstanding these commonalities, marked contrasts in socio-cultural, economic and political conditions around the world means that the form and extent of this 'negative reality' varies. Against this setting, the growth of the disabled peoples' movement has been a remarkable feature of the last two decades – in both 'developed' and 'developing' societies. In the more industrialized North, campaigns have focused on the achievement of 'independent living' as well as 'full participation and equality' for disabled people. In comparison, economic conditions in the South have led disabled people to emphasize a different strategy in their struggle for emancipation – notably, the significance of community-based initiatives for economic participation and equality.

Disabled people have engaged in increasing numbers in social and political campaigns against deeply entrenched prejudice and institutional discrimination. Yet without some major realignment in the balance of economic power between the North and the South, the prospects for further change, particularly in developing societies, remain bleak and many battles remain to be fought. Nevertheless, the paramount accomplishment of the disabled peoples' movement – including the DPI – is that the 'conventional wisdom' about the treatment and contribution of disabled people has been comprehensively attacked, with more and more governments in every continent forced to acknowledge that demands for basic human rights and empowerment in their everyday lives should no longer be ignored.

References

Abberley, P. (1987), 'The Concept of Oppression and the Development of a Social Theory of Disability', *Disability, Handicap and Society*, vol. 2, no. 1, pp. 5–20.

Albang, T.B. (1987), 'Disablement, Disability and Nigerian Society', *Disability, Handicap and Society*, vol. 3, no. 1, pp. 71–8.

Baird, V. (1992), 'Difference and Defiance', *New Internationalist*, July, pp. 4–7.

Barnes, C. (1991), *Disabled People in Britain and Discrimination*, Hurst and Co., in association with the British Council of Organizations of Disabled People, London.

———— (1992), *Disabling Imagery and the Media*, British Council of Organizations of Disabled People, Belper.

BCODP (1992), 'Centres for Independent Living', *Rights Not Charity*, vol. 1, no. 2.

Brandt, W. (1980), *North–South: A Programme for Survival*, Pan Books, London.

CAILC (1990), *A Guide to Independent Living Centres*, Canadian Association of Independent Living Centres, Ottawa.

Coleridge, P. (1993), *Disability, Liberation and Development*, Oxfam, Oxford.

Conference of Indian Organizations (1987), *Double Bind: To be Disabled and Asian*, Conference of Indian Organizations, London.

Davis, K. (1983), *Consumer Participation in Service Design, Delivery and Control*, Derbyshire Coalition of Disabled People, Derby.

———— (1993), 'On the Movement', in J. Swain, V. Finkelstein, S. French and M. Oliver, eds, *Disabling Barriers – Enabling Environments*, Sage, in association with the Open University, London.

De Jong, G. (1979), 'Independent Living: From Social Movement to Analytic Paradigm', *Archives of Physical Medicine and Rehabilitation* 60, pp. 435–51.

———— (1983), 'The Movement for Independent Living: Origins, Ideology and Implications for Disability Research', in A. Brechin, P. Liddiard and J. Swain, eds, *Handicap in a Social World*, Hodder and Stoughton, in association with the Open University, Milton Keynes.

Disability Now (1994), 'Mass Abortion Call on China's Monstrous Plan', February, p. 1.

DPI (1982), *Disabled Peoples' International: Proceedings of the First World Congress*, Disabled Peoples' International, Winnipeg.

———— (1992), *Equalisation of Opportunities: Proceedings of the Third World Congress of Disabled Peoples' International*, Disabled Peoples' International, Winnipeg.

Driedger, D. (1989), *The Last Civil Rights Movement*, Hurst and Co., London.

Driedger, D. and A. D'Aubin (1986), 'Disabled Women: International Profiles', *Caliper* XLI, pp. 16–19.

Enns, H. (1988), 'The Historical Development of Attitudes Toward the Handicapped: A Framework for Change', in A. D'Aubin, ed., *Defining the Parameters of Independent Living*, COPOH, Winnipeg.

Finkelstein, V. (1991), 'Disability: An Administrative Challenge?' in M. Oliver, ed., *Social Work: Disabled People and Disabling Environments*, Jessica Kingsley, London.

———— (1993), 'The Commonality of Disability', in J. Swain, V. Finkelstein, S. French and M. Oliver, eds, *Disabling Barriers – Enabling Environments*, Sage, in association with the Open University, London.

Helander, E. (1993), *Prejudice and Dignity: An Introduction to Community Based Rehabilitation*, World Health Organization, Geneva.

Helander, E., P. Mendis, G. Nelson and A. Goerdt (1989), *Training the Disabled in the Community*, World Health Organization, Geneva.

Hevey, D. (1992), *The Creatures Time Forgot: Photography and Disability Imagery*, Routledge, London.

Killin, D. (1993), 'Independent Living, Personal Assistance and Disabled Lesbians and Disabled Gay Men', in C. Barnes, ed., *Making Our Own Choices*, British Council of Organizations of Disabled People, Belper.

Lonsdale, S. (1990), *Women and Disability*, Macmillan, London.

Macdonald, J.J. (1993), *Primary Health Care*, Earthscan, London.

Malinga, J. (1992), 'Liberation: A Different War', *New Internationalist*, special issue: 'Disabled Lives: Difference and Defiance', no. 233, July.

Miles, M. (1990), 'Disability and Afghan Reconstruction: Some Policy Issues', *Disability, Handicap and Society*, vol. 5, no. 3, pp. 257–68.

Morris, J. (1991), *Pride Against Prejudice*, The Women's Press, London.

Oliver, M. (1983), *Social Work with Disabled People*, Macmillan, London.

——— (1990), *The Politics of Disablement*, Macmillan, London.

O'Toole, B. (1993), 'Community-based Rehabilitation', in P. Mittler, R. Brouillette and D. Harris, eds, *World Yearbook of Education: Special Needs Education*, Kogan Page, London.

Pagel, M. (1988) *On Our Own Behalf*, Greater Manchester Coalition of Disabled People, Manchester.

Stuart, A. (1993), 'Double Oppression: An Appropriate Starting Point' in J. Swain, V. Finkelstein, S. French and M. Oliver, eds, *Disabling Barriers – Enabling Environments*, Sage, in association with the Open University, London.

United Nations (UN) (1990), *Disability Statistics Compendium*, United Nations, New York.

——— Economic and Social Council, Commission on Human Rights (1991), *Human Rights and Disability*, Final report prepared by Mr Leandro Despouy, Special Rapporteur, July 1991, United Nations, New York.

Walmsley, J. (1991), 'Talking to Top People: Some Issues Relating to the Citizenship of People with Learning Difficulties', *Disability, Handicap and Society*, vol. 6, no. 3, pp. 219–31.

Werner, P. (1987), *Disabled Village Children*, Hesperian Foundation, Palo Alto, Calif.

West, J. (1992), *The Americans with Disabilities Act: From Policy to Practice*, Cambridge University Press, Cambridge.

Wood, R. (1991), 'Care of Disabled People' in G. Dalley, ed., *Disability and Social Policy*, Policy Studies Institute, London.

Zola, I.K. (1982), *Missing Pieces: A Chronicle of Living with a Disability*, Temple University Press, Philadelphia.

5

Empowerment and Ageing: Toward Honoured Places for Crones and Sages

Jenny Onyx and Pam Benton

Introduction

Ageing is often regarded, unproblematically, as a fixed transformation that is totally determined by the biological processes of decline leading to death. The 'problem of ageing' then becomes an issue of dependency and care. In fact, nothing about ageing is invariant. The experience of ageing varies from one cultural context to another, from one historical period to another, from one class or gender or race to another (Fennell, Phillipson and Evers 1988). Within a particular time and place, prevailing images of ageing impact on and are affected by dominant professional practices and public policy. But these are also dynamic. Within Britain, the United States and Australia, current discourses of ageing are in a process of change and the policy ground may be shifting quite dramatically. The argument of this chapter is that the experience of decline and dependency is largely a product of particular structures and discourses that serve to perpetuate regimes of disadvantage among older people.

This chapter critically examines some of these policies, practices and discourses. We deconstruct these, and move towards an alternative construction of the social meaning of ageing, suggesting that the key to change, as always, lies in providing the conditions of self-determination, or mutual empowerment by older people themselves. We are not looking for a more humane regime that treats the aged kindly within a continuing dependency, but for examples of good practice in all cultures that can in the future offer more positive constructions of ageing. We argue for the right to autonomous self-determination by older people, for an honoured place for our elders.

Politics and Policy

Recent discussions of ageing and social policy are critical of the assumptions underlying state policy in Western industrial countries (Fennell,

Phillipson and Evers 1988; Townsend 1981; Phillipson and Walker 1986). 'The problem' is usually couched in terms of demographic trends indicating rapidly increasing numbers of old, and particularly very old, people, both absolutely and as a proportion of the total population, into the twenty-first century (Rowland 1992). The economic implications of the expected increase in dependency ratio (the proportion of dependent population to active workforce) then engenders a reaction close to panic. For example, the New South Wales (NSW) State Government Office of Ageing states:

> The number of older people in Australia will almost double over the next 30 years. The rate of increase should far exceed that for the population as a whole.... In the OECD region as a whole, there is currently one older person for every five working-age persons. However, it is estimated that by the year 2024 this ratio will be two to one.... The ageing population will have a significant impact on the Australian economy. (NSW Department of Industrial Relations and Employment 1990: 3)

These stark statistics are then juxtaposed with other assumptions about what 'elderly' means. As Fennell *et al.* argue, most discussion rests implicitly on a pathology model of ageing. 'We focus unerringly on poverty, bereavement, social isolation, loneliness, role loss, illness, handicap, apathy and abuse' (1988: 7). In the context of these facts and perceptions, governments make decisions about the distribution of resources, about the establishment or disestablishment of services for the aged, and about solutions to perceived problems (Townsend 1981)

There is a certain circularity in this argument, and indeed in conditions prevailing for the aged. The aged are defined as dependent and therefore in need of various forms of care or support, which serve to reproduce the very conditions they are intended to ameliorate. As Townsend, and others (Blaikie 1990; Meethan and Thompson 1993) argue, the development of ageing policy is a highly political activity, in which sometimes the aged themselves take a high political profile in arguing their own cause (for example, Combined Pensioners). More often older people's own voices are lost as 'the problem of the aged' becomes either one of welfare (the issue of care) or, worse, of medicine (the issue of disease or pathology), older people being objectified into an undifferentiated 'other' whose fate is determined by professionals working within a state policy framework. In this, we do not dispute the valued and necessary task of caring for the small proportion of frail and sick aged, or the importance of medical and welfare services for the community at large.

Common Images of Ageing

State policy and prevailing social consciousness of the meaning of ageing are entwined. There are several competing and contradictory images, or mythologies, of ageing that operate. The practices that emerge or are created by, or for, older people will depend on the particular image of ageing that is explicitly or implicitly held; but reality is often quite difficult to disentangle, particularly as the images tend to generate their own dynamic, and to some extent create a reality which mirrors the image. Different interests within society have an investment in the dominance of particular images.

The dominant image, consistent with the 'problem' of ageing discussed above, is of frailty, helplessness and dependency. There are implications for social class and gender here as the prototypical person is female and poor. The health industry is the main beneficiary of this conception of ageing.

A second image about ageing has developed in many Western industrial nations over the past fifty years: that of the superannuant, prototypically middle class and male, accompanied by his wife. He is young for his age, fit, healthy, financially secure and enjoying a well-deserved leisured life-style following retirement from a successful career (Morse and Gray 1980). Governments concerned with the 'costs' of an ageing population, and the superannuation industry, have an investment in this image.

There is a third image of ageing, not current in modern industrial societies but once a dominant image in European society, and which still has currency in Third World societies: the image of the crone and the sage. The crone is a woman of age, power and wisdom; the sage is her male counterpart. There is growing evidence to suggest that the crone held an honoured and core role in most pre-patriarchal societies: the repository of the accumulated cultural stock of knowledge, much respected as teacher, healer, priestess and lawgiver. Her image, to be found in early Greek mythology, degenerated within the authority of the medieval Christian church, culminating in the massive witch-burnings of the fifteenth to seventeenth centuries (Walker 1985). The sage never had such a powerful image, but neither was his image under such strong attack; he maintained some currency through medieval times in such forms as Merlin the magician. Some vestiges of this image remain among indigenous peoples – within the old village cultures of Asia, for example. The aged are seen as a respected and valuable source of wisdom and advice. As tribal or village elders, they remain integral to social life. They no longer contribute heavy manual labour but are nonetheless crucial in maintaining the social and religious life of the community, and may command considerable social and material power. However, with the process of 'modernization', there is evidence of falling status and economic power (Phillips 1992).

These quite diverse images of ageing carry important implications for the empowerment of older people. Image one, the dominant image in our time, provides the least capacity for empowerment. The frail and helpless old woman is utterly dependent on others. Image three provides the reverse picture and the greatest potential for empowerment; indeed the crone is already empowered. Midway between the two extremes is the superannuant. He has considerable personal autonomy, though at the cost of reduced social power.

Some Realities

It is sometimes difficult to identify the realities within these myths. However a growing body of research within the USA, the UK and Australia suggests:

- The majority of older people enjoy good health. Fewer than 7 per cent of older people aged 65–75 experience a severe disability. Fewer than 5 per cent can expect to require institutional care (Johnson and Falkingham 1992).

- There is little evidence of consistent serious cognitive deterioration among older people. While there may be some reduction in the capacity to process new material rapidly, such losses are frequently compensated by the increased capacity derived from experience (Lovelace 1990).

- Income and wealth is disproportionately distributed. In Australia, 74 per cent of couples and 65 per cent of singles over 60 own their own home outright (Kendig 1989), while 75 per cent of couples and 80 per cent of singles rely primarily on a government pension for income (that equals roughly 25 per cent of a single average wage). Evidence for the UK and USA is similar.

- Older people, particularly those under 75, are more likely to give assistance than to receive it, making an active contribution to the life of the community. Older people as a whole give more financial assistance than they receive from their children (Kendig 1989). They also provide more personal care services than they receive (Arber and Ginn 1990). The greatest source of care for the frail aged is other aged persons, usually a spouse or daughter. The fit aged also provide personal care to the very young, the young sick or disabled.

The experience of old age is very different according to three intersecting factors. First, the experience of age varies with social class. Former professionals are likely to have higher incomes and know about available services. In the USA the middle class literally buys an additional seven years of life through health services (Ryan 1976). Australian statistics routinely show above-average mortality rates for manual workers, and below-average mortality rates for professional workers (Russell and Schofield 1986). The middle-class aged in Western industrial countries are more likely to own their own home, to have access to superannuation and other income support, to be able to enjoy an independent lifestyle (Johnson and Falkingham 1992). They are also more likely to form active lobby groups such as Grey Power. On the other hand, for the majority of older people who lack independent income support, ageing is associated with poverty.

Second, age is strongly gendered. Because women have, on average, lower incomes and more intermittent paid work throughout their lives, and live considerably longer than men, they are more likely to be poor in old age, to live alone, and on pensions rather than superannuation (Kendig 1989; Peace 1986; Fennell *et al.* 1988). They do more unpaid personal care work. They are more likely to suffer the effects of negative social stereotypes associated with the dominant, negative image of ageing, particularly about physical appearance. Men are more likely to have access to financial resources and to personal care support.

Third, the experience of age varies with ethnicity and race. This is partly a function of class, particularly where poverty is associated with migrant status (AIMA 1986). Older migrants from non-English-speaking backgrounds, living in an Anglo culture, are less likely to have the opportunity to learn English. While they may hold a secure place within the extended family, they are also isolated, economically vulnerable within the Anglo mainstream, and less likely to access mainstream services. In most Third World cultures (including indigenous Australia) life expectancy remains very low, more like the life expectancy of nineteenth-century Europe.

Empowerment in the Context of Community Development

The concept of empowerment is located within the discourse of community development, connected to concepts of self-help, participation, networking and equity. Empowerment is the taking on of power, at both the individual and social levels. According to Rappaport, 'empowerment conveys both a psychological sense of personal control or influence and a concern with actual social influence, political power and legal rights' (1987: 121). McArdle (1989) defines empowerment as 'the process whereby decisions are made by the people who have to wear the consequences of those decisions'. People who have achieved collective goals through self-help are also empowered, perhaps more so, as they have, through their own efforts and by pooling their knowledge, skills and other resources, achieved their own goals without recourse to an external dependency relationship. However, McArdle's definition implies that it is not the achievement of goals, as much as the *process* of deciding that is important.

Participation is also a vital component of self-help and of the empowerment process. People must be involved in those decisions that affect their lives, thus gaining confidence, self-esteem and knowledge, and developing new skills. The process is cumulative: the more skills, the more the person is able to participate, and the more s/he can gain. However, poorly structured or unstructured participation may have a negative, disempowering effect (Blakely 1979). Participation must be the sort that facilitates learning, action and the achievement of goals.

What remains ambiguous in most discussions of empowerment is the question of self-sufficiency. How much must people do for themselves? The achievement of personal goals may require at least the following steps:

- identification of need;
- identification of options or strategies;
- decision, or choice of action;
- mobilization of resources;
- the action itself.

The term 'empowerment' is used, however, differently in various contexts. At one extreme, the conservative use of empowerment may be restricted to situations of total self-help. According to this view, empowerment requires that all the above steps be completed by the participants themselves, with minimal outside intervention (or material support).

The use of such intervention raises the issue of equity. Those who are most in need, not already able to meet their own needs, are generally those with the least resources of knowledge, skill, money or physical strength. Kotze (1987) discusses this in relation to community development programmes in Third World countries; the observation is equally valid here. It was assumed that communities in poverty had the capacity to find their own resources once the opportunity arose. External assistance might be used occasionally, but this should remain uncertain, lest the community become dependent on external support. Yet this approach failed to recognize that no community can live and develop in isolation from others, or that it was precisely this element of uncertainty that created an attitude of passivity, an accommodation to poverty, in the first place. Most importantly, the self-help approach failed to acknowledge that often the community in question simply didn't have the necessary resources on its own.

At the other extreme is the view, implied in McArdle's definition, that the only thing required for empowerment to occur is participation in decision-making. In terms of the steps required to achieve a personal goal, empowerment might mean consultation with the person or community in the identification of needs, and over choice of options. Everything else is done on behalf of the 'empowered person' by other (professional) persons. This kind of approach to empowerment attracts the critique of tokenism. Such an approach is often used with people with disabilities. It fails to recognize that as long as the process is controlled by others who have access to resources, then the process is actually disempowering (Rose and Black 1985).

These distinctions are extremely relevant in dealing with older persons. Both extreme uses of the term 'empowerment' can be found in the rhetoric surrounding aged care services in Western countries. The conservative economic rationalist programmes of privatization are about returning responsibility for the care of the aged back to 'the community'. This is the rhetoric of self-help, of local decision-making and control of services, including finding the resources to carry them out. Yet within this rhetoric is also embedded the other approach. Community care programs are presented as giving the client a choice of services, tailored to his/her needs. But the way this process is carried out remains firmly under the control of the professionals, who have discretionary control over scarce resources. The frail aged client can hardly be more than the grateful recipient of care.

An Australian Example of Empowerment

The Older Women's Network (OWN) is a grassroots movement, directed and managed by older women themselves (Onyx, Benton and Bradfield 1992). Originating in an education programme within the Combined Pensioners Association (CPA) in 1985, the Network has since grown dramatically and established groups throughout Australia. One of its project reports noted:

> The Older Women's Network is a community based network run for and by older women. It was established to provide a means through which older women could meet others with similar interests and to challenge the stereotyped images of the older woman. (OWN 1993)

Action within OWN to fulfil these aims includes a monthly newsletter and a range of formal and informal meetings and social gatherings. An OWN theatre group writes and performs sketches based on the lives of older women, in a variety of educational, entertainment and political settings. In addition, seminar series are run both for the development of older women themselves, but also to provide consumer advice to governments. As stated in the OWN report:

> OWN has a commitment to the belief that older women are the real experts in matters concerning their lives. The ageing of society has lead to the emergence of 'experts' who claim to know best what older women need. This has made it even more important that older women have a base from which they can explore and develop their own perspectives and work towards making social changes.... This means a move away from passive entertainment to active participation in events and in decision making. It means opportunities for women to share their common experiences and to actively strive for change when services and government policies are inappropriate to their needs. (OWN 1993)

Two Examples of Co-option

While OWN is an example of empowerment in action, the more common story is one of co-option of community action by the state as with the Home and Community Care (HACC) programme in Australia (Onyx *et al.* 1992). Community Options projects have a community focus, developing packages of services in cooperation with client and community care organizations. Outcomes for clients specifically include 'determination of care requirements on equal terms' and 'enhancement of a sense of independence' (NSW Department of Industrial Relations and Employment 1990).

Services are locally managed and delivered. There is considerable reliance on local voluntary management committees, in some cases on voluntary service delivery. Nonetheless, the planning and location of Community Options projects is centrally controlled, using national demographic and other data. While government officers claim to use community consultation, in practice – at least in NSW – community consultation and development are often superficial and cursory. In one fairly typical case, a local area was identified through the central planning process as being a high-need area. A local community organization was 'invited' to establish a Community Options project. This was done in haste, with little community consultation and despite reservations expressed by the local organization. There was considerable local anger about the imposition of the service and about the lack of consideration for problems of local management and coordination.

Like HACC, the British NHS and Community Care Act (1990) is designed to incorporate the needs of users and their carers into the planning and delivery of local services. The concept of tailoring services to consumer needs requires that decisions be made as close to the user as possible. Meethan and Thompson (1993) trace the process by which a local decision was made to close a nursing home and replace it with more client-sensitive support services. They identify three separate discourses and practices. The initial concept stated in the Community Care Act used the discourse of community development, with its emphasis on 'local', on participation by a range of players, and on the implied empowerment of older people themselves. The actual decision was made within the local authority, and was entirely presented in terms of an economic rationalist discourse, with the emphasis on rational resource allocation, based on 'objective' data and formal criteria. The reality had more to do with the politics of negotiation and compromises concerning conflicting goals and expectations among a number of involved players. These included local politicians and concerned professionals, but bore almost no reference to the consumers themselves.

In cases like those described above, the discourse of empowerment remains embedded within a medical and/or derivative welfare model. The professionals speak on behalf of the client/consumers and control decision-making. Their expert knowledge is privileged over the clients lived experience, implying that older people do not know what is in their own best interests, or that basically the interests of the professional and the client are the same.

It may be argued that issues of power relationships are central in the provision of services for the aged, and that conflict of interest is inherent in the relationship between service provider and recipient. The *pretence* of consensus is the main way in which coercion, suppression and oppression are able to occur in the name of care and service. The real differences in power and resources between service provider and client, and the interest of the service provider in maintaining their own relatively privileged position vis-à-vis their clients, is ignored.

Examples of Empowerment

The literature provides examples of positive action being taken by older people on their own account, many appearing to operate within an adult-education discourse. Most have been initiated by professionals. However, control over all aspects of the action, from planning to implementation, remain with the older people themselves.

One well-known example is the University of the Third Age (U3A), which began in France in the early 1970s, involving a programme of lectures, study tours and cultural activities, developed and delivered by the universities for older learners. However, the model as developed in the United Kingdom and Australia involves minimal association with existing universities, and is almost entirely developed and managed by autonomous local branches, drawing on their own resources of skill, voluntary tutors and venues. The dominant reason for involvement is to obtain new knowledge, while important secondary reasons are personal satisfaction and the social stimulation involved. While the U3A is probably more attractive to older educated people, only some 21 per cent of the 16,000 Australian U3A members had university-degree-level qualifications (Swindell 1993). This seems an excellent example of older people mobilizing their own resources to fill a hunger for new learning.

Other examples can be found in the area of cooperative housing among older people. Friedan (1993) cites several projects in California which combine private quarters with shared living areas and shared responsibilities. As she notes, the inhabitants did not feel constrained by conventional images of ageing and, 'remarkably, *none of them* fulfilled the age mystique of deterioration and decline into senility before death' (p 359). Even more remarkable is Saegert's description (1989) of Harlem housing options for poor blacks. 'Unlikely leaders in extreme circumstances' is the story of old black women who have led the successful establishment and management of cooperative housing in abandoned Harlem tenements. In both instances, the old and very old are able to 'do for each other' in a way that maintains dignity and an active life within the context of inter-dependence.

Specific small, local, ethnic organizations or clubs have been specially designed by and for special-needs groups (Fullerton 1988). The Hen Co-op is a good example of the achievements of a womens' self-help adult education group (Hen Co-op 1993). Another example, the European Older Women's Project, links women across eight member states, and assists the development of skills and knowledge to participate in decision-making at local, national and international levels (Sclater, Paoletti and Kysow 1993).

Dilemmas and Ways Forward

It is interesting to observe the way in which mainstream services have responded to self-directed initiatives such as that of OWN. There is often an overt use of the rhetoric of empowerment which is simultaneously subverted through a series of covert messages, often played out in the minutiae of human interaction. To give a small example, the NSW state government held a much-publicized 'Forum on Ageing', in an upmarket Sydney hotel, with plush carpets and excellent catering. Yet the actual consultation consisted of groups of up to fifty people with several of these 'small' groups running simultaneously in the same large room, thus making both hearing and participation very difficult.

On a larger level, the NSW state government has adopted the slogan 'Age Adds Value' while simultaneously reducing funding to basic aged services. At the level of local services, professional workers emphasize the importance of encouraging increased independence of older people, while they continue to play the controlling role in the determination of options, in the provision of services, and in the judgement of value.

One of the most difficult contradictions that an organization has to deal with is that between the requirements of social action and the requirements of political lobbying. Both are necessary for social change and the empowerment of disadvantaged groups, and the two processes should be mutually supportive. The reality, at least for older people, seems to be the reverse. Social action is necessarily small, local, interactive and grassroots-based, directed by and for the members themselves. Lobbying, to have a concerted impact, needs to be large, centralized, nationally coordinated, directed towards the powerful, using the language and tactics of the powerful. Those organizations that have moved into a national, coordinated lobbying mode gain a high national profile, but may reduce the active participation of members at the grassroots. This seems to have happened to some extent with Combined Pensioners Association in Australia, and with the US Older Women's League. In the latter case, once the central lobby office was established in Washington, at least some local self-help groups ceased or reduced their own level of activity (Huckle 1991). It would appear that local self-empowerment groups continue to be dependent on local participation in all stages of the action process, and are very vulnerable to co-option by dominant national groups. In Australia, the recent establishment of a national organization (OWN Australia) raises similar concerns about the future of local OWN group action.

Perhaps even more disturbing is the danger of co-option from the state. As in the case of Community Options, the rhetoric of empowerment and community development is used to increase centralist control, while devolving responsibility for service delivery. The underlying agenda of conservative governments is about increasing control. Once community development initiatives become visibly successful, all sorts of blocks, subversion tactics, or co-options are set up. This leads to a discourse of despair. Community development always seems to fail at the point of its greatest success. To the extent that it succeeds, it challenges mainstream power structures. Those same structures then seek to block, or preferably co-opt, the energies of the initiative, bringing it under state control and using those energies to provide cheap services. But are organized empowerment strategies always doomed to co-option?

One potential answer lies in coalition politics, the potential links that may be developed with other progressive organizations which share common issues, and a concern for the empowerment of · disadvantaged groups. Unfortunately, the experience among older people so far has been of ageism within other progressive organizations. Older feminists, for example, bitterly complain of the ageism commonly expressed within womens' organizations (Anike 1991; Copper 1988). The potential for cooperative alliances may improve with increased awareness of the issues of ageism.

Within the discourse of community development, the case of OWN in New South Wales probably comes closest to the ideal. Older women are in control of the process of achieving their identified goals. They identify their own needs and the constraints that prevent their satisfaction. They determine alternative courses of action and carry out the actions. They draw on whatever resources are available to them that are relevant to their particular purposes, both from within the OWN membership, and from supportive alliances outside. Different members may participate at various stages of the process. OWN does not see itself as operating in a self-sufficient vacuum, but neither do the women adopt a dependent or helpless stance.

The women of OWN form and use networks between themselves and with other services and agencies. They are proactive in seeking to influence others, locating additional resources to do so, in developing their own skills and knowledge, self-confidence and mutual support. They are clearly empowering themselves. In the process they explicitly negate the image of the helpless, hapless, useless old woman. They have not yet all explicitly embraced the image of the honoured crone, the women of age power and wisdom, although some are moving toward that. But most are claiming a midpoint, a space of dignified independence and self-determined proactivity. They may be in danger of marginalization or co-option by the state. But equally they are in a dialectic position with reference to the state, and there is evidence that they have already had some impact on both public consciousness and official policy directions.

References

Anike, L. (1991), 'Women Over Sixty', *Refractory Girl* 39.

Arber, S. and J. Ginn (1990), 'The Meaning of Informal Care', *Ageing and Society* 10, Cambridge University Press, Cambridge, pp. 429–54.

Australian Institute of Multicultural Affairs (AIMA) (1986), *Community and Institutional Care for Aged Migrants in Australia Research Findings*, AIMA, Melbourne.

Blaikie, A. (1990), 'The Emerging Political Power of the Elderly in Britain', *Ageing and Society* 10, Cambridge University Press, Cambridge, pp. 17–39.

Blakely, E. (1979), *Community Development Research*, Human Science Press, New York.

Copper, B. (1988), *Over the Hill: Reflections on Ageism Between Women*, The Crossing Press, Freedom, Calif.

Day, A. (1991), *Remarkable Survivors*, Urban Institute, Washington DC.

Fennell, G., C. Phillipson and H. Evers (1988), *The Sociology of Old Age*, Open University Press, Milton Keynes.

Friedan, B. (1993), *The Fountain of Age*, Cape, New York.

Fullerton, M. (1988), 'An Asian Haven', in New Society, *Grassroots Initiatives*, Bedford Square Press, London.

Hen Co-op (1993), *Growing Old Disgracefully*, Piatkus, London.

Huckle, P. (1991), *Tish Sommers, Activist*, University of Tennessee Press, Knoxville.

Johnson, P. and J. Falkingham (1992), *Ageing and Economic Welfare*, Sage, London.

Kendig, H. (1989), *Background: Directions on Ageing in NSW*, Office on Ageing, NSW Premiers Dept., Sydney.

Kotze, D. (1987), 'Contradictions and Assumptions in Community Development', *Community Development Journal*, vol. 22, no. 1, pp.31–5.

Lovelace, E. (1990), *Ageing and Cognition*, North-Holland, Amsterdam.

McArdle, J. (1989), 'Community Development Tools of Trade', *Community Quarterly* 16, pp. 47–54.

Meethan, K. and C. Thompson (1993), 'Politics, Locality and Resources', *Policy and Politics* 21, University of Bristol, pp. 195–205.

Morse, D. and S. Gray (1980), *Early Retirement – Boon or Bane?*, Allanheld Osmun, Montclair.

NSW. Department of Industrial Relations and Employment (1990), *Directions on Ageing: Employment*, Office on Ageing, NSW Premier's Department, Sydney.

Older Women's Network (OWN) (1993), *OWN Health Report*, OWN, Sydney.

Onyx, J., P. Benton and J. Bradfield (1992), 'Aged Services in Australia: Community Development and Government Response', *Community Development Journal*, vol.

27, no. 2, pp. 166–74.

Peace, S. (1986), 'The Forgotten Female: Social Policy and Older Women', in C. Phillipson and A. Walker, eds, *Ageing and Social Policy: A Critical Assessment*, Gower, Aldershot.

Phillips, D. (1992), 'East and South East Asia: Issues of Ageing in the Region', in D. Phillips, ed., *Ageing in East and South East Asia*, Hodder & Stoughton, London.

Phillipson, C. and A. Walker (1986), *Ageing and Social Policy: A Critical Assessment*, Gower, Aldershot.

Rappaport, J. (1987), 'Terms of Empowerment/Exemplars of Prevention: Toward a Theory for Community Psychology', *American Journal of Community Psychology*, vol. 15, no. 2, pp. 121–48.

Rose, S. and B. Black (1985), *Advocacy and Empowerment: Mental Health Care in the Community*, Routledge and Kegan Paul, New York.

Rosenthal, E. (1990), *Women, Ageing and Ageism*, Harrington Park, New York.

Rowland, D. (1992), *Ageing in Australia*, Longman Cheshire, Melbourne.

Russell, C. and T. Schofield (1986), *Where it Hurts*, Sydney.

Ryan, W. (1976), *Blaming The Victim*, Random House, New York.

Saegert, S. (1989), 'Unlikely Leaders, Extreme Circumstances: Older Black Women Building Community Households', *American Journal of Community Psychology* 17, pp. 295–316.

Sclater, E., I. Paoletti and J. Kysow (1993), 'Older Women in Action', *International Journal of Community Education*, vol. 1, no. 4, pp. 1–7.

Swindell, R. (1993), 'U3A (The University of the Third Age) in Australia: A Model For Successful Ageing', *Ageing and Society* 13, Cambridge University Press, Cambridge, pp. 245–66.

Townsend, P. (1981), 'The Structured Dependency of the Elderly: A Creation of Social Policy in the Twentieth Century', *Ageing and Society* 1, Cambridge University Press, Cambridge, pp. 5–28.

Walker, B. (1985), *The Crone: Woman of Age Wisdom and Power*, Harper & Row, San Francisco.

6

The Voluntary Sector Challenge to Fortress Europe

Pauline Conroy

Introduction

The social restructuring of welfare in countries of the European Community (EC) has generated new manifestations of power among voluntary and charitable organizations in Europe, which are increasingly demanding a seat at social negotiating tables. In this chapter, this new social force is examined in the context of debates about the social and political character of citizen participation. The issue of participation in community and social development in European countries is frequently overshadowed, it is argued, by the emergence of a hidden disenfranchised class or social stratum of non-citizens forced to cohabit with large numbers of social outsiders surplus to the social and economic needs of contemporary societies. These developments give rise to quite differentiated strategies on community participation and empowerment, including renewed interest in representative forms of participation in the social sphere.

The revision of the European Treaties might have provided an occasion to extend the powers of the EC in the field of social policy and human rights, to the same extent that powers in relation to political and monetary union came to be greatly increased. However, despite persistent lobbying by forces such as the European Trade Union Confederation, the Member States split amongst themselves and failed to deliver a unified view on social policy or on increased powers in relation to human rights. The result was a fragmented Treaty, thickened with 'opt-out' protocols, and a lack of clarity as to what European citizenship and citizens' rights might mean in practice.

The UK's opting-out from the Social Chapter of the Treaty on European Union was surprising only in that its widely signalled intentions had not been taken more seriously in the lead-up to the signing ceremony in The Netherlands. The opting-out has deep ramifications not just for the UK but indeed for all Community institutions that must address the consequences in the wake of the final ratification of the Treaties of European Union in 1993 (Commission 1993b). Most importantly, it is unclear how the European Court of Justice will rule and interpret Community law subject to two free-standing but complementary frames of reference.

While the UK was the most publicized and significant case of opting-out, the fragmentation of social policy at the instigation of other states is visible in the various Social Protocols appended to the Treaty. In these Protocols, Member States agree singly or jointly to opt out together from selected social measures. For example, all the Member States together decided to remove an element of pension rights from the scope of Article 119 of the Treaty relating to persons employed prior to May 1990, unless they had already initiated legal proceedings in their own country. The purpose was to limit the effect of the Barber (UK) Decision of the European Courts granting equal treatment between women and men in occupational pension rights.[1] This was not the only use of an opt-out clause in relation to equal opportunities for women. In another example, all the governments agreed in a separate Protocol that the Maastricht Treaty would not have effect in relation to that article of the Irish Constitution which bans abortion. This followed several years of litigation in the European Court of Human Rights (Strasbourg) and the European Court of Justice (Luxembourg) on the issue.[2]

In addition to the constraints imposed on the social policy of an international treaty, global economic factors have subordinated social policy and the theme of community development and empowerment to a minor, even residual, role. The optimism with which improved employment forecasts were vaunted as a consequence of the process of creating an internal European market has proven ill-founded. The 1988 forecast on the effect of a single market had been to reduce the jobless rate by around one and a half percentage points. Between May 1992 and May 1993 an additional 1.78 million Europeans registered themselves as unemployed at their local labour exchanges (SOEC 1993). This represented a 1.1 per cent increase in the unemployment rate for Europe over a one-year period.

Widening inequalities between classes is mirrored in growing disparities in regional incomes in Europe. Regional data on comparative per-capita income and purchasing power in Europe between 1980 and 1991 (SOEC 1994) reveal that inequalities have increased. Thus some regions of The Netherlands, Greece, Portugal, France and Spain experience a substantial drop in per-capita income compared to the Community average. Others such as Lazio in Italy, Hamburg in Germany, the greater Paris region in France, whose per-capita income was already above the average, prospered even further. In the UK some 30 per cent of the population now have a per-capita income of only 90 per cent of the Community average.[3]

The Emergence of the Non-Governmental Sector

One innovatory development of the 1990s has been the coordinated representation of certain European community sector interests at European level. The non-governmental sector of voluntary, charitable, non-profit and community-based interest groups has emerged as a third strand in Europe, expressing the official voice of those not included in governmental, employer, trade-union or farmer dialogue. 'Non-governmental' is an accurate description for what is otherwise a most heterogeneous coalition of interests.[4] In 1991 a coalition of the charitable, voluntary and social lobbies combined in a General Assembly to form the European Anti-Poverty Network. The members share an explicit aim to 'empower people and communities facing poverty and social exclusion, to enable them to break their isolation and counter their social exclusion' (Network News 1994).

Funded under a vote of the European Parliament by the European Commission, this new force represents the first attempt by those working with the poor or deprived of Europe to insert themselves inside official European policy-making. A (non-binding) declaration attached to the Treaty of European Union pledges the European Community to 'cooperation with charitable associations and foundations as institutions responsible for social welfare establishments and services' (Treaty on European Union 1992).

A parallel development can be witnessed in the hundreds of citizen and non-profit groups from across Central and Eastern Europe seeking to enter the Democracy programme of the European Commission and establish themselves as NGOs or non-profit entities or in other forms which had not previously existed or been allowed.[5]

The arrival of the NGOs has not, however, altered their share of power in terms of resources. Following a scanning of European Community budgets, Venables (1992) concluded that a mere 1.5 per cent of the total EC budget might be available for the use of voluntary organizations. The considerable and continuing resistance to NGOs having an official voice in the social-policy dialogue in Europe suggests that the emergence of this social lobby is far from being an uncritical incorporation of the voluntary-charitable sector into a new social division of welfare.

The restructuring of the mixed economy of welfare (Mayo 1994), which is being undertaken by giving greater preference to commercial, private, voluntary and informal arrangements for welfare, has been accelerated by the push of some governments to achieve the goal of European Monetary Union and reduce their public debt by controls and reductions in social expenditure. Perversely, this has prompted a part of the non-statutory sector, charities, lobbies and service organizations, to reconsider their global relationships. 'Community development practice is about being present when and where it matters', according to Van Rees (1991). The when and the where for a considerable number is, in practice, inside European networks. If this is one of the key paths for the representation of the interests of citizens, where does this leave those who experience exclusion and are deprived of citizens' rights, and yet who are the alleged beneficiaries of social Europe?

The Citizens' Option

The concepts of citizenship and citizens' rights provide a framework for discussion of the status of the beneficiaries and consumers of a social Europe. They do not resolve the question of unequal relationships between state and individual, but they do enlarge choices. As Kleinman and Piachaud so aptly argue (1993), the European Community has been singularly lacking and has given little attention to developing citizenship rights: 'Issues of social justice and equity need to be pushed higher up the agenda' (p. 17). This would be a view shared by the UK Commission on Social Justice (1993), which views citizenship as an entitlement to responses to basic needs. But this is not the only view. Citizenship for the disenfranchised and non-nationals of Europe is also viewed as a broader absence of basic human rights (Cassese *et al.* 1989) or a narrower absence of basic freedoms of movement and right of residence (Commission of the EC 1993d). The Economic and Social Committee of the EC held seven meetings to try and grapple with the various manifestations of citizenship which might be advocated (ESC 1992). Indeed, it has been argued that 'a first priority must be to distinguish a sociological concept of citizenship from the specific legal and political definitions of citizenship' (Scott 1993). It has been the sociological concept of citizenship arising from the debate on social exclusion and solidarity that has risen up the agenda in a number of European countries, since it carries the notion of social membership and sharing, of participating in a social heritage, and of an activated society at a time of growing disenchantment with institutional politics.

Social Exclusion and Social Rights

If participation and the concomitant concept and practice of empowerment are not widely used in Europe, this is less due to a lack of interest in the mechanisms, than to a concern to understand and analyse the causes of the need to fill such a democratic deficit. Depending on the causes identified, somewhat different conclusions surface as to the strategies to be pursued, if any, to promote greater participation or empowerment among the more disadvantaged. Quite divergent views on the structural phenomena of social exclusion are apparent within and between European countries (Room 1993). In France, as in the Treaty of Maastricht, for example, social exclusion has no official, legislative, regulatory or statistical definition. For the European Commission, however, social exclusion is a dynamic mechanism that goes beyond income definitions of poverty and refers to processes whereby individuals and groups are excluded from social integration, social consumption, social transactions and daily life exchanges and are forced out to the edges of the economic life of their country or region (Commission of the EC 1993e). Among the consequences are the slow erosion of traditional social mechanisms, following which numerous forms of social problem begin to manifest themselves. It is only when the latter problems begin to impinge, usually spatially, on the rest of the population that public alarm is expressed at pregnancy among young girls, casual crime, substance abuse, visibility of street people and racial tension. The paradox of the situation can be perceived in the attitude of the former French Socialist Minister for Labour, Martine Aubry, who, having graphically described the exclusion emanating from a dual society, affirms: 'Social cohesion is still strong among us because it has its roots in a long history based on institutions to which the French are very attached: the State [and] Social Security. Let us take care to preserve these achievements'[6] (Aubry 1994).

Attachment to French institutions is precisely what is disputed by many analysts in a rather public debate in France. Pierre Bourdieu (1993) and twenty-two colleagues have gathered nine hundred pages of interview testimony from the alienated of urban society as evidence of disaffection. The issue of empowerment is not posed by the authors. According to Rouaud, this type of absence arises from a surfeit of consensus. 'France', he remarks, 'at the level of policy is characterized by political unanimity (except for the extreme right) around the rejection of exclusion (the principle) but by political divergences as to the lines of action and means to pursue (for example, immigration).'

In Belgium, in contrast, the question of participation and power on the part of citizens, residents and beneficiaries of state and non-profit programmes is more open. This openness arises in part from the political-federal and cultural diversity of Belgium itself. A long history of community work and socio-educational action has generated a dense web of associations, groups, campaigns and initiatives covering entire neighbourhoods and cities. Within this zone, there is a tendency for the Flemish community to prefer concepts such as 'poverty' and 'most disadvantaged' or 'poorest' and for the Walloon-French community to prefer the phrase 'the struggle against social exclusion' (Vranken and Geldof 1993). Across this social space, a minority but influential debate around issues of power and popular citizenship has surfaced between local associations and public authorities. This has been described positively as 'opening up a negotiating space' (Georis and Verzelen 1993).

Notwithstanding British and Irish enthusiasm for the political practice of empowerment in community development and Franco-Belgian explorations of the subject, there remains scepticism in Germany. A community worker from Hamburg describes these doubts:

> Participation is the counterpoint to exclusion and may be set against exploitation, injustice and oppression ... participation as a strategy in the face of growing complexity may not be the best way to replace decisions taken on a representative basis. Participation in the form of organised representation of interests is much better suited to politicising interests and turning them into political decisions. (Carstensen 1993)

A similar caution is expressed by Lange (1993), who argues that participation also needs to be curbed on occasions; otherwise every attack on a hostel for immigrants would be regarded as a form of participation inasmuch as individuals are involving themselves in issues which concern them, are organizing themselves and supporting each other. In identifying the relationship of participation and empowerment to the non-citizens of Europe, Lange has touched on a core issue of social development in Europe.

The Fortress

By 1 July 1987, the date of ratification of the Single European Act, problems were crowding onto the intergovernmental horizon with regard to the free movement of persons between EC countries and in and out of Europe itself; these problems would become real once the Treaties of European Union were signed and ratified. Indeed by 1991 the European Parliament had begun to express alarm at the proliferation of cross-government, bilateral, inter-governmental, Council of Europe and EC working groups devoted to the single subject of controls over the movement of persons between EC countries and in and out of the Community (Fontaine 1991: 33). The volume of transnational activity in this domain is all the more remarkable given the relative lack of urgency or working parties on major issues such as poverty, racism and unemployment. In June 1990, the governments of France, Germany, Belgium, The Netherlands, Luxembourg and (later) Italy joined each other in signing the Schengen Agreement to provide for passport-free movement between their states in addition to mutual assistance in relation to drug trafficking, police cooperation, crime and extradition. Schengen adds itself to the Trevi group of governments concerned with anti-terrorism and crime issues, which overlaps with the authority of the group of European ministers responsible for immigration. These, in turn, overlap with the responsibilities of the European Police Office (Europol), which figures under Article K.1 of the Maastricht Treaty and provides for cooperation in preventing and combating terrorism and drug trafficking, international crime and certain aspects of customs cooperation.

Similarly, political asylum is addressed by the 1990 Asylum Convention of Dublin, agreed by eleven states; it provides that an asylum applicant accepted in one Member State must be accepted in another. Or, looked at in reverse, refusal of political asylum in one country means refusal in ten others. Social exclusion as a structural phenomenon that forces out specific social groups has led to a renewed focus on the absence of political rights for minorities whose political citizenship is non-existent or in question. Included here would be:

- asylum seekers in Member States: 420,000 (1993);
- non-EC nationals immigrating into Member States: 274,000 (1992);
- irregular migrants in Southern Europe: 1,200,000 (1989);
- Rom, Sinti and gypsy peoples: 2,000,000;
- foreign prisoners in Member State prisons: 29,000 (1990);
- displaced persons in former Yugoslavia: 21,000 (1993).[7]

The figures in the categories above are a measure at a fixed moment in time; they are subject to rapid and sometimes sudden fluctuations resulting from legal political changes. The size of the population in question is just under 4 million people (this does not include legally resident non-nationals living in Europe without the right to vote). Thus, in addition to the evident existence of a social underclass, one can speak in terms of a political underclass in Europe.

Spatial Ghettoes

The majority of the non-citizens attempting to enter and reside in fortress Europe would not be included in data gathered on those living in situations of poverty. Data on the latter include estimates of 52 million people living on below-average income (1988) and 20 million registered unemployed (January 1994). While the enforced mobility of the former would appear to contradict the fixed nature of the latter, there is in fact a forced coexistence of the two states. Non-citizens and poor together are increasingly compelled to share the same space and territory, the same informal and unofficial labour markets, and the same small hand-outs from social and economic integration programmes.

The internationalization of labour markets and capital have created new heterogeneous metropolitan zones of population in already undermined and economically surplus communities. In the absence of employment plans for the 20 million registered unemployed and the invisible non-registered unemployed women, there is a real danger that the informal labour market and economic integration programmes will be fused as a policy option among North European governments.

In a detailed appraisal and preliminary critique of Danish experiments with workfare, activation policies and 'everyone is needed' programmes,

Andersen and Larsen (1993) come down in favour of a renewal of the Danish welfare model with a stronger rights safety net for weaker groups. What they call the 'market conforming' model of social development, involving a reduction in transfer incomes, has already prompted street riots in France in 1994. A proposal to reduce the training allowance/ wages of young people entering employment programmes to a level below that of the official minimum income provoked outrage among graduates and had to be withdrawn. The introduction of taxation on social-employment-scheme training allowances attracted criticism in Ireland following the 1994 budget. Warnings against the serious difficulties that will arise from the 'topping up' of income from work with social-security benefits have been made in relation to the UK (Bennett 1994). In all of these developments, one observes serious attempts to welfarize the labour market for categories of citizens for whom no real jobs are available. Empowerment through the right to a job and wage is substituted with the right to a semi-job on a semi-wage. Research into the implications of these plans for states to intervene in the informal labour market does not appear to exist. The process itself will undoubtedly create new forms of discrimination and exclusion as the failure to obtain a job for the un- and non-employed is reinforced by failure to find a place in the integration scheme.

Conclusions

Despite a renewed interest in social policy emanating from European Community institutions, budgetary resources devoted to social policy remain relatively symbolic, thereby challenging the reality of a social Europe. All of the twelve Member States agreed to tolerate the UK's decision to opt out of social policy, and to accept the addition of other specific opt-out protocols on social affairs. The next occasion to revise this arrangement will be the intergovernmental review of the Treaty in 1996, for which some European social networks are already preparing.

The refusal of a strong European institutional involvement in social policy has not reduced the scale of social restructuring in relation to welfare in Europe, and in particular the re-weighting of the voluntary sector as a provider of welfare. This has created new and complex resistances and exposed the heterogeneity of the non-governmental sector. The strongest and most coordinated sector has been that of the voluntary and charitable organizations acting as a third voice amongst social partners. Community-based, locality-based and self-help groups and associations are in a weaker position, without the representational forms to articulate the multiple interests of their populations. Thus, category-based alliances, such as those related to HIV/AIDS, or to disability, have better opportunities of being heard and participating in European and national-level decision-making than geographically based more numerous populations.

The issue of the power and rights of non-citizens and yet-to-be-enfranchised residents has become a touchstone of rights in Europe in general. This is all the more paradoxical as European citizenship rights are extended to new Member States but denied to those resident.

The debate on social exclusion has begun to impinge on decision-making in national social affairs and social welfare; but a surface reading of the conclusions in national policies suggests that economic integration through individual insertion is frequently an unresearched strategy proposed in response to the arguments about the process of social exclusion. It might be equally valid to propose a strategy of social rights or a strategy to revitalize collective forms of local democracy. There is a risk that well- and long-evaluated strategies of community development will be drowned under waves of ever-changing local economic development and enterprise programmes.

In an era of extreme dissatisfaction and withdrawal from institutions, the concepts of citizen participation and empowerment of communities may well need to be tempered by new formulations of democracy and justice, including forms of representation, commissions, working parties, tribunals and citizen platforms.

Notes

1. See the case of *Barber* v. *Guardian Royal Exchange*, 17 May 1990 in Case 262/88 before the European Court of Justice, reported in *Official Journal of the European Communities*, no. C.146 of 15 June 1990, p. 8.

2. See Commission Européen des Droits de l'Homme, Requètes Nos 14234/88 et 14235/88, Open Door Counselling Ltd et Dublin Well Woman Centre Ltd et autres contre Irlande, Strasbourg, Conseil de Europe. See also: *SPUC* v. *Grogan*, Case 159/90 (1991), European Court of Justice, Luxembourg.

3. For example, per-capita income in Cumbria, Lincolnshire and Grampian was lower than that in central Macedonia (Greece) or the Balearic islands (Spain).

4. The coalition includes amongst others, Association of Charities, Caritas Europa, ATD Fourth World Movement, European Network of Women, European Network of the Unemployed, the EMMAUS movement, European Council of ADIS Service Organizations, the Salvation Army, the Quaker Council of European Affairs, the International Council on Social Welfare, the International Federation of Settlements and many others, as well as national networks from each Member State.

5. The PHARE Democracy programme (1993–97) of the Commission covers Poland, Hungary, the Czech Republic, Slovakia, Albania, Lithuania, Bulgaria, Latvia, Estonia and Slovenia. It includes support for newly developing NGOs and the development of anti-poverty measures.

6. Author's translation.

7. Author's calculations from various reports, including EC Immigration and Asylum Policies 1994; Council of Europe, Prison Information Bulletin 1992; EC Social Europe.

References

Andersen, J. and J. Larsen (1993), *Towards a New Welfare Model*, Forlaget Sociologi, Copenhagen.

Bouget, D. and H. Nogues (1992), *Observatoire des politiques nationales de lutte contre l'exclusion sociale*, A & R, Lille, France.

Bourdieu, P., *et al.* (1993), *La misère du monde*, Editions du Seuil, Paris.

Carstensen, M. (1993), in P. Conroy and N. Yeates, eds, *Beyond the Wall: Papers on Participation*, A & R, Lille, France.

Cassese, A., A. Clapham and J. Weiler (1989), *1992: What Are Our Rights? An Agenda for a Human Rights Action Plan*, European University Institute, Florence.

Commission of the EC (1993a), *Community Structural Funds 1994–1999*, Revised Regulations and Commentary, OOPEC, Luxembourg.

—— (1993b), *Employment in Europe 1993*, DGV. OOPEC, Luxembourg.

—— (1993c), *Communication Concerning the Application of the Agreement on Social Policy*, COM(93)600, Brussels.

—— (1993d), *European Social Policy*, Options for the Union, DGV. COM(93)551, Luxembourg.

—— (1993e), *Medium Term Action Programme to Combat Exclusion and Promote Solidarity: A New Programme to Support and Stimulate Innovation*, COM(93)435, Brussels.

Commission on Social Justice (1993), *The Justice Gap*, Institute for Public Policy Research, London.

Economic and Social Committee (ESC) (1992), *The Citizen's Europe*, Brussels.

Fontaine, P. (1991), *A Citizen's Europe*, Commission of the EC, Luxembourg.

Georis, P. and W. Verzelen (1993), *Projets Européens de lutte contre la pauvreté en Belgique*, Fondation Roi Baudouin, Bruxelles.

Kleinman, M. and D. Piachaud (1993), 'European Social Policy: Conceptions and Choices', *Journal of European Social Policy*, vol. 3, no. 1, pp.1–19, Longman, London.

Lange, D. (1993), 'Partizipation and Politikverdrossenheit', Department of Social Education and Policy, Paper of the Fachhochschule für Socialwesen, Reutlingen.

Mayo, M. (1994), *Communities and Caring in the Mixed Economy of Welfare*, St Martin's Press, New York.

Network News (1994), Newsletter of the European Anti-Poverty Network, no. 18, March, Brussels.

Room, G., ed. (1993), *Observatory on National Policies to Combat Social Exclusion*, Second Annual Report, European Commission and A & R, Lille, France.

Scott, J. (1993), 'Wealth and Privilege', in A. Sinfield, ed., *Poverty, Inequality and Justice*, New Waverley Papers, no. 6, Edinburgh University.

SOEC (1993a), *Unemployment in the Community*, no. 7, Theme 3, Series B, 1 July 1993, Eurostat, Luxembourg.

—— (1993b), *Statistiques Rapides* – Régions, no. 2, 5 February 1993, Eurostat, Luxembourg.

—— (1994), *Statistiques Rapides* – Régions, no. 1, Eurostat, Luxembourg.

Treaty on European Union (1992), Council of the European Communities, OOPEC, Luxembourg.

Van Rees, W., ed. (1991), *A Survey of Contemporary Community Development in Europe*, Opbouwteksten, The Hague.

Venables, T. (1992), in *Combating Social Exclusion*, Report of a Conference, 2–3 April, Brussels.

Vranken, J. and D. Geldorf (1993), *Armoede en Sociale Uitsluiting Jaarbook 1992–1993*, ACCO, Leuven.

7

The University and Empowerment: The European Union, University Adult Education and Community Economic Development with 'Excluded Groups'

Peadar Shanahan and John Ward

Introduction

University Adult Education (UAE) in Ireland, north and south, is fundamentally no different from UAE elsewhere in the so-called developed
world, being mainly concerned with continuing education and with those
who have sufficient resources to use university facilities in part-time courses
to better themselves as individuals. As Zwerling (1982) and Thomson
(1980) have suggested, adult education is mainly for the 'haves' in society.
The main beneficiaries are the universities, colleges and consultants which
serve their needs. The most disadvantaged social strata and countries
receive least resources for adult education. The vast bulk of UAE in
Ireland is directed centrally on individualization and reflects the structures
of society uncritically. There is little or no appreciation in mainstream
university adult and continuing education in Ireland, north and south, for
the warnings sounded by people like Zacharakis-Jutz (1988) that individualization is a tool by the dominant culture to foster utopian visions, riches
and glory, and personal freedom and power. Yet in reality, focusing on the
individual only to the exclusion of the role to which the person plays in
his/her social groups, and to the exclusion of the system and the structures of society which ascribe those roles in the first place, leaves most
people, particularly those marginalized by society through poverty and
unemployment, profoundly powerless relative to the state or dominant
institutions. Through the process of individualization, so dominant in
contemporary 'developed' society, collective resistance to dominant values,
institutions and structures is dissipated. UAE practice, like adult education
generally, in Ireland, the UK and North America is largely concerned
'with designing techniques that will change the individual learner's behaviour and inculcate coping skills to make up for what are claimed to be
objectively identified deficiencies' (Collins 1991).

Changes in European Union (EU) policies in relation to adult education, higher education, community development and interregional cooperation provided opportunity for resource-starved adult educationalists in Irish universities to look to Europe for funding (Shanahan *et al.* 1989). Thus, since 1987, Irish university adult education has developed programmes with 'excluded groups'[1] aimed at enabling 'community economic development' in both urban areas and rural areas with substantial assistance from the EU and the universities. To date, this intervention on the part of four university campuses has cost in the region of £5,000,000, of which 55 per cent originated from the EU. The programmes are organized by adult educationalists in University College Galway (UCG) and Maynooth University (Maynooth U) in the Republic of Ireland and on the Jordanstown Campus (UU Belfast) and the Magee College (Derry) Campus (UU Magee) of the University of Ulster in Northern Ireland. The intervention has created the Inter-University Partnership for Community Development (IUPCD) between the four university adult-education partners. (Shanahan 1993a).[2]

This chapter looks at the above phenomenon, focusing on the question of 'empowerment' of the 'excluded'. It is premissed on a critical view of 'advanced' capitalist society and on the contrasting natures of the economic and political systems within it and assumes that higher education in particular plays a pivotal role in the interaction between those two contrasting systems (Shanahan 1992a).

Theoretical Perspectives on Participation and Empowerment

University-validated programmes aimed at social change may be ideally and critically interpreted in terms of an attempt to create a 'knowledge democracy'. Knowledge, like capital itself, is in the hands of the few and is, in this information society, a most important form of capital. In such study programmes, it has been argued, 'excluded groups' and activists involved in local expressions of social movements acquire the various university resources (time, economic and educational and space, skills and so on) and cultural capital to access and create knowledge by and for themselves which empowers them in terms of increased resources, participation, and the assertion of their economic, socio-cultural and educational interests (Gaventa 1988; Fals-Borda 1991; Rahman 1993).

Excluded groups and the EU: participation as an issue

The global restructuring processes involved in 'the re-capitalization of capital' (Marris 1983) are reflected in the implementation of the Single European Act. These dramatic changes aim to promote the free movement of capital, goods, services and people throughout the EU and the world in order to encourage competitiveness and growth in the economy; but their effect, plus the additional effects of the deregulation and dismantling of public services, on certain population groups has been staggering. By July 1993, there were 17 million unemployed persons in the EU, and of these, 16 out of every 100 unemployed people were under twenty-five years of age while 45 out of every 1,000 had been unemployed for more than a year. (Commission of the EC 1993b). Compounded by structures of disadvantage like class, race, religion, age, disability and gender, the disadvantage of geographic peripherality leaves many regional population groups excluded from realistic participation in society.

In response, the more recent EU programmes are designed for 'participation' and for the 'integration of the excluded' (Commission of the EC 1989). A Background Report to the Commission of the EC in March 1993 (Commission of the EC 1993b) outlines the problem of social exclusion and proposes a new action programme to combat the problem. 'One of the main factors [in social exclusion] is poverty, but [it] also refers to inadequate rights in housing, education, health and access to services' (Community of the EC 1993b). However, while the metaphors of 'participation' and 'integration' signify notions and actions of a laudable nature and carry with them moral connotations of 'goodness', they also carry with them the potential of being used effectively for manipulative purposes (Rahnema 1992). They are based on the assumption that the 'excluded' want to come into this particular societal system. And while it is conceded that many individual unwaged and excluded people are grateful for anything from the system that has rejected them, it is assumed in this project that many other 'excluded', if given a chance to reflect and act collectively, would want to change that system and 'to make it their own' by addressing structural issues of their choice. In line with the radical tradition in adult education, our approach assumes that the traditional concentration on the individual further alienates many who find themselves, after 'going through' these programmes, without the 'promised' job.

Despite the substantial work done by the Council of Europe on adult education for community development in the late 1970s and 1980s, comparatively little effort is made in mainstream EU-supported education and training programmes to enhance and augment the power, knowledge and skill of the individual through collective/cooperative discussion and action with other 'excluded individuals' in similar predicaments.

Identifying an Adult-Education Model for Empowerment

The university unit from which this programme is organized was influenced by the adult-education/training approaches of the Quaker Self-help Housing Pilot Scheme at Chawama, Zambia in the mid-1970s and by its sequel, the World Bank-supported Squatter Settlement Upgrading Schemes in Lusaka (American Friends Service Committee 1975; Narine 1986). However, this tradition of 'enablement' was adapted and tempered both by praxis (people coming on to the Magee programme in the mid-1980s were 'looking for jobs') and by the dramatic international changes brought about by the 'recapitalization of capital'. A new model of adult education was needed, which allowed socially committed adult educationalists to argue effectively with authorities by using systems theory and new phraseology like 'enterprise'. The model which seemed to 'fit' best was that which emerged from the Council of Europe Project No. 9: namely, Adult Education and Community Development (CDCC 1986).

In order to clarify this type of university adult education, we use an adapted version of this EU model. We can speak of four 'tendencies' in UAE in general and in Ireland in particular, the word tendency being used to denote that all four categories derive from a unified source and that they overlap in many ways. They are established using two criteria:

(1) whether UAE is isolated from day-to-day practical concerns of 'excluded' people or whether it deals with and is integrated with such realities;

(2) whether UAE is geared towards changing those realities of 'excluded' people or whether it is not geared to changing those realities.

From this analysis we can make four distinctions in UAE in general.

	Cut off from Life	Integrated with Life
Not aimed at changing the socio-cultural and politico-economic environment	Tendency 1 'Academic'	Tendency 2 'Training'
Aimed at changing the socio-cultural and politico-economic environment	Tendency 3 'Professional education'	Tendency 4 'Empowerment'

Tendency One is characterized as 'academic' in the sense that it would appear to be 'cut off' from everyday life and is not deliberately aimed at changing society in any way. It is seen in (i) very academic and aesthetic exercises and artistic and leisure programmes of UAE and (ii) to a lesser extent in the curricula of access courses where the emphasis is placed on the acquisition of specific disciplinary skills of an academic nature, skills which will assist the individual in his/her aspirations for social mobility and the attainment of a degree.

Tendency Two is characteristically related closely to life, as in industrial training in the repetitive type of industrial production process. It is not aimed directly at changing the environment. This is seen in UAE in the training of people to operate specialized and sometimes prestigious prefabricated jobs of high complexity. Its counterpart in industrial training for operators is based squarely on behaviourist psychology. Basically, the individual is 'fitted' to a predetermined and specific task.

Tendency Three is characterized by professional education/training whereby the adult student is trained to act on other peoples' environments, not his/her own. This is UAE for professional development. It is oriented towards changing environments, but the environments it aims to change are those of other peoples – the clients who will pay for the service.

Tendency Four is characteristically involved in life and is directly aimed at changing the socio-economic, political, educational and cultural systems and structures in which the disadvantaged individual lives. This tendency has less to do with UAE aimed at encouraging meaningful recreation, broadening the quality of life for people, preparing people to advance in academic life or to prepare people for highly predetermined tasks, and more to do with facilitating social change through some form of collective-personal learning (Dunn 1971) by attempting to create an educational environment which enables individuals – and, through them, the 'excluded groups' to which they 'belong' – to empower themselves. The contention is that 'excluded' groups may be enabled to empower themselves if the UAE provision for them *primarily* exhibits the principles underpinning Tendency Four: that is, if the attitudes of tutors, the methods of learning, the organization of the programme and criteria for evaluation of project work reflects these principles. In this way, 'learning', teaching, training becomes capacity-building. In the words of a Southern African people, 'learning' becomes *uakana*, 'building each other', or *uglolana*, 'sharpening each other' (Rahman 1993).

The Magee Community Development Studies Unit

Magee College (UU) is situated in Derry (population 100,000) on the northwest periphery of Europe near the disputed and highly-militarized border with the Republic of Ireland. In the neighbourhoods from which students are drawn to this Unit, state and para-military violence has long been an almost daily experience. Neighbourhoods are divided between nationalists and Unionists, making the practice of adult education uniquely exciting as well as problematic (Shanahan 1992a and 1993b; Oliver 1989). Unemployment in Derry (particularly amongst nationalists) is endemic and historical. When the rest of the UK had unemployment of 0.6 per cent, Derry had unemployment of 5 per cent. The unemployment figure now stands at about 20 per cent rising to 70 per cent male unemployment in the Magee catchment area. Participants on the programme have their fees and basic expenses for child care (more than half the participants are women), travel and food paid for when they attend the programme three days a week. The programme allows the person to remain on unemployment benefit.

The Magee Course is a mixture of critical education with basic vocational training, validated by the University of Ulster and responsible to an external examiner. This curriculum 'concoction' is advocated by the Council of Europe for adult education with the long-term unemployed (Engelhardt 1990). It incorporates social sciences and Information Technology in its curriculum. It seeks not only to encourage critical thinking but to bring knowledge to bear on operational, organizational and managerial realms so that the tutors 'can move from the functions of advisors or evaluators to the actual execution of development plans and to daily problem-solving' (Cernea 1985). Forty unwaged people (mostly voluntary community workers) attend Magee for forty weeks each year. Three days are spent in the College and two days in the community, where it is the responsibility of Training and Development Officers to supervise and advise on their project ideas for development. In the College they take five compulsory theoretical study modules, one compulsory module on research skills, and choose from ten optional skills courses. In addition, they have joint education/training with University College, Galway; and an ERASMUS student mobility programme with twenty-one EU universities is available.[3]

The practical project (50 per cent) by the participant is a basic exercise in Participatory Action Research: that is, an effort by the disadvantaged group, through the participating person, to investigate reality in order to change it; an effort by unwaged persons, and the community group to which they may be attached, to gain control over their own lives, drawing on models of intervention offered elsewhere (Rothman and Tropman 1987). This is evaluated both by the tutors and by the external examiner. To date, the actual presentation of the project has been offered in different modes: written report/proposal, drama, video or photographic material. Criteria for evaluation include motivation, relevance to the group/neighbourhood, personal change and development, as well as the usual academic criteria.

Students and their projects

Three phases of the Unit's development reflect different types of student project. The Cinderella Phase of the Unit represents that period prior to EU support (1982–87) (McCartney 1988). The Innovatory Phase (1987–89) represents the pilot action-research project operated by the Magee Unit and the local Regional Technical College across the border in the Republic of Ireland (McClenaghan and Shanahan 1989). The Inter-University Phase (1989–94) is ongoing and incorporates three EU supports: ESF, INTERREG and ERASMUS (Shanahan 1990 and 1993a).

By the end of 1993, a total of 260 unwaged voluntary workers from urban and rural areas of the northwest of the province had passed through the Magee Unit, and more than 100 were involved in the rural development training in the west of Northern Ireland through the INTERREG-subsidized programme also organized by the Unit.

The Community House: a prototypical community economic development organization

The Magee Unit has formal and informal links with many community development/enterprise organizations (Shanahan and Crilly 1992) in its catchment area, developed since 1982. From our experiences of these organizations, we set out below a case study (within a case study) of a prototypical organization and the thematic issues, both operational and ideological, confronting it. For reasons of space, we concentrate largely on issues associated with resource management; but this is not to underrate the significance of other overlapping issues such as organizational structure, the planning cycle and the 'Troubles'.

The Community House is a registered charity, managed by a voluntary committee, traditionally providing a range of social ('self-help') services, including advice on welfare rights, debt counselling, basic home and garden maintenance for the needy, visitors for the housebound, recreational and catering facilities for the elderly. The House is funded largely under the ACE (Action for Community Employment) scheme, offering employment for up to a year to the previously unemployed.

The scheme funds the wages for most of the House employees and associated overheads, roughly equivalent to 10 per cent of the relevant wage bill. ACE funding has been frozen for some time, and it is becoming increasingly difficult to pay wages at rates which are acceptable to trade unions (the ACE scheme requires liaison with trade-union representatives). Members of the management committee of the House are sensitive to possible allegations that the House is becoming a medium for 'self-exploitation'. In addition, some members have deeper reservations about the nature of the scheme itself, which they regard as a political device for deflating unemployment statistics. They also argue that the continued reliance on government funding which the scheme entails leads inevitably to self-censorship. This, in their view, stultifies its potential advocacy role, locking it into the present socio-political status quo.

The House is unable to rely on the ACE scheme to cover all its overheads, and in addition it has to fund five permanent non-ACE staff. The House also 'employs' many volunteer workers who are reimbursed their expenses only. On the one hand, this amounts to a notional donation of extra resources which can increase the effectiveness of the organization. On the other hand, it creates a need for further actual cash resources to fund the extra overheads involved. The House has sought external – government – funding for, amongst other projects, its debt-counselling services, but has run headlong into the socio-political orthodoxies that require approved projects to achieve *financial* self-sufficiency in the longer term, irrespective of the value of their contribution to the local community as a whole.

The freezing of ACE funding, combined with real doubts about its long-term durability, constitutes a major strategic problem for the House, given its heavy financial dependence on the scheme. The management committee is considering ways of diversifying its sources of income, and in particular the prospects of accepting contracts under the 'care in the community' programme. The ideological misgivings which attach to the ACE scheme resurface in this context in acuter form. Many committee members believe that the community should be allowed to define its needs and priorities, that by cooperating with state agencies the House will become an active agent of *disempowerment*, and that the economics of the contracting arrangements will result again in self-exploitation, primarily through the rehiring of existing care workers at lower wage rates. The House policy of 'empowerment' means that it only provides employment to those who would otherwise be excluded from the labour market. However, its experience indicates that following such a policy of self-empowerment without access to appropriate training and consultancy support may be over-idealistic. There also exists, amongst both staff and members of the management committee, ideological resistance to 'costing' the House's activities, a concept characterized by them as the asocial dictates of accountancy. This play between operational and ideological motive is unsurprising, given that accounting practices are, by their very nature, highly ideological (Montagna 1986).

The House has also been responsible for the establishment of a self-standing community business, involving the provision of computer network services, for community groups. The business has grown steadily, but in the manager's view it now requires substantial capital investment if it is to realize its full potential. However, he is finding that many funding agencies do not 'speak the same language'. The fulfilment of the business's 'social goals' means that the pursuit of profits and/or job creation does not take *absolute* priority; rather, there is a deliberate cross-subsidization between 'market-based' and community-orientated activities, as well as an emphasis on job satisfaction for employees and the provision of 'reasonable' wages as opposed to cost minimization. The funding agencies accordingly regard the project with some suspicion, and indeed a certain degree of incomprehension. The manager also feels (rightly or wrongly) that his working-class background and attitudes are the subject of prejudice, and is left with the familiar dilemma: to what (if any) extent should he compromise his 'ideological' commitment in order to secure the 'operational' viability of his project?

The EU and UAE for Empowerment: Contradictions and Tensions

The substantial funding of the Magee Unit is arguably related to EU policies on education and training and to interregional development; to the exigencies of mass unemployment, particularly in the nationalist community; to educational mission statements by the university and educational concerns; to cut-backs in higher education during the Thatcher years. It is also related to politics: to the predicament of a government faced with a crisis of legitimacy and the consequent establishment of the Anglo-Irish Agreement (Shanahan 1994). Given that background, we can describe the Unit's work as a dramatic working out of contradictions in practice.

With dual funding, the programme incorporates two almost contradictory purposes. The purpose of the EU funding is to train unwaged people in a skills programme and so enable them *to acquire jobs (as opposed to creating jobs)* as quickly as possible – even if they must drop out of the course to acquire those jobs. Although the university, too, is imbued with a 'business ethos', it is also concerned with standards, academic rigour and substance; programme coherence for validation; administration; and, above all, the number of students graduating. In addition, two other forces may be mentioned: the agenda of the staff to create curriculum space for the creative and critical involvement of the 'excluded'; and the socio-economic and political environments of the Magee Unit, which are in constant flux. These four forces, at least, impinge on the development of the curriculum over time. One lesson is that an advisory committee drawn from wide sections of the disadvantaged communities is important.

From radical action to voluntarism for the state?

The adult-education tradition from which the Magee Unit draws its sources is twofold, consisting of: (i) the 'largely autonomous (UK) tradition in adult education and social action with its roots deep in working class history' (Martin 1987); and (ii) radical 'Third World' perspectives and practice in adult education. With this background, the Magee Unit illustrates the possibility of developing validated, non-individualized UAE programmes with EU support. It does so in neighbourhoods of extreme poverty, and in a situation where the state has a serious problem of legitimacy. When substantial EU funding began in 1987, the Unit made a concerted attempt to maintain a base in dynamic movements in the Derry community and the northwest of Ireland. To this end, and in line with James (1986), six full-time staff were appointed to the Innovatory Project (1987–89) (McClenaghan and Shanahan 1989), all of whom had immediate activist backgrounds (four locally, two internationally) and strong credibility with activists in local social movements – the women's movement, the alternative planning/social action movement, the cooperative movement and the ethnic revival movement. These staff in turn recruited many activists with whom they had credibility. There is little doubt, then, that in the first years of the project, particularly, the Unit opened up university resources to people 'attached' to these movements, and can reasonably say that it contributed to these movements without attempting to interfere with their ongoing locally defined aims.

However, the vast majority of groups using the Unit 'exist to obtain a better deal from the state bureaucracy rather than possess a commitment to radical social change' (O'Neill 1992). The same observer further implied that the Magee Unit is simply a training course funded by the EU, and one which acts 'as an appendage to the academic establishment'. While the observation is fundamentally sound, this does not apply to *all* groups who have used the Unit. Many of the most energetic 'radical' groups who continue to use the Unit address structural issues of class, gender, ethnicity and ecology.

Nevertheless, as a serious effort in Participatory Action Research, the Unit has failed. It can only claim that it facilitated what we might call *preliminary* PAR. The Unit has shifted substantially from a position of radical action to voluntarism for the state: that is, it has shifted from a position resembling Tendency Four (of direct involvement in issues of development with the 'excluded', some of which would be critical of the state) to one of Tendency Two (of providing uncritical social and other services for the state). It is also probably true to say that the Unit has come to be seen by some participants as an access course to third-level education; that is, it has shifted slightly from a position resembling Tendency Four (of direct involvement in immediate developmental needs of collective initiatives) towards Tendency One (of preparing *individuals* for mainstream education, a laudable, though non-essential objective of the Unit) (Shanahan 1993b).

UAE for community economic development with the 'unwaged' is built on two foundations, or two 'legs': the college-based education/training for many different groups together (the 'Blunderbus Programme'); and the community-based training for specific groups (the 'Rifled Programme'). The function of the Blunderbus Programme (leg one) is not only to enable self-confidence and impart technical skills; it must also enable community organizations to understand and manage the fraught balancing acts required of them in an unsympathetic socio-economic and political environment. In addition, the college-based curriculum must provide the educational space and time for adults to create networks, reflect on their own power and previous experiences of community development and unemployment, and come to conclusions on the local, regional and international socio-political contexts of unemployment and 'business in the community'. We now see the best way forward as coming about through collaboration between adult educationalists and sympathetic academics from the 'business and management' field. The function of the Rifled Programme (leg two) is to organize and provide informal developmental support and tailor-made training in specific skills for specific groups which are 'represented' on the college-based course.

The Unit has failed to contribute *directly* to regional development in the northwest. The fragmentary nature of community groups; their suspicion of state and local government funding; the power of political parties at grassroots level; the highly centralized nature of the NI 'statelet' and its need for control; the divided nature of the population – all made it impossible to create a regional 'Northwest Community Council' or 'Forum', tied into the EU. Such a grouping might have generated pressure from below to change policies and practices of government and its institutions in the interests of the groups and their constituencies. Nor was it possible for the various agencies (of which the CDSU was one) to cooperate together in the interests of their 'clients'; they too were fragmented, possibly for the same reasons indicated above. The result is that a new, embryonic 'Northwest Regional Development Authority' is being created by local politicians with the endorsement of the EU. These community groups had no *direct and organized* part in its creation.

Acting locally and thinking globally?

One of the most energizing developments for staff has been the development of EU and interregional and international links. This university intervention in adult education has involved the interregional collaboration of the four academics responsible over the years and has led Irish university adult education into the larger EU network group in adult education. Magee, Galway and Maynooth have been involved with twenty-one other EU universities in the development of a postgraduate common curriculum, and in student exchange. Within the European network, the three Irish universities have been accepted as specialists in 'adult education for community development', and links have been made with other networks in the 'Third World'.

The university as the arena for change: the real EU agenda?

EU policies on the role of higher education in the integration of the 'excluded', on higher education and training and its role in regional and interregional development, have all been operationalized in the Unit's work (Commission to the Council 1991). The Unit, too, set as one of its goals the change of the university itself. In Freire's words, the formal education sector itself was seen as an arena of change. We intended the university to 'become less closed, less elitist, less authoritarian, less distanced from the common people' (Poster and Zimmer 1993). There is strong evidence to suggest that the Magee Unit has assisted in such a process, attested to by the 'spread' of the Innovatory Project in Magee (1987–89) to four other campuses. Many people involved in collective activities would not have had the benefit of such resources prior to the intervention. With the attraction of almost £4 million of external funds to these universities, UAE for community economic development has 'come in from the cold' in terms of adult education and training. There is evidence to suggest that the Unit's programme has had some effect on the bureaucratic, administrative structures of the university institution in line with the notions advocated by Korten and Klauss (1984) and the World Commission on Environment and Development (1988). However, the Unit's work still remains marginal to the life of the university, despite winning a prestigious award and despite recognition from the university that the Unit 'has done much to enhance the partnership between Magee College and the community' (Partnership Awards 1990).

Conclusion: Evaluating Magee's Impact

It is beyond the scope of this article to examine the complicated question of evaluation (Eisenschitz and Gough 1993; O'Cinneide and Keane 1990). The Unit is presently piloting a methodology to evaluate such work. However, Shell UK Assessment Team, who evaluated the Unit's work, concluded that the programme enabled unwaged participants to develop confidence in their ability to influence through social change and 'to organise community projects into stand-alone co-operatives' (Partnership Awards 1990). This is a judgement with which we would concur: many community initiatives which created jobs have used the Unit over the years. However, like all small (and large) businesses, their longevity is often problematic. In addition, and on average, about 25–30 per cent of unwaged participants find some paid work within six months of the course, albeit of a temporary and low-status nature. At a less tangible level, the programme contributes to a more egalitarian society through the redistribution of cultural capital in the forms of knowledge, resources and skills in a validated programme of study with high academic standards.

On the negative side, the continuation of this EU, interregional and inter-university intervention is always in doubt, for it is largely dependent on external EU funding; the pressures towards job training and job 'acquisition' (of temporary and badly paid jobs) inhibits more creative approaches to mass unemployment; the work lacks prestige within the university and needs to be integrated into postgraduate programmes in development; the intervention, too, needs to develop a more strategic approach to the fragmentation of community economic development groups, if it is meaningfully to address the real questions of 'exclusion', 'participation' and 'empowerment'.

However, there is little doubt that this EU 'leverage' intervention in university adult education, in a situation of militant insurgency and a state crisis of legitimacy, has opened third-level educational resources to 'excluded' groups in Magee and elsewhere. It has provided opportunity 'to make both formal and community education increasingly democratic and creative'. The innovation has responded to what Freire calls 'a matter of fundamental importance': that is, the task of making education less distanced from the masses. And it has done so while upholding the standards of a validated university course.

Notes

1. 'Social exclusion refers to the multiple and changing factors resulting in people being excluded from the normal exchanges, practices and rights of modern society. One of the main factors is poverty, but social exclusion also refers to inadequate rights in housing, education, health, and access to services' (Commission of the European Communities, December 1993). See also Shanahan *et al.* 1989.

2. The support for the work can be seen in the context of EU policies of interregional cooperation; local or community economic development; poverty strategy for the integration of the 'unwaged' and the excluded; and EU policies on education and training. Its existence is also a response to the politico-economic situation in Ireland: the alienation of the nationalist population after the hunger strikes in the early 1980s; the establishment of the Anglo-Irish Agreement in 1985; and the many policy statements and funding arrangements associated with cross-border cooperation for development. At the time of writing, more than twenty full-time-equivalent action-researchers/Training and Development Officers/ Research Officers and academics are employed in community development education/training for the 'socially/economically excluded'.

3. Given the maturity and the responsibilities of the students on the programme, and given the fact that people are on the dole, we find it difficult to exploit fully this ERASMUS facility. Two of our (unemployed) students have, so far, taken up the exchange: one to Leiden University, one to Pau University.

References

American Friends Service Committee (1975), *Chawama Self-Help Housing Project*, AFSC, Lusaka.

CDCC (1986), *Adult Education and Community Development*, Final Report, CDCC, 29(86), Council of Europe, Strasbourg.

Cernea, M., ed. (1985), *Putting People First: Sociological Variables in Rural Development*,

Oxford University Press, Oxford.

Collins, M. (1991), *Adult Education as Vocation: A Critical Role for the Adult Educator*, Routledge, London.

Commission of the EC (1989), *Employment in Europe. Luxembourg*, Ch. 10, Brussels; see also Eurostat (1988), *Definitions of Registered Unemployed*, Brussels.

—— (1992), *Memorandum on Higher Education in the European Community*, Task force Human Resources, Education and Training, Luxembourg.

—— (1993a), *Guidelines for Economic Renewal in Europe: Frontier-free Europe*, July–August, Office for Official Publications, Luxembourg.

—— (1993b), *Background Report on Social Exclusion and Poverty: New Action Programme 1994–1999 and Report of Action Programme 1989–1994*, ISEC/B34/93, Jean Monet House, London.

Commission to the Council (1991), *Memorandum on Higher Education in the European Community*, Brussels.

Dunn, E. (1986), *The Nature of Social Learning*, in D. Korten and R. Klauss, *People-Centred Development: Contributions towards Theory and Planning Frameworks*, Kumarian Press, Hartford, Conn.

Eisenschitz, A. and J. Gough (1993), *The Politics of Local Economic Policy*, Macmillan, London.

Englehardt, J. (1990), *Adult Education and Long-term Unemployment*, DEC S/EEs (90) 4, Council of Europe, Strasbourg.

Fals-Borda, O., ed. (1991), *Action and Knowledge: Breaking the Monopoly with Participatory Action Research*, Apex Press, London.

Gaventa, J. (1988), 'Participatory Research in North America', *Convergence*, vol. 21, no. 2/3.

James, W. (1986), 'Tomorrow Is Another Country: Alternative Scenarios for Work, Leisure and Learning', *Changes in Working Life Opportunities for Learning*, Council of Cultural Cooperation, Strasbourg.

Korten, D. and R. Klauss (1984), *People-Centred Development: Contributions towards Theory and Planning Frameworks*, Kumarian Press, Hartford, Conn.

Marris, P. (1983), *Community Planning and Conceptions of Change*, Routledge and Kegan Paul, London.

Martin, I. (1987), 'Community Education: Towards a Theoretical Analysis', in G. Allen *et al.*, *Community Education: An Agenda for Educational Reform*, Open University Press, Milton Keynes.

McCartney, F. (1988), *The Extra-Mural Certificate in Community Studies at Magee*, MA thesis, University of Ulster.

McClenaghan, P. and P. Shanahan (1989), *Report on the Cross Border Community Economic Development Innovatory Training Project*, Magee College, Derry.

Montagna, H. (1986), 'Accounting Rationality and Financial Legitimation', *Theory and Society* 15, p. 103.

Narine, D. (1986), 'Urban Development: Housing and Community Involvement', in J. Midgley *et al.*, *Community Participation, Social Development and the State*, Methuen, London.

O'Cinneide, M. and M. Keane (1990), 'Methodological Considerations in Evaluating Local Economic Development Initiatives', 'European Seminar on Evaluation Approaches and Methods of Programmes and Projects Aiming at Economic and Social Integration', Associacao in Loco/CCE, DGV.

Oliver, Q. (1989), 'Community Development in Areas of Political and Social Conflict: The Case of Northern Ireland', *Community Development Journal*, vol. 25, no. 4, October, pp. 370–76.

O'Neill, G. (1992), 'Adult Education, Community Studies: Transformational Themes and Perspectives', unpublished report to the Magee Community Development Studies Unit, University of Ulster.

Partnership Awards (1990), The Reception for the Winners, Innovation in Teaching and Learning in Higher Education, The Partnership Trust.

Poster, C. and J. Zimmer, eds (1993), *Community Education in the Third World*, Routledge, London.

Rahman, M.A. (1993), *People's Self-Development: Perspectives on Participatory Action Research: A Journey through Experience*, Zed Books, London.

Rahnema, M. (1992), 'Participation', in W. Sachs, *The Development Dictionary: A Guide to Knowledge and Power*, Zed Books, London.

Rothman, J .and J. Tropman (1987), 'Models of Community Organisation and Macro Practice Perspectives: Their Mixing and Phasing', in F. Cox *et al.*, *Strategies of Community Organisation*, F.E. Peacock, New York.

Shanahan, P. (1989), 'The Cinderella/Fairy Godmother Factor in Adult Education: A Case Study', in W.E. Morgan, ed., *Power Policy Enterprise International*, SCUTREA Proceedings, University of Nottingham.

—— (1990), 'Inter-regional Coordination for Development at the Periphery: A New Role for University-based Adult Education in a New Europe', in *Towards 1992: Education of Adults in the New Europe*, SCUTREA Proceedings, University of Sheffield.

—— (1992a), 'Social Movements and the University', *Essays on Class and Culture in Ireland*, Community Development Studies Unit, University of Ulster.

—— (1992b), 'Towards a Knowledge Democracy?', *Studies in the Education of Adults*, vol. 24, no. 1.

—— (1993a), 'The EC, Irish Universities and Community Development on Both Sides of the Border: The Story of the Inter-University Partnership for Community Development', *Europe File, EH266*, Open University, Milton Keynes.

—— (1993b), 'Ireland: Serving a Divided Community', in L. Brook, ed., *Serving Communities*, The Staff College in association with The Association of Colleges, London.

—— (1994) 'Opening Address' and 'The Restructuring of University Adult Education in Ireland, North and South' in P. McClenaghan, ed., *ILSCAE Dimensions of 1992 Conference Report*, International League for Social Commitment in Adult Education and the Community Development Studies Unit, Magee College, Derry.

Shanahan, P. and A. Crilly (1992), *Between Street and State: Some Derry Co-operatives*, video, Elgin Productions and Community Development Studies Unit, University of Ulster.

Shanahan, P., *et al.* (1989), 'Between Popular Movements and Professional Manners: A Transborder Community Economic Development Training Project', *Community Development Journal*, vol. 24, no. 2, pp. 136–44.

Thomson, J. (1980), *Adult Education for a Change*, Hutchinson, London.

World Commission on Environment and Development (1988), *Our Common Future*, Oxford University Press, Oxford.

Zackarakis-Jutz, J. (1988), 'Post-Freirean Adult Education', *Adult Education Quarterly*, vol. 39, no. 1.

Zwerling, L. (1982), 'Adult Education Breeder of Inequality', *New York Times*, 22 August.

8

Self-Organization and Older People in
Eastern Germany

Prue Chamberlayne

This chapter describes the main organization for older people in East Germany from the late 1980s in the state-socialist German Democratic Republic (GDR) through the process of unification with the Federal system. Since few organizations associated with the old regime remain, its survival through the transition is remarkable. In the former GDR, Volkssolidarität (VS – People's Solidarity) aimed to strengthen social networks and mutual self-help among older people, whilst building intergenerational solidarities by involving youth and neighbourhood organizations in meeting older people's needs. 'Citizen participation' was mobilized through 'mass organizations', designed to integrate all sections of the population into the political life of the state.

The chapter interrogates broader claims and counterclaims of 'citizen participation' and the characterization of pre-unification GDR as 'fully-statized'. Such questions relate to issues of empowerment and democracy in Central and Eastern European state-socialist societies more widely, despite great and often underestimated differences between those countries. 'Totalitarian' theories of Eastern European societies centre on the absence of independent organizations of civil society, whereas 'pluralist' perspectives point to forms of interest-representation necessary to the maintenance of legitimacy and sometimes unrecognized by Western political science (Nelson 1980; Lefort 1986).[1]

'Totalitarian' and 'pluralist' views of such societies promote opposite prognoses for the transition to capitalist democracy. The totalitarian view implies a 'blank field': market structures, civil society and democratic culture have to be built from scratch, based on imported Western, liberal models. According to the pluralist view, social infrastructures were in place at both formal and informal levels, capable of developing into democratic forms, onto which imported structures should be carefully grafted. The 'blank field' approach has been characteristic of the West German approach to East Germany, espoused by many Western advisers in Central and

Eastern Europe and widely adopted by the new liberals, backed by popular illusions about the 'market'. The radical discontinuity implied by such a break may be responsible for a large part of the disorientation, loss of identity and insecurity which underpins the new nationalist authoritarianism in Central and Eastern Europe.

Spanning old and new regimes, VS is in a rare position to test the viability of 'GDR ways of doing things'. We describe its work under the GDR, when it boasted a membership of 2 million in a population of 17 million, organizing 197,000 active volunteers (Volkssolidarität 1991). This points to VS's strengths and its strong potential for self-organization; however, these were constrained not only by a centralized apparatus and political power, but by a chronic lack of resources and a legacy of adverse attitudes to old age. We then trace developments in the self-organization of older people in Leipzig since unification, contrasting VS activities with the new initiatives of the East German 'Spring' of 1989/90, following the removal of the Wall in 1989. Despite the enormous impetus for self-organization through the process of political change, and despite maintaining extensive social infrastructures, VS still suffers both from its bureaucratic legacy and from new forms of 'contextual disempowerment'. The chapter principally focuses on Leipzig, the second largest city in Saxony, one of the five Länder (regions) in East Germany, where the author has been researching 'cultures of care'.[2]

Volkssolidarität: The Old Regime

In 1989 Leipzig VS had 66,000 members organized in 250 local groups; the surrounding area had 11,000 members in 144 groups. Local groups met in clubrooms and organized social and cultural activities; they also ran the meals service for the elderly and a system of neighbour help for shopping, carrying coal, chatting, delivering birthday greetings. While neighbouring was voluntary, club leaders and those delivering meals were paid. Another section of the organization ran the poorly paid system of home-helps. From the standpoint of community development in the West, VS's situation seemed enviable. Partly financed by member contributions, it also received state funding, and was surrounded by numerous neighbourhood-level organizations pledged to helping the elderly. Young pioneers in the schools ran errands; house collectives and neighbourhood organizations helped with repairs and renovations; whilst local social commissions watched out for elderly people in particular need. These infrastructures were embedded in a society with a strong culture of 'helping each other out'.

Another positive feature of VS lay in the interweaving of formal and informal services. According to VS spokespersons, home-helps often began as neighbour helpers, their caring activities based on long-standing friendships. Moreover, volunteer neighbourhood helpers provided feedback on the home-help system. Abrams's inevitable 'distance' between neighbours, in protection of self-respect and against gossip, seems not to have pertained in East Germany (Abrams 1984; Bulmer 1987). 'We lived closely together and knew far more about each other than people do in the West, for instance in our work collectives.' Despite the known extent of surveillance, informal networks in house and work collectives exhibited a high degree of solidarity and intimacy. East German commentators have argued that alienation in the public sphere made relations in the private sphere more meaningful – local arenas offering welcome opportunities for relatively unpolitical forms of social engagement (Poldrack 1992). However, the potential of VS's locally rooted structures for effective community action was severely constrained.

Lack of resources

From the 1950s spending priority lay in production, though with great emphasis on health, education and child-care provision as facilitating services. The early 1970s, following (Brezhnevite) Soviet Union policy, brought 'the unity of social and economic policy', with a stress on well-being and consumption. The GDR, with its relatively strong economy, implemented this policy more fully than its neighbours, especially with regard to families and children. However, as the GDR economy went into serious decline in the 1980s, the widely proclaimed social improvements became seriously undermined, although the extent of disadvantage of minority groups, such as the disabled, remained hidden behind 'the veil of equality propaganda' (Hofmann 1991: 16).

Voluntary effort could not substitute for the professionalization of services for the most needy, and the growing numbers of elderly people only seemed to widen the gap between needs and provision, creating a situation in which VS was bound to 'fail'. Moreover, low living standards and poor services meant that a great deal of paid or voluntary effort was needed to effect basic tasks: carrying coal in buildings without central heating; carrying meals 'in the basket' for lack of transport; 'slopping out' because toilets were on half-landings; laundry for lack of incontinence pads.

VS depended on 'voluntary' contributions, collected through an openly recorded door-to-door system, as well as state funding. This was deeply resented. No household dared give less than the first sum recorded; and some allege that there was inadequate accounting for these funds. Motivation for generosity was also curtailed as local groups could only retain 30 per cent of the funds raised. Shortages of resources also restricted the scope for local activities.

Centralization

The self-proclaimed 'developed socialist state' of the GDR laid great stress on participation. 'Join in working, planning, ruling' was a prominent slogan, recognizing the need to promote individual engagement at all levels of society. But centralized control militated against the development of meaningful community action. For despite its alleged autonomy and system of internal elections, VS, like other mass organizations, was pledged to accept 'the leading role of the party', and chairpersons at district, city, region and national levels of the organization were invariably Socialist Unity Party (SED) members.

Centralized control reached down to local levels of organization, although it affected the paid service sector more directly than the voluntary side. In the late 1970s, for example, appointment of staff and allocation of clients in the home-help service were summarily removed from local to county level. Decisions were thus made without the personal knowledge of the individuals concerned. The constant stream of instructions from above sapped the energy necessary to pursue local initiatives: a residential home organizer spoke of demands for weekly reports on 'flu immunizations and of never-ending directives to mobilize voluntary activities by young people'. But she also claimed there was scope for those with initiative to work around these limitations.

This determination to circumvent bureaucratic impediments to participatory action illustrated the regime's dilemma. On the one hand, it espoused lower-level initiatives, since it needed to find ways of promoting more active engagement in social goals; on the other hand, it attempted to monopolize control. In local government, officials were exhorted to 'leave the green table' and establish 'closer' relations with citizens. Various local working groups were established in an attempt to improve service coordination. These included, for older people, representatives from every conceivable organization: enterprises and trade unions, mass organizations, local functionaries, and members from various tiers of local government. This model of 'complex care' for the elderly was pioneered in 1973 to achieve more differentiated, sensitive and coordinated services and to encourage self-help (Kondratowitz 1988). This could have been an effective instrument for promoting local planning and new approaches, as in Leipzig. But in the absence of resources from above, and if dominated by bureaucratic political figures, its output could only take the form of exhortations, bearing heavily on the hapless implementers.

Critics, inside and outside the party, many of them reform communists, saw in participation and higher educational levels in the population an inevitable dynamic towards politicization and democratization of the system, views widespread amongst academics and professionals. Other critics were more cynical, believing that the depoliticization of society through the retreat into the private sphere of 'niche' society had destroyed all sense of social responsibility and the will for collective solutions. For them, 'citizen participation' meant 'citizen exploitation' by an ailing regime. (Hankiss 1990; Meuschel 1992). The more cynical of these views appears to have prevailed, as expressed in the overwhelming majority vote for the Christian Democrats in the 1990 elections and in an upsurge of nationalism and neo-Nazism. However, disappointment with 'market' solutions and the experience of mass unemployment is causing many in Eastern Germany, as in Central and Eastern Europe generally, to reconsider their political choices. Collectivist values and solutions, and demands for more meaningful forms of democracy than the ballot box, are now manifest.

Ideology of old age

Despite the greater emphasis on social policy and on sociological perspectives in the GDR of the 1970s, the medical model, with its patronizing and dependency-inducing attitudes towards older people remained dominant. These attitudes had long, complex roots. In the immediate postwar view, all older people – unless clearly identified with party and anti-fascist activity – were depicted as victims of capitalism, redundant in the building of the new society. Their one political relevance was their witness to the evils of prewar existence under bourgeois society.

The GDR was imbued with a 'youth cult', as was clear in patterns of social spending. In 1989 average pensions still only reached 45 per cent of average net income, 55 per cent with the voluntary supplement, with a big disparity between male and female levels (Winkler 1990); and whereas spending on the 'baby year' for mothers and on children's benefits rapidly escalated in the 1980s, spending on older people remained stable. Negative attitudes to older people were internalized. 'Old people were treated like children or objects rather than as autonomous personalities', said one interviewee, who also objected to the paternalism inherent in the emphasis on 'care' of the elderly. 'They felt they had to be thankful...' Such negative attitudes perhaps crystallized round VS. Groups with higher political status and more education had access to different meeting grounds, whereas VS club users were mostly women on minimum pensions, too old to be capable of active participation, effectively constituting a social circle of the most helpless. Since home-help and meals-service pay was more a fillip to voluntary effort than real pay, it attracted women on minimum pensions or with small children. The service was unreliable: there was no back-up in the case of absence, and home-helps' wages were so low as to generate pilfering and dishonest accounting of hours worked. Condemnation of VS intensified after 1989. One (professional) informant said her sister-in-law had been 'literally slated with contempt' within the family when she took a position with VS.

By contrast, VS spokespersons estimated that 60-70 per cent of their paid helpers were deeply committed, helping out at weekends, often on the basis of genuine friendship or partnership, and tolerating appalling conditions. They maintained that only people with a feeling for old people would take on such work; that it took dedication to maintain friendly relations in many of the situations encountered. One VS spokesperson spoke of loyalty: older people knew that the state was unconcerned by their plight whereas VS stood by them, waging a persistent fight for better resources.

Some of the negative attitudes towards VS probably arose from the low social status of its workers and members, even though it represented the majority of older people. Commentators point to the homogeneity, even classlessness of East German society (Meuschel 1992). This over-looks deep divisions of age, exacerbated by low educational levels among older people as compared with younger age groups. Nevertheless VS built a widespread social infrastructure, mobilizing younger old people to help the more frail, and offering social activities and purpose to many retired people. Its structures held potential for local self-management, but this was undermined by the factors analysed above. At the 'turning point' of East German politics in 1989/90, its fate hung in the balance.

German Unification

Despite a huge fall in membership, in 1992 VS in Leipzig retained 15,000 members (compared with 66,000 before), and the neighbouring town of Halle 9,260 members. Leipzig maintained 150 out of 250 local groups, with 2,000 voluntary helpers, and it ran fifteen clubs, offering meals, social activities, welfare rights advice and travel opportunities. By 1993 in both cities the organization reported a reinvigoration following the low point of 1990. Halle, for example, had formed ten new local groups since 1990, making a total of 100, and produced a lively monthly newspaper. In both cities, VS had taken its place amongst the major welfare organizations,[3] providing meals, domiciliary services from 'social stations', old people's homes, and was taking on children's facilities. Its role among the statutory services was uncertain in 1990/91. During 1990 local elections, for in-stance, while a concerted effort was being made to discredit candidates associated in any way with the PDS (Party of Democratic Socialism, the former SED), and while VS was fighting for the right to stand candidates, the Western press ran a campaign accusing it of being a 'terrorist' organi-zation because it had given funds to Nicaragua. Its application to join one of the main Federal welfare organizations, the DPWV (German Parity Welfare Association), was hotly contested. Having joined, however, it became dominant within the DPWV, with prominent positions at regional level and much more administrative expertise than the other new member groups in East Germany. To many of these other groups, however, formed in the heyday of 'citizens' initiatives' in 1989/90, VS remains overcentralized and patronizing.

VS straddles incompatible camps. First, it aims to perpetuate the positive values of the former GDR, such as localized forms of mutual support. Second, it claims to counter the patriarchal nature of state socialism through 'self-determination', a key theme among the new parties and independent initiatives in the events of 1989/90 (Henrich 1989; Dölling 1990). Third, it has a place in the archaic Federal system of welfare organizations.[4] As a result, whilst freed from many of the old constraints, VS is subject to new forms of disempowerment endemic to the Federal system, and remains shackled by its own internal contradictions.

Internal divisions

The speed and terms of unification have not been favourable to the democratic process in East Germany. In the initial 'Spring' period there was the beginning of an open confrontation with the past, of grassroots-level debates within organizations, with open competition between reform communists in the party and oppositionists who had been under the umbrella of the Church. There was a process of diversification and inter-penetration as opposition groups broke away from party and Church, and for the first time came into dialogue with each other (Rink 1993; Wielgohs 1993; Pollack 1993).

The decisive vote for the Christian Democrats in 1990 and Chancellor Kohl's early offer of currency union led to a swift process of unification – effectively an absorption of East Germany into Federal structures. In this process any association with the old regime was vilified. As one commentator put it, 'everything that counted for something before is suspect now.' Many respected reform figures were discredited through links with the state security system: even critical reform communists became defensive. This created an unfavourable climate for debate in such organizations as VS, which continued to suffer from unclarified guilt and mutual suspicion, and whose personnel were unpractised in dealing openly with political and professional conflict. VS in Halle prides itself on having shaken free of the centralizing tendencies of its parent body. It has formed a legally and financially independent association, terminated and renewed membership by re-application, and dedicated 80 per cent of membership dues to local groups. But even in Halle, allegations of an inadequate grasp of the principles of self-organization persist.

VS is undoubtedly constrained by its own elderly membership, which feels comfortable in authoritarian structures. Moreover, its policy of recruiting staff from its own membership serves to build in conservatism

(Angershausen *et al.* 1993). VS organizers regret their failure to attract younger age groups forced into early retirement. The Halle organization is trying to break out of its social straitjacket of association with lower-status groups by collaborating in a higher-education scheme directed at 50 year olds.

Independent initiatives

Leipzig has offered a particularly favourable setting for independent initiatives since 1989/90. The proud originator of the Monday marches which led to the collapse of the old regime, the city boasted a wealth of new initiatives, which the incoming Social Democratic city council supported, boosted by its determination to be more radical than the Christian Democratic regional parliament. In the period of dual power between the Round Table and the old regime in spring 1990, independent initiatives exerted considerable local influence. The appointment of a range of equal-opportunities posts, including for gays and lesbians, date from that time, and many of the city-council personnel came from these new social movements. Lack of professional expertise is compensated for by enthusiasm and the lack of administrative bureaucratism. As one informant said in 1993, 'decisions which would take months in West Germany, can be made in minutes'.

Pensioners' organizations have figured prominently among independent initiatives in Leipzig and in city-council policy. The sixty-strong Leipzig Committee for Elderly People helped organize a demonstration for a 'pensioner-friendly state' in 1990, and has since held public discussions on health, housing and pensions, each attracting 400–500 older people. The European Year of the Elderly was celebrated in Leipzig, with an open day featuring facilities and organizations for older people. In 1993 the deputy director of the Office of Health supported twenty-six self-help groups, and the Disability Officer ran a workgroup of thirty-three independent and self-help organizations. Leipzig City Council prioritized grants to independent initiatives, and the Federal policy of encouraging temporary job creation posts assisted such developments. A new programme entitled 'Action 55' was planned for 1994, offering 'top-up' monthly payments of 200DM (£80) to those in early retirement undertaking voluntary work.

By 1993 none of this had made much impact on the primary problem of housing. Elderly people lived disproportionately in the worst housing, putting up with a lack of central heating, no lifts, even shared landing toilets. Lack of suitable housing means that many older people in residential homes who could live independently are not able to; and the privatization of housing has seemed to slow down purpose-built provision. Moreover, the energy of independent initiatives has been sapped by financial uncertainty and by the weight of administrative and legal requirements. The Disability Association of Leipzig, an umbrella group for a multitude of organizations, shrank from twenty-nine job-creation posts to thirteen full-time posts, and was struggling to fulfil Federal labour requirements and cope with procedures such as planning permissions. Many activists had exhausted their energies, or moved into city council posts. Mutual recriminations abounded, particularly between party and Church or independent oppositionists. One informant saw the problem as a failure to think big and seize opportunities: 'We are small and we think small.' The élan of the new politics had gone; new activists were not forthcoming.

From the inception of unification, Western commentators predicted that East German civil society would not be able to 'carry' the democratic process. Offe (1991) argued that West German institutions would fail to take root for lack of social infrastructures; others blamed West German welfare organizations for failing to recognize and graft themselves onto infrastructures already in place (Backhaus-Maul *et al.* 1992; Poldrack 1992). Prime examples of vanishing infrastructures were workplace-based welfare and social facilities, which included meals, holiday and social activities for pensioners, and polyclinics offering flexible, coordinated specialist local-level care.

Thus, although independent parties and initiatives abounded in the 'Spring' period of 1989/90, their energies have been sapped in the ensuing unification process. The emergent civil society remains weak. Many of the key activists are now in the city administration, from which much of the impulse for reform now comes. Thus ironically, the historical German tradition of reform from above by an 'enlightened' state has been reproduced, at least in Leipzig. For all the many benefits of support from above, this syphoning off of community activists inevitably weakens the impulse for self-organization.

The welfare organizations

In principle welfare organizations were well-placed to support and develop the independent initiatives.[5] But in West Germany they have a reputation of operating as a corporatist cartel inasmuch as they determine their tariffs with their main financiers, the insurance funds, as well as with regional and local government, and are accused of having elbowed out the 'alternative' movement of self-help groups which blossomed in the early 1980s. The DPWV has a tradition of sponsoring more radical initiatives; but in Saxony, as noted, it is dominated by the insufficiently radicalized VS, and has the insuperable task of supporting two hundred inexperienced member groups.

Welfare organizations did not consider how they might recast themselves in the new conditions of East Germany. While this is undoubtedly due to conservative and monopolizing tendencies, it is also true that the speed of unification left little opportunity to rethink their approaches, and that East German institutional structures, such as polyclinics or workplace-based services, were incompatible with Federal funding patterns. The accommodation of East German infrastructures would have required a considerable adjustment of West German welfare arrangements. In fact the opportunity for long-overdue modernization has been missed. In Leipzig in 1991–93, welfare organizations all felt overstretched by demands that they take on more domiciliary, residential and day-care services, family centres and drugs projects. Like the independent initiatives, the new apparatuses suffered from the weight of novel bureaucratic procedures. They dreaded the administrative complexity of impending means-tested charges and the enforcement of relatives' contributions in line with the principle of subsidiarity. They also feared that increased charges would lead to a fall in demand, and that financial controls would dehumanize the service. The days of home-helps chatting with their clients ended as home-help activities became tightly scheduled; only one hour would be allocated for a community nurse to make three visits. Lifts, invalid beds and disposable needles would speed up the work, squeezing out the opportunity for socializing. Sociability in work situations was greatly valued in GDR society, with little regard given to the 'low productivity' it might entail. VS and other professionals were acutely aware that in the arena of welfare services, tightened work norms would leave service users feeling more isolated and vulnerable.

Since VS could only preserve its organization and maximize its members' employment by joining with the Federal welfare organizations, it was not likely to present itself as a challenging force. In addition to taking responsibility for domiciliary services and residential homes, it offered an infrastructure of clubs and services to be maintained and utilized, and which could fit into the new welfare system. Its acceptability among traditional welfare organizations therefore took priority over its potential for community-action work and for improving its credentials with the new initiatives.

Conclusion

Volkssolidarität in Leipzig still dominates independent initiatives in terms of membership, its 15,000 vastly outnumbering the 1,000 of the 'Active Elderly' or the 300–400 of the Grey Lions. But it has not been prominent in developing a new politics of self-organization in East Germany. Cultural change has come from independent initiatives and the city administration. Nevertheless the broad infrastructures of VS are invaluable for the potential self-organization of older people. Doubtless the principles and practice of self-determination, inasmuch as they are realizable in Federal structures, will percolate through into VS, aided by the gradual ageing of a more educated population.

The interweaving of professional and voluntary systems formerly achieved by VS remains an important model for wider attempts to strengthen social networks and mutual self-help. So far in Leipzig, no formal relationship exists between VS clubs and neighbourhood help systems, on the one hand, and the social stations on the other, not even where the social station is within VS competence, although the social clubs do a lot of welfare rights and referral work. However, many former VS meals and home-help workers have gone to work for other welfare organizations, taking with them their knowledge of local networks and needs.

Most informants in 1992 roundly denied the possibility of the 'helping' culture of the old GDR surviving in the newly competitive and individualistic society, though by 1993 comments were less pessimistic. In general, unification dealt a blow to voluntary activity, since people became passive or engrossed in their own survival. Generational divisions became much sharper. But recession and mass unemployment have provoked nostalgia for the old securities, a new appreciation of the old solidarities. Thus it seems possible that the informal networks which were vital to the service sector in the former GDR will survive (Chamberlayne 1994), eventually contributing to a capacity for self-organization. In East Germany at least, the maintenance of VS's social infrastructures, with their commitment to egalitarian principles, together with the culture of self-determination and respect for difference emanating from the new initiatives, give grounds for cautious optimism. However, the danger of 'self-organization' being used for exclusionary racist and nationalist purposes must be recognized, especially in the wider context of Eastern and Central European politics.

Notes

1. The main mass organizations were for trade-union members (FDGB), women (DFD), youth (FDJ) and elderly people (VS). There were a number of special interest groups for sport, culture, Soviet friendship, gardeners, consumer cooperatives, and so on.

2. This project (R000 23 3920 – 1992–94), financed by the ESRC, centres on interviews with home carers. The chapter is based on the author's previous work on neighbourhood systems in the GDR (Chamberlayne 1990) and on interviews conducted with officials and organizers of VS and other welfare organizations in 1992–93. Several later interviews, including those with city-council and regional-level officials, were conducted by Frauke Ruppel. I would like to thank Holger Backhaus-Maul and Detlev Pollack for informative discussions.

3. The five major welfare organizations in East Germany are Caritas (Roman Catholic), Innere Mission (Evangelical – that is, Protestant), Arbeiterwohlfahrt (Workers' Welfare Organization), Deutsche Paritätische Wohlfahrtsverband (DPWV

– an umbrella organization), the Red Cross. In West Germany there is also the Jewish Welfare Organization. The DPWV is the 'newest' of the welfare organizations, and was formed in 1927.

4. 'Archaic' because religious organizations, on which others are based, derive from feudal society. Corporatist in structure and culture, they do not conform with the structures of modern parliamentary democracy. They have no system of direct accountability, and the Church organizations are exempt from employment legislation. Moreover, responsibility for caring lies explicitly with families, to the detriment of women.

5. The Federal principle of 'subsidiarity' places responsibility with the lowest level of organization capable of bearing it, creating a hierarchy of care consisting of the individual, the family, the welfare organization, the municipality, the region and the federal government. The 'social state' is obliged to enhance the capacity for self-reliance, which should include self-help initiatives and voluntary effort.

References

Abrams, P. (1984), 'Realities of Neighbourhood Care: The Interactions between Statutory, Voluntary and Informal Social Care', *Policy and Politics*, vol. 2, no. 4, 1984, pp. 413–29.

Angershausen, S., H. Backhaus-Maul and M. Schiebel (1993), 'Interessenvermittlung durch die Wohlfahrtsverbände? – Verbandliche intermediäre Organisationen im Sozialbereich der neuen Bundesländer', paper delivered at the DFG workshop 'Entstehung und Funktion intermediärer Organisationen in den Neuen Bundesländern', Zentrum für Sozialpolitik, Bremen, pp. 1–28.

Backhaus-Maul, H. and T. Olk (1992), 'Intermediäre Organizationen als Gegenstand sozialwissenschaftlicher Forschung – Theoretische Überlegungen und erste empirische Befunde am Beispiel des Aufbaus von intermediären Organisationen in den neuen Bundesländern', in W. Schmähl, ed., *Sozialpolitik im Prozess der Deutschen Vereinigung*, Campus, Frankfurt am Main, pp. 91–132.

Bulmer, M., ed. (1987), 'Privacy and Confidentiality as Obstacles to Interweaving Formal and Informal Social Care: The Boundaries of the Private Realm', *Journal of Voluntary Action Research* 16, pp. 112–25.

Chamberlayne, P. (1990), 'Neighbourhood and Tenant Participation in the GDR', in B. Deacon and J. Szalai, eds, *Social Policy in the New Eastern Europe*, Avebury, Aldershot.

——— (1994), 'Transitions in the Private Sphere in East Germany', in W. Lee and E. Rosenhaft, eds, *The State and Social Change in Germany 1970–1990*, 2nd edn, Berg, Oxford.

Dölling, I. (1991), 'Between Hope and Helplessness: Women in the GDR after the Turning Point', *Feminist Review*, no. 39.

Hankiss, E. (1990), *East European Alternatives*, Oxford University Press, Oxford.

Henrich, R. (1990), *Der Vormundschaftliche Staat*, Kiepenheuer, Leipzig.

Hofmann, M., ed. (1991), *Aufbruch im Warteland – Ostdeutsche soziale Bewegungen im Wandel*, Palette, Bamberg.

Kondratowitz, H-J. von (1988), 'Zumindest Organisatorisch Erfasst… Die Älteren in der DDR zwischen Veteranenpathos und Geborgenheitsbeschworung', in G.-J. Glaessner, ed., *Die DDR in der Ara Honecker – Politik, Kultur und Gesellschaft*, pp.

514–28, Westdeutscher Verlag, Opladen.

Lefort, C. (1986), *The Political Forms of Modern Society: Bureaucracy, Democracy and Totalitarianism*, Polity Press, Cambridge.

Meuschel, S. (1992), 'Revolution in a Classless Society', in G.-J. Glaessner and I. Wallace, eds, *The German Revolution of 1989*, Berg, Oxford.

Nelson, D. (1980), *Local Politics in Communist Countries*, Lexington, Kentucky.

Offe, C. (1991), 'Die Deutsche Vereinigung als "Natürliches Experiment"', in Giesen and C Leggewie, eds, *Experiment Verinigung: ein soziales Grossversuch*, Rotbuch, Berlin, pp. 77–86.

Poldrack, H. (1992), *Bürgerschaftlich-Soziales Engagement im Transformationsprozess: Biographische Bezüge, soziale Typen und Potentiale*, Berichte aus Forschung und Praxis, no. 18, Institut für Sozialwissenschaftliche Amnalysen und Beratung, Köln-Leipzig.

Pollack, D. (1992), 'Zwischen alten Verhaltens-dispositionen und neuen Anforderungsprofilen – Bemerkungen zu den mentalitätsspezifischen Voraussetzungen des Operierens von Interessenverbänden und Organisationen in den neuen Bundesländern', *Probleme der Einheit*, vol. 12, no. 2, Halbband, pp. 489–508.

——— (1993), 'Die Entzauberung des Politischen Bürgerinitiativen und Bürgerbewegungen in Ostdeutschland', paper delivered at the DFG workshop 'Entstehung und Funktion intermediärer Organisationen in den Neuen Bundesländern', Zentrum für Sozialpolitik, Bremen, pp. 1–31.

Rink, D. (1993), 'Von Milieu zur Bewegung: Die Bürgerbewegungen von 1989/90', in S. Benzler and U. Bullmann, eds, *Bürgerbewegungen und Kommunalpolitik in Ostdeutschland*, Deutschland Ost vor Ort, Opladen.

Volkssolidarität (1991), *Die Volkssolidarität – Kurzinformationa*, May.

Wielgohs, J. (1993), 'Auflösung und Transformation der Ostdeutschen Bürgerbewegung', *Deutschland Archiv*, vol. 26, no. 4, pp. 426–35.

Winkler, G. (1990), *Frauenreport '90*, Die Wirtschaft, Berlin.

9

Community Work and the State:
The Changing Context of UK Practice

Marilyn Taylor

The future destiny of community work, like its present and its past, will be inextricably bound up with that of the state.

P. Waddington 1979

Community work began to flourish in the UK in the 1960s when, despite growing criticism of the delivery of state welfare, the principle of state responsibility for its citizens' welfare was largely undisputed. Thirty years later, it operates in a very different environment with the state withdrawing from welfare and seeking ways of transferring responsibility for both delivery and financing of welfare to the market, family, community and individuals. The implications of this ideological shift for community work are fundamental. To effect change in the 1960s and 1970s meant tackling state institutions – mainly a still-expanding local government, which, as employer, educator, service provider and regulator, had a profound effect on most areas of people's lives. Now, community organizations are invited to become 'agents' of the state, to take over services that an increasingly disempowered local government used to provide, and to do so in a climate of financial restraint.

The Roots of Community Development

Community work in the UK can be seen as a direct descendant of the colonial community development and education that British governments carried out from the 1930s onwards, first as a colonial power but increasingly as a reaction to political movements for independence (Craig 1989). Its roots, however, lie further back. They can be traced in the working-class mutual-aid traditions of the last century, the rent strikes of the First World War, mainly led by women (Smith 1992), unemployment struggles between the wars, and the postwar squatters' movement (Craig 1989). Community work interventions also derive from the settlement movement of the late nineteenth century, which aimed to give the rich 'a greater understanding of the poor and their problems by living among them' (Johnson 1981: 27), and in the development of working-class and women's education throughout the current century.

Making the state work better

The postwar growth of community development was piecemeal. The term gained currency in the UK in the social-work field, following a report in 1959 (Younghusband) which borrowed from US experience to establish new directions for this growing profession. But much of the actual work before the 1960s was concerned with youth, leisure and education – as a new approach in the still-surviving settlements, in community centres, and on newly built but inadequately resourced postwar housing estates (Thomas 1983).

By the 1960s, criticisms of the welfare state suggested that a rapidly expanding government machine was dominated by inflexible bureaucracy, yet still failing to meet need. Pockets of deprivation remained, often concentrated in particular localities. Postwar house-building programmes which owed more to the architectural fashion for high-rise development than to tenants' needs were beginning to show the effects of dislocation, lack of facilities and inappropriate design (Power 1987).

At the same time, a generation educated under the welfare state had expectations that reflected this upbringing. A new political consciousness was shaped by civil-rights movements and opposition to the Vietnam war in the US and revolutionary movements in Europe. New campaigning organizations from the late 1950s onwards focused growing concern about nuclear disarmament, apartheid, homelessness, poverty and the environment. At the same time, young volunteers were mobilized by new organizations to work in developing countries abroad and disadvantaged communities at home. A new impetus was given to community-based organizations, especially those concerned with play and public housing.

Following signs of growing social unrest and racial tension, the government was provoked into action. Borrowing from the US War on Poverty and other programmes, the UK government established programmes to combat deprivation, principal among them the Educational Priority Areas, the Urban Programme and the Community Development Project (CDP), the last of which setting up local teams of community workers and researchers (Edwards and Batley 1978; Loney 1983). Local authorities sought to pre-empt problems by encouraging participation in planning (Dearlove 1974).

The models of community work applied at the end of the 1960s – and underpinning government initiatives – were overwhelmingly consensus models. Community problems were seen in terms of *individual* or *community pathology*, that is, the breakdown of family and community ties or as the teething troubles of rapidly expanding local government (Boaden *et al.* 1982). The late 1960s, despite emerging problems, were still characterized by economic growth and optimism. Public social services expenditure continued to increase in the early 1970s (Knight 1993) and governments worried by urban unrest could still buy off the discontented. It was possible to conceive of a society with no losers, if only the 'disadvantaged' could be given assistance in making their case. Empowerment was scarcely on the agenda.

The 1970s: Opposition

The 1970s witnessed a 'flowering of local initiative ... tenants' groups, community arts groups, advice centres, play centres, environmental pressure groups, good neighbour schemes and citizen action groups' (Knight 1993). This rush of activity owed much to the support of the central government programmes already mentioned and to growing interest in community work from more powerful service departments within newly reorganized local authorities.

For a while, Craig argues, 'the interests of the state in engaging the potentially dispossessed and disaffected seemed to accord with those who were attracted by the political possibilities offered by working more directly in contact with working class activists at a neighbourhood level' (1989, p. 9). But the consensus was soon to break. The 1973 oil crisis signalled an end to economic prosperity, bringing recession and its own version of structural adjustment to the UK as increasing pressure on public expenditure and the international restructuring of industry took its toll particularly on working-class communities. Communities themselves were becoming more militant as rent strikes spread across the country in response to legislation to increase rents. There was growing resistance to housing redevelopment and road-building policies as people took action to save their communities from the bulldozer.

The influential analysis of the CDP, emerging at a time of growing political tension, challenged the assumption that local action alone could tackle problems which had their roots in much wider economic forces. Deprivation was seen as structural: not as a function of community pathology or even system failure, but of the interests of international capital and the state's role in securing these interests. CDP's analysis was based on class interest and urged communities to link with the central struggle at the workplace, especially through alliances with the trade unions.

As the economic recession tightened its grip, the CDP analysis was widely adopted, offering a theoretical model which explained the gap between achievement and ideals. But critics such as Waddington (1979) have suggested that it was 'longer on analysis than on applications' (p. 126).

More generally, Peter Marris (1982) commented on the growing frustration of community planners and workers who found that their increased
understanding of the wider forces affecting the urban environment made
it more and more difficult to identify any viable local strategy to tackle
problems.

One response to this frustration was a renewed interest in education
(although in Scotland community development had always had an educational rather than social-work base). Some looked to the work of Freire
for a bridge between a wider structural analysis and local action (Lovett
1983), seeking to 'rebuild socialism' from below (Fleetwood and Lambert
1982). Feminists began to assert the links between the personal and the
political and to stress the importance of work around issues which had
been regarded as politically 'soft', such as play and health. Even those
who were critical of CDP's highly political stance and adopted a more
pluralist approach, working with rather than against the state, still identified political education as a key element in that strategy (Thomas 1983).
Another way of linking action in the neighbourhood to a wider structural
analysis was to build federations at regional and national levels, especially
around housing issues (Taylor *et al.* 1986). There were precedents for this
in the Association of London Housing Estates in the 1960s and in a
variety of Play Forums that had been set up around the country.

Meanwhile, the state itself was becoming a major employer and funder
in the community development field. Waddington (1979) describes its initial
interest as one of 'pragmatic urban buffering or mediation'. But, with
Craig, he sees it developing as a strategy for social control: 'managing
deprivation and urban dissent' (Craig 1989: 13). In fact, few local authorities then had a strategic approach to community development. Many of
their community workers were relatively isolated, struggling with the
ambiguities of working within the system that their communities were
organizing against.

The dilemmas involved in accepting state funding were graphically
illustrated in the programmes of the central government Manpower Services Commission. With economic recession, unemployment became, for
the first time since the war, a significant problem. Government, locally
and nationally, committed more resources to economic regeneration. Central government's job-creation and training policies, the subject of fierce
debate, provided a significant new pool of resources for the development
of community action. Many argued that community organizations would
be impossibly compromised by becoming agents for the provision of low-
paid, non-unionized, short-term employment, even if, initially, funds were
available for jobs of community benefit (Addy and Scott 1988). But these
programmes nonetheless became a major funding source for emerging
minority ethnic organizations and also led to the employment of significant numbers of working-class people as community and advice workers.

The 1980s: Defence

In 1979, a radical right-wing government was elected, committed to rolling back the welfare state. Its programmes of privatization and market reforms took time to become operational, but it soon became clear that local public services would bear the brunt, particularly through the sale of public housing. Local-government finances were subjected to 'capping' – a mechanism which put a limit on the amount of money they could raise through local taxation.

Local authorities had to respond both to the attack from central government and to widespread public dissatisfaction with the services they provided (Taylor and Lansley 1992). They sought to gain public support for their services and role, some developing decentralization policies and new opportunities for participation in local decision-making in order to bring their services closer to their constituents. Many authorities provided resources to community organizations, while left-wing authorities in particular developed equal opportunities policies to improve access both to services and jobs for marginalized groups.

Community workers, past and present, were among those attempting to make these policies work – as councillors, senior officers, leaders of new decentralization or equal-opportunities units. Even those who had in the past adopted a conflict model saw the new possibilities of working through local government: 'The political logic of this seemed clear, that of taking control of the local state and reshaping it to serve the interests of the working class' (Craig 1989: 15). Across the board, community workers and organizations found themselves defending the very services they had previously criticized.

If the state, with its increasing tensions between central and local government, was no longer seen as a monolithic entity, 'community', too, was unravelling as a concept. Community development had in the past assumed an identity of interest within communities. While local groups largely comprised women, community work rarely examined the implications of this (Green and Chapman 1992): power often still lay with men. At the same time, black and minority ethnic organizations challenged the racism within predominantly white community organizations. It was becoming clear that 'the emancipation of the working class', even if it were achievable, would not of itself 'bring an end to social divisions and conflicts' (Butcher and Mullard 1993).

Meanwhile the need to tackle persistent unemployment led to new approaches to empowerment. Community workers inevitably found themselves in areas where rising unemployment was taking its greatest toll. What people in these communities most wanted was economic power and jobs. Community enterprise strategies, especially in Scotland and Wales, and a range of training and economic development projects, especially for women and minority ethnic groups, sought new ways of delivering jobs under local control.

The 1990s: Agency and Substitution

By the beginning of the 1990s, the battle for the defence of local government was in difficulties. The Greater London Council and the other 'metropolitan counties' (the upper tier of local government in major UK conurbations) had been the arena for the most creative partnerships with local government, but their abolition in the mid-1980s signalled the determination of the central state politically to subdue local government. While campaigns against the reform of local government taxation (the 'poll tax') at the beginning of the 1990s attracted huge public support, they may have been as much a last valiant effort as a taste of things to come.

The election of the third Thatcher government gave it a mandate to introduce across-the-board market reforms, which until then had been largely rhetorical. Legislation to allow schools, hospitals and public housing estates to be removed from local or health authority control ('opting-out'); the introduction of compulsory competitive tendering for some local authority services and the encouragement of 'welfare markets' in others; the introduction of internal markets to the national health service; the reform of local government finance; the enormous increase in the number of non-elected public bodies set up by central government to take on public responsibilities (often recruiting their leadership from business): a new managerialism which aimed to import business values into the public sector – all these have challenged traditional views of the role of the state. Under considerable financial pressure, local authorities are now under pressure to sell public assets (for example, buildings, land), cut back services and adopt the language of cost centres, purchasing and commissioning.

Diamond and Nelson (1993) claim that community workers in the 1980s overestimated the room for manoeuvre in the local state. Instead of a re-empowered local government, what these market-oriented policies have created is a new institutional environment at local level, with a much wider range of organizations – central government quangos (quasi-autonomous national government organizations); local government; opted-out hospitals, schools and housing estates; voluntary organizations; private organizations entering new fields and taking on new public responsibilities; and various hybrid ventures. Boundaries between public and private are becoming increasingly blurred, and the extent of the central state's sphere of influence is masked by a diversity of players whose accountability is unclear.

Nonetheless these policies offer community work a number of possible roles. It can develop and support the capacity of the community to take on services as agents for the state: a *market development* role. It can capitalize on the current emphasis on service user involvement and help user organizations to develop their own services, to make sense of the new institutional environment, to offer advocacy and to take up new opportunities for participation in service planning (for example, in community care): a *consumer development* role. A third role has been alluded to, that of *'managing deprivation and urban dissent'*: to participate in government programmes to address the dislocation caused by economic change, particularly crime and urban decay.

How far will these roles empower people? The new welfare market offers community organizations the chance to take more control over the production of the services they need – an opportunity with particular attractions to groups who have consistently been excluded in the past. It offers more stable funding and status for those community-based services which government defines as priorities. But investment is needed if relatively fragile community organizations are contracted to deliver services. And for many community organizations, the reality of the changed policy environment has been cuts in grant-aid and a struggle to survive. Where they are providing contracted services, evidence shows that funding fails to provide overheads or development costs and places considerable administrative pressure on organizations ill-equipped to carry this load (Lewis 1992). If this continues to be the case, the costs of provision will be borne more by communities in most need, employing people on the margins of the labour market. Further, as the balance of funding shifts from grants to purchase of service, there will be less money for the range of support, advice and capacity-building activities which communities have developed, both complementary to and supportive of mainstream provision.

If the transfer of service delivery is something of a mixed blessing, is there much to welcome in the government's recognition of the need to give service users more power? The new emphasis on consumerism should offer opportunities, for example, to the rapidly growing disability movement in the UK. People with physical impairments or learning difficulties, survivors of mental health services, people with HIV/AIDS and carers have set up their own organizations and demanded that their voice be heard, not least by community workers and community organizations themselves. Mainstream service providers are being forced to re-examine their practice and management structures.

But again there is a problem of resources. Although advocacy appears to be one area where it is possible to find new money, many user organizations are small and fragile and the support they receive is minute in relation to spending on provision and to the demands on them. As community organizations have found before them, consultation processes initiated by the state can absorb a tremendous amount of energy, divorcing the few people who have the expertise and confidence to participate from the rest of their constituency. Most of those doing the consulting are paid for their time. Those who are consulted are seldom compensated. Tight budgets and constant demands mean there is little time for stretched organizations to reach out, involve their constituencies, be held account-able and develop their own agendas.

Disabled people are clear that they wish to be empowered as citizens and not just seen in terms of their use of specialized (and segregated) services. The danger with the move towards the market is that citizenship is a concept which is disappearing from public policy. Empowerment in the welfare market is the empowerment of the customer. The term 'citizen-ship', meanwhile, has been used in two ways by the state. 'Active citizenship' was the first. Promoted by government briefly in the 1980s, as a response to what it saw as an overemphasis on rights under the welfare state, its emphasis was on citizens taking more individual responsibility for welfare and security. While this kind of citizenship has an important part to play as a facet of social responsibility, at the time it was seen by many as an attempt to substitute individual for public, collective, responsibility.

More recently, central government has introduced citizens' charters for services still provided by the state and therefore not subject to market disciplines. But as this description suggests, these are consumer rather than citizens' charters, giving procedural rather than substantive rights. Citizenship in the sense of people contributing to political debate about the way society allocates its resources, defines its priorities and meets its needs, receives considerably less attention. As society is privatized, access to that process is increasingly constrained. The key relationship becomes one between the individual and the market.

One area where people have opportunities to participate as citizens is that of urban and estate regeneration. Throughout the past thirty years, a consistent thread in government policy has been the promotion of pro-grammes to fight crime and counter urban unrest. Riots in inner cities and outer estates during the 1980s kept this on the agenda, and these programmes continue to provide opportunities to develop new initiatives in communities under severe pressure. People in marginalized communities are highly vulnerable to both crime and unemployment, and these funds have been used to meet a range of community needs. The introduction of a City Challenge programme in the early 1990s, where urban areas competing for money under the programme were *required* to involve the community, built on earlier regeneration initiatives and brought with it the opportunity for community organizations to have both significant representation on boards involving local authorities and business, and a role in designing and implementing major local economic regeneration programmes.

Funds for the organizational development and social regeneration programmes that underpin economic regeneration have been, however, increasingly hard to obtain as central-government programmes emphasized employment and training rather than social goals. The special employment programmes dropped their funding for jobs 'of community benefit' in the mid-1980s, and the long-running Urban Programme, which provided support for many locally-based activities, changed its emphasis over the years to economic projects before being scrapped altogether in 1993. Urban regeneration now subsumes the City Challenge programme, whose impact is awaited; however, there is little sign that support will be available to build the capacity that will make community involvement work.

Towards 2000: Reinvention

Harman argues that 'the world economy in its present form has as one of its main products *marginal people*: the unemployed, the underemployed, the disenfranchised – people who lack what traditional society provided, a sense of belonging and of having a recognised role' (1993: 106). Paradoxically, technological advance has increased this marginalization. In the UK, divisions between rich and poor have widened both financially (Donnison 1993) and physically. Those who can do so move out of the areas that show most signs of stress. The considerable reduction in social rented housing means that it is now the refuge of those who have no other choice – except, of course, homelessness.

People's lives have been privatized. Many things which used to be done collectively can or have to be done individually: entertainment and leisure pursuits are perhaps the most obvious examples. There seems less need for any kind of public or even collective involvement. Meanwhile, as democracy is rediscovered with difficulty in Eastern and Central Europe, it is in need of revival in many Western countries, with many people distrustful of the political system. While the European Union may offer a source of appeal above the UK government for some campaigns, the democratic deficit there offers no effective alternative political model.

In discussing urban regeneration, Donnison suggests that 'what we should be talking about is not just a few research programmes, not just community development. It is a new pattern of government replacing old patterns of government' (1993: 298; see also Osborne and Gaebler 1992). If this is to happen, ways must be found to engage people and convince them that there is a point in making a commitment to a public sphere which they feel has failed them or is simply seen as irrelevant in a consumerist age.

The contribution that community work can make to this may be limited but can be significant. It can act as a laboratory for change in providing bottom-up solutions to the crisis that democracy is facing at present. But if it is to do so, there are a number of challenges it must face.

How to release people's energies without exploiting them

New forms of service provision and production are required which not only release resources rather than exploit them (on the environmental as well as the human front) but also change the power relationship between provider and user, recognizing that service users are producers of their own welfare and not passive recipients. These would take their place in the development of a distinctive 'social economy' operating as a third force between state and market (Paton 1991). Models are most likely to be found in other countries with more current traditions of cooperative and mutual action than the UK and where industry itself is developing more flexible ways of working (Piore and Sabel 1984). But local exchange trading systems, credit unions, cooperatives and the intermediate technology movement could provide a foundation on which to build.

How to respect 'difference' whilst organizing around common interests

Community work in the UK has moved from a belief in common community interest and traditional representative structures to more disparate forms of organizing around different identities. This has been an important development in allowing excluded groups to gain power. But empowerment strategies now run the danger identified by Meekosha (1993) of being 'set adrift on a sea of relativity'. Identity politics, she argues, have a capacity for infinite fragmentation and for trapping groups into the expression of opposition or disadvantage – an ironic mirror of the increasingly competitive world which most community development workers wish to change. Paradoxically, this could make it easier for the community to be suborned as a substitute for the state, with community development becoming 'a mode of work in which ever-more tightly delineated minorities and sectors of society experiencing discrimination are channelled into organising the provision of specific, usually volunteer-operated services' (Meekosha 1993) or are sucked into systems of participation where their separate interests are highly vulnerable to manipulation, dissipating their potential to take power.

The difficulty for community development is to reconcile the paradoxes between the values of solidarity and identity. It has struggled over recent years with the need to recognize and value difference; but with increasing fragmentation across the globe, the challenge is to give people enough confidence and sense of strength in their own identity to recognize and come together on their common interests. If this project fails, the way will be open for further fragmentation and fundamentalism. The political movement which stands most to gain from this is fascism.

How to make local action relevant beyond the neighbourhood

This has always been an aim, albeit problematic, of community work. There is now growing interest in networks in the community-work field (as indeed there is in business), and organizations like the UK Federation of Community Work Training Groups have demonstrated the value of loose structures in the support of local action. The success of social movements across the globe provides an even more persuasive model. Power is more difficult to locate and address than it once appeared. The march on the town hall, or even parliament, is no longer viable as a central strategy. The future for work which links the neighbourhood to the wider world is likely to lie in looser and more flexible networks, which are light on their feet and on resources – the women's movement or the cooperative movements in Europe provide examples. But issues of transparency, accountability and access will need to be addressed if these networks are to be grounded in the needs of people in communities and in acknowledged democratic processes.

Conclusions

Community work in the UK has tried to empower people in a number of different ways: restoring community spirit; trying to make government more responsive to people's needs; engaging communities in the class struggle; organizing around identity; political education and consciousness-raising; organizing around service use; developing economic power and alternative forms of provision to the state. Its relationship with the state in this process has taken several different forms: making it work better and seeking to extend its provision, attacking it, defending it, and now either acting as its agent or seeking to find the cracks in the system through which empowerment can be drawn. Different relationships have reflected different analyses of power and the state: from consensus and system failure, to conflict and class interest, to a recognition of conflicts of interest within both state and community.

Capitalism, as Sternberg (1993) notes, is undergoing several different and contradictory transformations at once. Centralization of power goes hand in hand with increasing fragmentation of sectarian conflict and identity politics. Rigid fundamentalism has emerged as one response to the instability of modern society and culture. In a society where polarization, fragmentation and privatization have challenged traditional understandings of the state, accountability and citizenship, community work will need a more sophisticated analysis of the operation and meaning of power and how it can be addressed at a local level. But it is likely that in a more fragmented 'postmodern' environment, networks and alliances will be the foundation on which empowerment is built. Community work needs to

develop a practice which can work with allies across the institutional map
to find the possibilities for change in an increasingly turbulent environment.

References

Addy, T. and D. Scott (1988), *Fatal Impacts? The MSC and Voluntary Action*, William
  Temple Foundation, Manchester.
Boaden, N., N. Goldsmith, W. Hampton and P. Stringer (1982), *Public Participation
  in Local Services*, Longman, London.
Butcher, H. and M. Mullard (1993), 'Community Policy, Citizenship and Democ-
  racy', in H. Butcher, A. Glen, P. Henderson and J. Smith, eds, *Community and
  Public Policy*, Pluto Press, London.
Craig, G. (1989), 'Community Work and the State', *Community Development Journal*,
  vol. 24, no. 1, pp. 3–18.
Dearlove, J. (1974), 'The Control of Change and the Regulation of Community
  Action', in D. Jones and M. Mayo, eds, *Community Work One*, Routledge and
  Kegan Paul, London.
Diamond, J. and A. Nelson (1993), 'Community Work – Post-Local Socialism',
  Community Development Journal, vol. 28, no. 1, pp. 38–44.
Donnison, D. (1993), 'The Challenge of Urban Regeneration for Community
  Development', *Community Development Journal*, vol. 28, no. 4, pp. 293–8.
Edwards, J. and R. Batley (1978), *The Politics of Positive Discrimination*, Tavistock,
  London.
Fleetwood, M. and J. Lambert (1982), 'Bringing Socialism Home: Theory and Prac-
  tice in a Radical Community Action', in G. Craig, N. Derricourt and M. Loney,
  Community Work and the State, Routledge and Kegan Paul, London, pp. 48–58.
Green, J. and A. Chapman (1992), 'The British Community Development Project:
  Lessons for the Future', *Community Development Journal*, vol. 27, no. 3, pp. 242–
  58.
Harman, W.W. (1993), 'Rethinking the Central Institutions of Society', *Futures*,
  December, pp. 1063–70.
Johnson, N. (1981), *Voluntary Social Services*, Blackwell and M. Robertson, Oxford.
Knight, B. (1993), *Voluntary Action*, Home Office, London.
Lewis, J. (1992), 'Developing the Mixed Economy of Care', *Journal of Social Policy*,
  vol. 22, no. 2, pp. 173–92.
Loney, M. (1983), *Communities Against Government: The British Community Development
  Project 1968–78*, Heinemann Educational Books, London.
Lovett, T., *et al* (1983), *Adult Education and Community Action*, Croom Helm, London.
Marris, P. (1982), *Community Planning and Conceptions of Change*, Routledge and Kegan
  Paul, London.
Meekosha, H. (1993), 'The Bodies Politic – Equality, Difference and Community
  Practice', in H. Butcher, A. Glen, P. Henderson and J. Smith, eds, *Community and
  Public Policy*, Pluto Press, London.
Osborne, D. and T. Gaebler (1993), *Reinventing Government*, Penguin, New York.
Paton, R. (1991), 'The Social Economy: Value-based Organization in the Wider
  Society', in J. Batsleer, C. Cornforth and R. Paton, eds, *Issues in Voluntary and
  Non-profit Management*, Open University Press, Milton Keynes.

Piore, M.J. and C.F. Sabel (1984), *The Second Industrial Divide: Possibilities for Prosperity*, Basic Books, New York.

Power, A. (1987), *Property before People*, Allen and Unwin, London.

Smith, J. (1992), *Community Development and Tenant Action*, Community Development Foundation, London.

Sternberg, E. (1993), 'Transformations: The Eight New Ages of Capitalism', in *Futures*, December.

Taylor, M. and Newcastle and Sheffield Tenants' Federation (1986), 'For Whose Benefit? Decentralising Housing Services in Two Cities', *Community Development Journal*, vol. 21, no. 2, pp. 126–32.

Taylor, M. and J. Lansley (1992) 'Ideology and Welfare in the UK: The Implications for the Voluntary Sector', *Voluntas*, vol. 3, no. 2, pp. 153–74.

Thomas, D. (1983), *The Making of Community Work*, George Allen and Unwin, London.

Waddington, P. (1979), 'Looking Ahead: Community Work into the 1980s', *Community Development Journal*, vol. 14, no.3, pp. 224–34

Younghusband, E. L. (1959), *Report of the Working Party on Social Workers in the Local Authority Health and Social Welfare Service*, HMSO, London.

10

Community Action in the United States

S.M. Miller, Martin Rein and Peggy Levitt

The United States continues to experience considerable community organizing activity. The positive interpretation is that a surprising range of activism occurs, the negative that its impact is limited. Both conclusions are valid. Important shifts in the focus and terms of community action occurred in the last three decades. Organizers work now on a broader set of issues, using more varied, sophisticated strategies. Most striking is the erosion of boundaries separating conventional community organizing from coalition-building and electoral politics.

The terms 'organizing' and 'social movement' have many variations. Purists would reject the inclusion of many current activities under citizen or community action. This chapter is ecumenical, delineating seven forms – and blends – of 'organizing' of current importance in the USA.

Organizing Approaches

The organization of organizations

This approach brings together several organizations in one area to act collectively on a particular issue. Often, the drive for such action comes from a council of social agencies or a church group. Saul Alinsky inspired much organizing along these lines. The original Alinsky model – his successors in the Industrial Areas Foundation (IAF) and in other organizations changed it considerably – has been poorly understood. This model started with a request by a leading community organization, usually a church group, for help from Alinsky. Initially, inviting communities were usually white and working class; later, African-American and Latino communities enlisted the IAF's assistance. Alinsky's approach was to bring existing community organizations into a coalition. An issue was chosen which was visible, winnable, would yield concrete results and mobilize people by focusing on a villain. Then, clever, publicity-winning tactics were deployed. Many Alinsky tactics have been important in approaches which do not build around the organization of organizations. Alinsky's work was confrontational and usually disturbed public officials (and private employers), but didn't move to electoral action.

This approach, though common, is used in ways that contrast frequently with early Alinsky methods. His influence is also felt in other community organizing strategies. For example, most of the state affiliates making up the national network Citizen Action are coalitions of community-based organizations, sharing progressive/populist outlooks, pursuing a political and electoral strategy, influencing legislative decisions and electing like-minded people to political office.

The organization of residence

This 'grassroots' approach brings together individuals residing in the same geographic community – 'grassroots' implying both closeness to ordinary people and distance from elite power groups. Recent grassroots organizing was influenced by the model developed by Fred Ross, who worked with Alinsky and later organized Latino Californian agricultural workers. Since these migratory workers had not sustained ongoing organizations, Ross organized them from scratch at each new picking site through 'house meetings' where new leadership would emerge.

The grassroots approach differs from the organization of organizations in that it mobilizes individuals into some form of collective action. It is also more likely to be class-based in that residents from the same neighbourhood share comparable incomes, household characteristics and employment status. However, the organization of organizations tends to draw on the better-off of a particular area. That situation affects the representativeness of grassroots organizations, for non-members may differ on issues. Grassroots organizing does not occur only in lower-income neighbourhoods; nor is it necessarily progressive. Those with higher incomes will protect themselves against what they view as threats to their way of life. Right-wing groups are often effectively organized to fight on school, library reading material, anti-tax or abortion issues.

Grassroots organizing can be initiated by a local sponsor such as a local service bureaucracy, an interest group or a residents' group. For example, public housing authorities may support tenant organizations promoting resident participation in property maintenance or anti-crime efforts. An environmental organization's campaign in a neighbourhood may inspire residents to organize against industrial polluters. Often, grassroots efforts develop spontaneously around some specific irritation bringing residents together.

The catalyst behind the organizing efforts influences the issues addressed and levels of militancy developed. At one extreme are issues arising from an immediate local grievance such as organizing to obtain a traffic light for a crossing where several accidents occurred. When the goal is achieved, the organization disappears. Residents also organize around more enduring issues. For example, in Massachusetts, where state law limits annual property tax increases, some residents work successfully each year to win a tax override.

Nationally, ACORN (Association of Community Organizations for Reform Now), developing from the 1960s welfare-rights movement, organizes lower-income neighbourhood residents around housing and other issues. ACORN takes a more militant, direct-action approach than comparable national and regional organizations. It is largely sustained by membership subscriptions, though it still requires foundation funding and door-to-door canvassing in non-poor localities.

Organizing is now a fine art, a trainable skill. A well-trained organizer can go into any community and promote citizen activity. Several provisos are involved: the particular focus of organizing is neither identified in advance nor limited to anything more specific than an important neighbourhood complaint; the organizer is supported by outside funds for at least six months, therefore not having to rely on raising his/her salary from the community being organized. Despite grievances and organizing skill, community-based grassroots organizing declined in recent years: Reagonomics demoralized communities more than it mobilized them. In some localities faced with the major factory shutdowns, however, workers and the communities organized to block the shutdown or develop an alternative, democratic plan for the factory. Unfortunately, few campaigns succeeded.

The main positive action is the considerable growth of local environmental groups, working on issues like hazardous waste disposal, clean water legislation, and recycling. To some extent, the environment has become an issue cutting across class lines. With the emergence of the concept of 'environmental racism', identifying many areas inhabited by African-Americans that are the locale of dangerous waste dumps, white-dominated environmentalism has become racially aware.

Organization around consumption

The weakness of unions and their limited attention to organizing non-public workers result in organizing activity centring mainly on consumption issues (the problems of residents; the spending of income) rather than on production issues. This is disappointing since unemployment is high, job insecurity widespread, and median real wages have stagnated for two decades.

From the late 1960s the National Welfare Rights Organization (NWRO) organized women welfare recipients to demand larger grants. In the late 1970s groups were organized to prevent utilities from raising their rates by pressure on regulatory public agencies. The environmental movement, especially that part concerned with toxic dumps, can be regarded as a consumption-oriented activity, seeking to improve neighbourhoods as places to live in, not places to work in. Citizen Action's current emphasis on health questions is another example of a consumption issue, as is tenants' organizing. In the 1950s such organizing largely took place in low-income neighbourhoods. Now with college-educated persons living on moderate incomes, it has expanded beyond a low-income constituency, generating state and national federations of tenants' organizations. Some analysts see such organizations as exemplifying 'the new social movements' promulgated by European intellectuals. That interpretation seems inappropriate, for most of these consumption-oriented activities are responses to immediate, small-scale, concrete disturbances, seldom leading to ideological demands for larger changes, let alone transformative shifts. Even organizational leaders only vaguely identify the more fundamental social changes they would like to see and how they might bring these about.

Organizing around identity

Organizing around race/ethnicity and gender has become a major focus, often as part of broader social movements using extra-institutional channels to challenge attitudes or institutions. Organizing around identity seeks to break conventional ways of 'conducting business' by reframing issues along new principles of justice or equality. Examples are the 1960s civil-rights movements and, recently, Chicano and women's rights movements. Gays and lesbians, disabled persons and AIDS sufferers have also constructed political and movement identities built on their definitions of self.

Organization around identity differs from grassroots organization in that it does not rely on geographic location. In the organizing of identity, 'who you are' is the axis for mobilization. For example, Latinos from a broad geographic area will travel to use a Latino community-based service delivery organization. Identity groups are made; they are not simple reflections of common distinguishing characteristics. The new social identity of 'Asian Americans and Pacific Islanders' is particularly interesting: nationalities with long histories of enmity (for example, Vietnamese and Chinese), with different languages, cultures and religions, have forged alliances in response to common political, legal and community needs. Some assert that a similar conglomeration occurs within the African-American identity group, contending that important place-of-origins variations among Blacks in New York City are greater than the ethnic differences among all New Yorkers. In reality, identity groups may be less uniform in their outlooks (because of cultural backgrounds or class position) than rhetoric suggests.

Often, the national movement grows out of local initiatives without a central national focus. For example, many African-American organizations struggle against local discrimination but lack strong connection to national organizations or agendas. The politics of identity has a strong value character which pervades most issues. It may also limit the scope of the identity group. The abortion issue became the prime organizing link for women as well as the litmus test to determine endorsement of candidates. Although the abortion issue is not settled as it moves increasingly to the level of the states, there is considerable effort to move women's groups to a broad agenda concerning economic and family support issues which can enlist wider local support.

Sometimes ethnic identity is organized by middle-class professionals who shape the agenda; at other times it can be framed by the interests of lower-income groups. For African-Americans, organizing appears focused more often on the provision of public services than work issues. In the women's movement, issues such as abortion, the equal-rights amendment and equal pay for equal work seem more central and have led to criticism that it has neglected the concerns of women of colour or low income.

The politics of identity can be extended to include 'value-based organizing', seeking to affect participants' view of the world, their organizations, their community and their roles. It goes beyond 'issue-based' organizing although issues are involved; for example, building an organization of organizations can transform their and their members' outlook by expanding notions of democracy, justice and participation. This does not reflect left–right ideological splits but conveys a democratic ideology which transcends traditional political dichotomies. The goal is transformational change, not only specific improvements in community or nation. Many IAF projects share the contention that value-based organizing is in a better position to promote fundamental change than is issue-based organizing. It can more openly discuss philosophy or ideology than can issue-based organizing that must minimize internal dissension by avoiding disturbing value-laden questions. For example, even during the height of its considerable popularity, the now-defunct Massachusetts Fair Share deliberately avoided discussion of abortion and school busing issues as being too divisive.

Self-help and mutual aid organizing

The objective is to encourage individuals in similar, difficult situations to help one another and only occasionally to change the external world impinging on them. The form has spread rapidly, including groups organized around various addictions (drugs, eating), severe health difficulties, or similar traumas (for example, MADD – Mothers Against Drunk Driving). Those who directly consume the service are involved in organizing the group. Despite their name, they are mutual aid groups.

Many analysts of organizing would not consider self-help and mutual aid as citizen organizing, but the numbers involved makes them significant and they have the potential to go beyond mere comfort or re-education functions. To date, the hope that mutual aid activities would take a more directly political role has been disappointed. Two notable exceptions are MADD, which campaigns vigorously against drunk driving, and organizations of parents of children labelled mentally retarded, who moved from mutual support to influencing relevant policies. By far the largest self-help/mutual aid group is the original one – Alcoholics Anonymous (AA). Organizers of activist groups can learn a great deal from its organizational skill at stimulating local development and autonomy within a national framework.

Advocacy organizing

Another important form often excluded from the rubric of community organizing is that of advocacy organizing. What distinguishes this form is that it is done by one group on behalf of another presumed to need help. Coalitions for the homeless are made up of professional and volunteer advocates joining together to represent the former's interests. The advocate speaks in the name and interest of a population but is not responsible to it. Advocacy organizations, proliferating in the 1980s when social conditions worsened for many, are not membership organizations of consumers or clients themselves but work for their interests. With the relative silence of the poor, advocacy groups such as the Children's Defense Fund play an essential role in speaking out for poor children. This group's substantial influence is surprising because it lacks a direct, active constituency. Its strength lies in its ability to marshall evidence of the effects of funding cuts on low-income children, present a compelling moral case, and lobby effectively in Congress and state legislatures.

Mixed models

Many organizations combine some of the approaches described above or link organizing with service delivery or politics. The IAF's Nehemiah project in a poor area of New York mobilized African-American residents by working through church and community organizations and produced low-income housing. Two other IAF projects have received attention for their broad actions: COPS in San Antonio has been important in local elections, and BUILD has played a major role in education in Baltimore. The independent Dudley Street Neighbourhood Initiative in Boston also combines organization with development. This multi-ethnic resident coalition was so effective that it was the first community group to be awarded the right, usually reserved to the state, to acquire city-owned property and turn it into parcels for development.

Many community organizations evolve from an exclusive grassroots organizing outlook into providing needed services, sometimes also to secure a funding base. They seek to carry simultaneously both a service function and an organizing role. With the great need for services in low-income areas, the mixed model is likely to grow. It is also spurred by the increasing move toward electoral politics, discussed later.

Developments since the 1960s

What influenced the growth of these approaches to organizing? From the 1960s much organizing opposed American involvement in the Vietnam war and racial discrimination. In addition, low-income, primarily Black, women organized for greater welfare benefits through the NWRO, which grew from local welfare-rights efforts. A key link to this period is that many leaders of today's community and citizen-action organizations were activists in those anti-war, welfare-rights or feminist actions. They have drawn lessons from their earlier experiences and have responded to the changing terrain of economic, social and political life. Some tried to build bridges with working-class and lower-middle-class people alienated by anti-Vietnam protests. Many modified their political outlook, becoming more pragmatic and adopting a more traditional liberal programme of extend-ing governmental activity, a stance differing from the 1960s view that government was the source of difficulties.

In most localities, some organization is addressing a community issue. For example, even in remote areas of the mountainous Appalachian region, associations have formed around concerns about streams overflowing during the spring and threatening homes. Inner-city residents have formed groups to oust drug pushers and educate young people about their dangers. Recently, concern about AIDS and inadequate government responses prompted residents in numerous cities to organize demonstrations and form groups to assist AIDS victims.

In the 1980s a distinct turn toward electoral involvement occurred. Influencing legislation, endorsing candidates and even running candidates associated with community movements became increasingly common, with – in the early 1990s – some success. Many state legislatures, notably in the Northeast, not only have progressive representatives but also caucuses of progressive members. The Northeast Coalition has effectively organized legislators in the region as well as in individual states. The model is influencing developments in other regions.

Leaders of issue- and residentially based organizing express concern that their efforts do not transform ideology and political attitudes, nor create viable long-term organizations bringing about durable social change. In many cases, after the major issue around which they are created is resolved, the organizations lose support. Forced to operate with limited finances and personnel, these groups have few prospects of stability and longevity.

Unfortunately, most people who support a local action are little changed by the organization and action. This lack of deep impact on participants is a major limitation of efforts to democratize American life through grassroots involvements. Nevertheless, the number of community organizations that have survived despite obstacles is impressive. Some lower-income community groups are associated at the national level with the National Training and Information Centre; some are chapters of ACORN. But the overwhelming numbers of surviving community groups are unaffiliated at state or national levels. Local independence breeds national weakness. However, places where organizing took place in the past, even if apparent somnolence followed, are easier to rouse to deal with a current difficulty than are communities which lack an earlier organizing experience. Organizing thus can provide a legacy even when it is not transformational in immediate impact.

The women's movements concentrated on the passage of the Equal Rights amendment by organizing state-by-state campaigns. That valiant but unsuccessful effort gained them members but led to criticism that they were not working directly on economic issues important to low-income women and women of colour. The eroding of the right to have an abortion mobilized large numbers of women. Since the abortion issue is unsettled as Supreme Court decisions give states leeway in regulating abortions, it is likely to lead many women into involvement. Many politicians have learned that an anti-choice position may lose them more votes than they would gain.

Economic pressures are driving many women and particularly mothers into the labour force. That trend is likely to lead to a renewed emphasis on economic questions, centring particularly on pay gaps between women and men and the need to ease family and work burdens.

Organizing among African-Americans is more complicated. The enormous activity around the civil-rights and Black Power movements of the 1960s and 1970s has largely dissipated. National organizations are weak and few local chapters are active. The level of anger in many African-American communities is very high; some of the agitation is channelled into neighbourhood groups, churches and Black Muslim organizations tackling severe local problems involving schools, jobs, poverty, police or drugs. But the broad feeling of those outside is that most low-income African-American neighbourhoods lack effective organization.

Some Challenges

Proliferation and fragmentation

De Tocqueville's observation of the 1830s that Americans tend to form associations certainly applies today where 'single-issue' and civic organizations appear (and often disappear) in the community and political scenes. The variety of organizations and issues engaging people can be a strength – people finding some involvement in the public arena. It is also a great weakness. Fragmentation and competition grow with proliferation, as progressive organizations compete for attention and funding.

First, there is competition among issues. Is one more interested in environmental depredations than the abortion or homelessness issue? Second, within any issue, organizations vie for support. For example, which environmental organization is most worthy of attracting interest – is it conservationists protecting threatened animals; those concerned with toxic wastes in communities; or those clamouring for measures against water pollution? Attempts at limiting competition range from an informal code to speak no evil of people on 'our side', to formal meetings of leaders of competing and overlapping organizations or occasional joint action. The diffusion of support weakens possible impact. While electoral coalitions can bring together organizations in political campaigns, fragmentation prevails. Divisions within the Democratic Party have not made it a strong coalescing force, although electoral coalitions invariably support Democratic candidates.

Empowerment

The route to empowerment is through involvement and participation. This usually takes place because of self-interest, whether economic, as in the case of tenants combating rent increases, or protecting one's neighbourhood against the disruption of bulldozers. One study reported that activists felt more capable of public speaking, accosting politicians and the like. This kind of involvement may lead people to become concerned about other issues and to feel and act empowered. It is striking how many recently elected Congress members, particularly women, first became involved in an action of immediate family interest, like a concern about local schools.

When interest participation does expand to what might be considered generalized empowerment, it is likely to result from linking broad values or ideology to interest. This is clearly the situation for women's groups, which have empowered many women, not only by emphasizing interests (for example, abortion, gendered wage differentials) but also developing women's consciousness. They provide a way of thinking about issues that affects what many women do in their local communities.

In many organizations, educational activity which might develop a broader view and expand empowerment is weak. The strains of maintaining organizational activity while staying within tight budgets undoubtedly contribute to this situation. Also, the staff of these organizations are usually more radical than rank-and-file participants and may become reluctant to espouse positions which may antagonize members with a limited organizational agenda.

A disturbing conclusion of some well-informed activists is that many organizations have a leadership but not much of a following. As a result, the possibility of empowerment is remote. The relationship between leaders and members is tenuous. That weakens the organization politically and limits what members gain from it. However, it is important to recognize that there are degrees and kinds of empowerment. People engaged in what one might term rightist action programmes also can become empowered. Certainly, those involved in 'Not In My Back Yard' actions, banbooks-from-libraries campaigns, or in anti-abortion protests may feel empowered by involvement and move to greater participation in electoral politics and other community issues. Empowerment has to be specified. Unless one is unusually ecumenical, populist and/or democratic, believing that any kind of action is always to the good, one must be concerned about *whose* empowerment to do *what?*

Fundraising

Organizations raise money from membership dues, foundations, canvassing and government. Those relying on subscriptions and contributions are usually large associations with devoted memberships and fundraising skills. Canvassing refers to door-bell ringing and telephone calling which solicit funds from people. Progressive activist foundations provide important parts of organizational budgets. Obtaining government funds usually requires performing some local social service (though in the 1970s, Carter's VISTA programme placed young community service internees with community organizations).

The notion of a self-supporting movement, gathering in funds from membership subscriptions or door-to-door canvassing, is appealing. Few action organizations having a national presence do not rely on some foundation support. Since the people actually doing the canvassing have to be motivated financially as well as morally to carry through their assignments, the net of the 'take' can be only half of the gross. However, the canvassers can 'educate' many of the canvassed people about issues and the organization.

An occasional criticism is that the canvass determines the organization's policy decisions rather than the other way around – the choice of issue may be influenced by its potential effectiveness in attracting donations. But those organizations which do not rely on a canvass for funding may be dependent on foundations or churches. Relying on local contributions is perilous and limits what an organization can do. Soliciting funds from foundations, however, often requires tailoring the organization's activities to meet a foundation's interests. Gaining government funds may turn an organization into a service agency rather than a combative community action force; and, with growing competition for funds, the uncertainty of funding is a constant threat.

Impact

Both Citizen Action and, to a lesser extent, ACORN seek national impact. Citizen Action seeks to influence local, state and national elections. Through its energy affiliate, it attempts to influence policy and has also turned to the politically controversial health issue. ACORN has tried to influence national affordable housing policy and, recently, to highlight the savings-and-loan crisis which is important in the Southwest, its main site. So far, the IAF has not sought national impact but has significantly influenced developments in several cities where it has strong organizations.

However, community and citizen groups overall do not have substantial impact at the national level and it is important to ask why. One obvious reason is that they are not national organizations but state and local ones. Because of the separation of federal and state powers, to be a national actor an organization has to revolve primarily around a national agenda. The strength of the constituent organizations of, say, Citizen Action is in their state or local actions. Second, these national organizations rarely have national spokespersons – seen as a disadvantage by the American media.

Third, groups with dissident outlooks tend to be treated by the media as leftovers of the countercultural 1960s rather than as significant new forces. Consequently, when populist forces gain attention, it is not always in a positive light. Fourth, community action and other citizen organizations are so divided that their sum is less than their individual parts. The consequence is that as a *national* force, they are not only unable to act but often are not even perceived as an effective agency of change.

Finally, groups seeking progressive social change are at a distinct disadvantage. Government funding and/or regulation are needed to improve community operations and citizen participation. Neo-conservative and liberal populist feelings against government have penetrated political and intellectual life. Issues such as increasing taxation to pay for desperately needed social programmes are difficult to pursue today. Any proposed governmental action is in disrepute seen as likely to be overly expensive and incompetently performed.

What of the Future?

Many community action organizations like Citizen Action and its state organizations have diminished hope of changing people's consciousness through their activities. Rather, they seek electoral power: the election of enough candidates, including some drawn from their staff and participants, can gradually shape decisions which affect the lives of people, especially the non-participating poor. This contrasts sharply with the 1970s when many of the New Left disdained traditional politics, focusing on the possibilities of local community organizing. Increasingly, that is regarded as a false dichotomy, particularly since much of what can be done to improve localities depends on national legislation and funding.

The constituency of active groups will probably continue to move up the social class ladder. In the 1960s and early 1970s the aim was to organize the poor; in the late 1970s and early 1980s organizing occurred among the upper working class and lower middle class (the Citizen Action base). With increasing job insecurity and low pay rises, it is likely that middle-class groups will be seen as organizable and effective.

The politics of identity will grow in importance. Crucial issues will be the bridging of differences within and between identity groups. Almost half African-Americans, for example, are low income; more than half are not. Of the latter, almost a quarter are at or above median household income but working longer hours to attain it. The political context is less favourable to helping the poor than it is to criticizing them and pressing welfare systems into operating as employment programmes. Where the notion of a last resort 'safety net' supersedes the prevention of destitution, little hope is possible for a positive response to organization and unrest. Advocacy groups of various kinds will continue to play central roles in attempting to improve the situation of low-income households.

The plight of so many will engender short-term generous gestures but not the kinds of structural changes that require sizable public funding. The public strategy will increasingly be twofold: pushing families off 'welfare' by forcing them into low-paid, insecure jobs or revolving from one 'training' programme to another; half-heartedly promoting individual social mobility by providing incentives for some of the children of the poor who show talent and motivation. But profound changes to improve the prospects of many will not occur.

Unfortunately, the African-American poor currently seem unlikely candidates for an aggressive community and political role. Whether working- and middle-class African-Americans will play a strong, continuing role in communities, maintaining concern for the Black poor, will depend on the politics of the locality, divisions within African-American communities, the availability of federal and state funds to support programmes and the state of ideology and solidarity among African-Americans. The more likely role is in electoral politics, both at local and national levels, as more African-Americans are seen as electable to public office. Election campaigns can be built on and contribute to community organizing, as occurred to an important extent in the successful campaigns of Harold Washington for mayor of Chicago.

The emergence of 'Black conservatives', critical of the African-Ameri-

can poor or of affirmative action or who seek African-American empowerment through a call for community economic development, may not be
a minor tendency. The political impacts of various nationalist, separatist
and Muslim movements active at local levels are unclear. In some big
cities they are not a minor force, influencing at least the rhetoric of Black
leaders. However, there is no single voice that can authoritatively speak
for African-Americans.

Hispanics, Latinos, the Spanish-speaking (terms used interchangably
though misleadingly) are growing rapidly in both legal and illegal migration.
In the Southwest they are gaining political power, led by a strong get-out-
the-vote organization. In some Western and Southwestern states, community organizations will continue to be important in their electoral work.
Increasing economic widening may split Latino communities as a sizable
middle class grows, leaving many others in deep poverty.

The enormous immigration of the last decades will give rise to a new
ethnic politics. While the new Asian and Latin American ethnics have a
diverse politics because of their current geographic locations and past
national base, some issues may bring them together. These issues may
move beyond immigration and citizenship questions to common economic
and social concerns. The role of an expanding new ethnic middle class
will be crucial. Overcoming strains between African-American and Latino
communities is important. They often see each other as competitors for
limited public resources, or, as in Miami, feel that one group is favoured
over the other. In some places, alliances may be forged, at least for a
while, but the more general situation breeds distrust.

A long-held progressive hope is that poor and low-income groups can
become a cohesive political force because of common economic interests.
Identity groups cut across such class lines. It will require great skill and
goodwill among at least the leaders of community and identity groups to
forge a coalition. The more likely occurrence is temporary joint actions
on immediate issues rather than strong, enduring alliances. Environmental
groups which started with higher socio-economic and white groups may
move down the class ladder and expand support if they emphasize toxic
and pollution issues which affect more directly lower-income persons. If
environmental racism becomes an important theme embraced by more
mainstream environmental groups, that would offer important organizational possibilities.

Like environmental groups, women's groups are also faced with questions of constituency. They have been largely, though not exclusively, made
up of younger, better-off, higher-educated women. The concern with 'the
feminization of poverty', the continuing wage differential between male
and female workers, the awareness that women after marital break-up
suffer declines in their income while men improve theirs, the increasing
recognition that troubled coping with work and family is not a sign of

individual inadequacy but of remediable societal obstacles and inattention, all point to the broadening of issues and constituencies for women's organizations. The upsurge in women running for elective office will highlight the issues that are important to a growing number of women. Male as well as female candidates have learned that strong support on women's issues will bring out a sizable number of women to donate and to work in their campaigns.

Some labour unions, faced with declining numbers, are moving toward community involvement, seeking linkages with community groups. The most advanced in this regard are some service-based unions which have more progressive agendas than do production-based unions. But even some of the latter are using community issues to promote the organizing of unorganized firms. If this tendency is strengthened, both union and community organizing may benefit.

The vital community activity of the 1990s may be about women's and environmental issues. Both movements face questions of constituency or class which structure their issues and actions. We believe that the force of events in the United States – increasing distress for many, substantial gains for others – will lead to a broadening of constituencies and issues.

A vital issue is the likely deepening of electoral action by community-oriented groups. Electoral politics can produce a sense of influence but also result in feelings of manipulation and disillusion. If 'politics is the art of the possible', many hopes will be dashed as progressive officials compromise in order to win some gains, or politicians confuse their personal political needs with the wider good. Trust in leaders is at a low ebb and accountability needs to be restored.

In the 1990s, the most difficult question is: What does organizing seek to achieve? The traditional New Deal liberal emphasis on expanding the public sector was adopted by many progressive leaders of social movements at the time that the ideological assault on government programmes and regulation grew in effectiveness. It may be that the attack has peaked and people understand that an active government is necessary if the USA is to meet domestic and foreign challenges. Will the effort aim at supporting governmental programmes as they have been conducted in the past, or will the goal be to *defend and change* social programmes as they are expanded? To what extent will the organizing community seek to have important functions undertaken by community-based groups rather than government?

The mixed model of providing service while building organizations may expand. Direct, sustainable organizing is more difficult these days, while providing a service is a way of organizing in that it pulls people together in a common interest. If the dearth of governmental funding at federal, state and local levels continues, it would limit the move toward the mixed model.

Self-help/mutual-aid organizations will have limited expansion of political activities centring on legislative and administrative action around immediate organizational concerns. The concerns which underlie mutual aid might seep into other organizations. Working together to help one another as well as to achieve the larger external objectives could become more avowed goals of organizations. Mutual aid may gain support as people weary of individualism. Difficulties faced by recent immigrants should also promote mutual-aid activities.

One formidable need is a way of transforming local issues into a cohesive national agenda and integrating effectively many forms of organizing into the electoral process. Can stable political coalitions be formed? Whether a populist or anti-corporatist or traditional New Deal liberal ideology and agenda can succeed in doing this is an open question. A second need is to maintain the openness, flexibility, spread and vitality of local organizing – particularly important in appealing to younger people. Since these two needs somewhat crisscross, what may continue is the multiplicity of organizing endeavours and occasional coalitional activity. That situation could produce some important changes, develop a sizable number of very attractive and sophisticated leaders, but have a blunted impact.

The capacity of American society to encapsulate pressures for change is extraordinary. Despite spectacular talent and dedication, organizing efforts have not yet escaped from marginalization. That is the challenge of the next years.

Note

We have benefited – not as much as we should have – from the observations of Lisa Peattie, Janice Fine and Carin Schiewe.

11

Community Development Organizational Capacity and US Urban Policy: Lessons from the Chicago Experience 1983–93

Wim Wiewel and Doug Gills

Introduction

In his first year in office, President Clinton talked more about community development than any previous president, often citing the extensive experiences of community development organizations throughout the country. The new Empowerment Zone programme, the most significant neighbourhood revitalization initiative since the Model Cities programme of the 1960s, is based on approaches designed by neighbourhood development activists working in central cities. Additionally, the administration talks about a vision of one hundred community development banks located across the country: making loans, underwriting urban partnerships, stimulating housing and job generation.

In Chicago, as in other cities, many community development organizations are engaged in grassroots efforts to revitalize low- and moderate-income neighbourhoods through housing development, economic stimulation, job training and advocacy. Increasingly, these efforts occur in close cooperation with the private sector and local governments. The Chicago experience has much to offer, since it is the largest city in which community development has had a real chance at involvement in local government. We review that experience, attempting to draw out lessons regarding the applicability of this approach across the nation. Thus, our objective recalls the hopes of the British Labour Party, which intended to implement the lessons from local initiatives in cities such as Sheffield and London at a national level once Labour won the 1992 election (Benington and Geddes 1992). Of course, Labour didn't win, and the local experiments atrophied. With Clinton's presidency, the progressive movement, while hardly in charge, has at least earned a place at the table. In this chapter we assess what community organizations have to offer in regard to the role of such organizations vis-à-vis government; what compromises are made and how this affects the participatory, grassroots base of the organizations; the tensions between professional, political and grassroots leadership; and the extent to which local efforts combine or carry over into national policy arenas.

The relevant Chicago experience occurred primarily during the administration of Harold Washington in Chicago (1983–87), which represented a new political coalition mobilizing the relatively poor population groups that formed the bulk of the urban electorate. But mobilizing the poor alone was not enough. The coalition also included other progressives who had opposed the machine domination of mayor Richard Daley, and the Hispanic and black bourgeoisie. It was also necessary to maintain sufficient confidence and legitimacy with the city's business elite so that economic growth could continue, thus providing some of the resources to distribute. The administration managed to juggle the demands for redistribution made by its poor constituents with the need for broader support for government reform and citizen participation. It did this by expanding participation and adopting a new economic policy agenda, evolved over a decade of work by the leadership of the city's neighbourhood organizations. In the process of implementing this agenda, the rules of the game and the nature of the political structure of the city were significantly altered. How did the Chicago neighbourhood movement grow to achieve such influence? For this we need briefly to turn to the history of neighbourhood development organizations.

Chicago's Neighbourhood Movement[1]

The history of this movement starts with the nineteenth-century settlement house movement, evolving through the often racist neighbourhood conservation groups of the early part of this century. The strongest organizational influence can be traced to Saul Alinsky's work in the 1930s. His coalitions of churches, fraternal organizations, block clubs and other groups emphasized immediate, easily identifiable, and winnable issues as the route to creating power for ordinary citizens. The fundamental orientation was to accept the basic rules of the game, arguing for democratic inclusion in resource allocation.

The 1960s anti-poverty programmes and the northern civil-rights movement brought a second type of neighbourhood-based organization into prominence in Chicago. Unlike 'Alinsky' organizations, these new groups provided services or channelled citizen participation in the planning process, around issues of 'urban renewal', desegregation and housing code enforcement. The focus was on tenant organizing and welfare-rights reform. These programmes created an organizational infrastructure of

trained organizers and leaders, especially in poor and minority neighbourhoods, interacting regularly with government agencies.

As federal funding for these programmes diminished, the organizations
that survived became more diverse. Some became involved in housing
rehabilitation; others developed into purely protest and advocacy organizations, or remained involved in social-services delivery. A few combined
all these elements in a search for a comprehensive approach to the
problems faced by many of their constituents.

The ability to mobilize support and organize around a wide range of
issues was necessitated by the growing social and economic dislocation in
urban communities. The recognition of these problems was strengthened
by the ever-growing number of neighbourhood organizations. The urban
programmes of the Carter administration provided a temporary surge in
federal resources, and under Mayor Jane Byrne (1979–83) neighbourhood
organizations involved in commercial revitalization and economic development began to receive city funding. By the end of the 1970s, then, activities
had shifted toward development, policy advocacy and electoral politics,
and away from protest. Many organizations were aligned with a 'protest'
organization or advocacy group, or they would 'spin off' a respectable,
mainstream community development organization. This balance between
institutional and insurgent politics was a major contribution to community
organization practice until recently. This period, extending into the early
1980s, also saw the birth of half a dozen coalitions and technical assistance
providers, coupled with more favourable foundation support. This brought
community-based organizations a new level of expertise, resources and
legitimacy. In 1982, there were some 150 community-based groups seeking
delegate agency status – that is, getting funded to deliver city services.

Leadership, professionalization and grassroots control

Community organizations had also become alternative paths for a new
stratum of political leadership to emerge, particularly from the late 1970s.
Thus community-based organizations became a part of the political
process. This was based on the reality that blacks, Latinos and poor whites
constituted the new majority in Chicago. This demographic shift fuelled
the major political upheaval of Harold Washington's election. Byrne had
been elected in 1979 as a reform candidate who talked about the interests
of Chicago's neighbourhoods. But her campaign was not rooted in either
the neighbourhood movement or the black and Latino movements. Not
surprisingly, shortly after her election she came to an accommodation
with the old machine politicians. When her term came to an end in 1983,
the stage was set for a candidate who could bring together the disaffected
liberals who had long opposed machine politics with the neighbourhood
movement and the new black and Latino majority.

The 1983 election itself was marked by a level of intensity and mobilization not seen before or since, featuring extensive grassroots participation in the formulation of the agenda. Since Chicago was in the depths of the most serious recession since the Great Depression, the issue of jobs became central to the campaign. This created the opportunity for the work of the community organizations in economic development to become the centrepiece of Washington's development agenda. Not surprisingly, many of the neighbourhood activists went on to take positions in Washington's administration, and a variety of programmes were created which included community organizations more closely in planning and governance (Wiewel and Rieser 1989; Mier *et al.* 1992).

The increased professionalization of the movement also resulted in a loss of grassroots control over community organizations. Their resident boards were still nominally in charge of enacting policy, but most organizations became staff-driven. Even among the few that remained board-driven, the central character of the leadership tends to be middle class by function, orientation, accumulated experience and training. The staff became more professionalized and bureaucratized. This development, already underway before the Washington election, accelerated after 1983 through the capacity-building strategies of city policy makers. The Department of Economic Development alone increased its number of delegate agencies from a dozen to almost one hundred, and by 1986 all departments together funded over three hundred neighbourhood-based agencies. As delegate agencies, organizations received $15,000–40,000 per year to market city programmes, reach out to business in their areas, do housing rehabilitation, or engage in other neighbourhood development work.

Government–community organization relations

To be a delegate agency of local government is to be given credentials by the government to act on its behalf. To some extent community organizations were constrained by these legal relations; their independence and initiative were circumscribed, in part by the contracts they entered into, and to a larger extent by the self-imposed constraints inherent in a partnership arrangement (Brehm 1991). However, there remained a similarity between the reform neighbourhood development agenda and the core demands of the black and Latino empowerment movement for fairness, open government and equitable practices. The neighbourhood movement demanded equitable resource allocation to black and Latino communities, enforcement of affirmative action and minority set-aside mandates, access to government policy-making, and accurate information. They also wanted the elimination of patronage with respect to public employment, contracts and provision of public services. One reason for this compatibility of

interest was that the core demands of the community development movement originated out of the nationality movements among black and Latino
population groups, and then were pursued in Harold Washington's agenda.

The other aspect of the role of community organizations during the
Washington administration relates to their role as part of the political
reward structure. The need to institutionalize a base of power is something that is central to American politics and to any regime. Patronage
control over public jobs had been the cornerstone of Daley's machine
politics, but had been ended by a consent decree Harold Washington
signed, prohibiting political hiring and firing except for a small number of
top positions. Nevertheless, there remained a need for a political structure
that would serve to secure continuity of power and reward supporters.
The community-based organization provided an excellent alternative form
for regime maintenance. It may not have provided direct patronage, but
it was possible to build up a patronage-type army without the individual
payoff. It was possible to use the new neighbourhood agenda as a framework within which access was given to neighbourhood-based actors without the corruption that is associated with the under-the-table deals of the
previous regime of the ward bosses. One of Washington's first acts – one
that increased the technical and political capacity of neighbourhood-based
groups – was to transfer $13 million of community development block
grant money to delegate agencies who contracted to provide public services
to low-income, disadvantaged residents and communities.

There were a number of other results for the neighbourhood organizations as well. They received greater access to decision-making, implementation and evaluation, and basic information. Under Washington, it
was possible to find out what was happening in regard to city planning
and expenditures to a far greater extent than ever happened before
(Kretzmann 1991). There was more equitable resource distribution across
Chicago. Under Mayor Washington, partnerships were created where public-
sector resources were used to leverage private-sector investments of benefit to the low-income population. Public services and capital development
expenditures were distributed more equitably, without political patronage
being the primary factor in distribution (Mier and Moe 1991).

There was also a downside for the community organizations, with some
loss of independence and initiative. Activists within the neighbourhoods
became more complacent, taking for granted both the accountability of
elected officials and administrators within the government and the relations
among the community organizations themselves. They operated as if all
that they had to do was to proclaim movement politics or profess to be
a supporter of black–Latino or black–white unity and … Presto! Instant
unity! But unity has to be struggled for and then tested in battle. During
the Washington mayoralty, it was more frequently proclaimed at a press
conference in the midst of a policy issue, and quickly dissipated once an

issue was resolved. Community activists had clamoured for access and inclusion. They received both under Washington and Eugene Sawyer, his immediate successor. However, when they stopped pressing for action, they lost both. In the absence of this thrust, organizations lost independence and initiative at the same time. The movement also lost fighters in the trenches to City Hall. Once they carried the 'agenda' into City Hall, some of them stopped listening to the neighbourhood base. They took the reproduction and further development of the movement for granted. The dialogue became uni-directional. Frustration generated intolerance; fervour gave way to indifference.

The price of partnership

One question to ask is whether, given the administration's relations with its base and its accomplishments, it was worth community organizations investing significant resources in Washington's campaign and administration, thus deviating from their previous, very limited involvement in electoral campaigns? The community movement as a whole appears to have answered the question positively. For instance, during 1990, all the major coalitions banded together to formulate a 'Neighbourhood Agenda' aimed at the 1991 mayoral and aldermanic races. The work culminated in a 'Community Congress', which established the lasting stake of the neighbourhood movement in the electoral process alongside the enduring emphasis on community organizing practice. It also demonstrated the advances made during the previous eight years in the community development movement's organizational strength, the sophistication of community organization work, as well as growth in their understanding of the political process.

We think that entrance into electoral politics by the neighbourhood movement was not a mistake. There certainly were costs, and the benefits would have been greater if Washington had stayed in office longer. But the neighbourhood movement made it possible for the city administration to innovate in city governance, in public policy orientation, and in programmes and service delivery. The enduring elements of the legacy of the Washington–Sawyer era (1983–89) are that it demonstrated that a progressive coalition can be built which pushes forward the material, democratic and communal-egalitarian interests of most of the city's residents; it also demonstrated that significant changes can take place in the political culture of governance, embracing broad citizen participation. This era represented an unique attempt at fusing expertise with social activism in decision-making and implementation on the basis of shared values about fairness, equity and openness.

One lasting effect of these changes is the school reform effort that has taken place in Chicago over the past few years. Its cornerstone is the decentralization of control from a highly centralized bureaucracy to popularly elected Local School Councils for each school. Similarly, citizen concerns over the lack of relation between infrastructure planning and neighbourhood development led to the formation of the Neighbourhood Capital Budget Group (NCBG), a coalition of community organizations and technical assistance providers. NCBG has argued for neighbourhood planning councils which would set priorities for public capital expenditures. Its proposal for a city-wide Capital Improvement Advisory Board was approved by the mayor in 1990, and an annual capital budget process was established similar to the citizen input and review processes established by Mayor Washington for the city's corporate budget and the community development block grant. Taking involvement one step further, NCBG suggested the city issue a $100 million-plus Neighbourhood Infrastructure Bond for public transportation and infrastructure improvements throughout the city. Helped by low interest rates, the city issued the bond in 1992 and NCBG is now involved in efforts to make sure proceeds are indeed spent appropriately.

The experience during the Washington–Sawyer years also shows the problems caused by the lack of strategic or tactical discussions between the administration and the movement base. It would seem important for a progressive administration to maintain communication networks that would make such discussions possible. This would also clarify the distinct roles of the administration and the outside organizations and make clearer that, while the neighbourhood movement had representatives within the administration, it was not the whole of the administration.

Implications for the Clinton Presidency

The foregoing discussion suggests that social movements within specific communities of place and condition can be important sources of progressive public policy innovation. However, what would it take for community-based development organizations to make significant contributions to national domestic policy? There are four key issues, discussed below.

Capacity

There appears to be real potential for policy impact in the sense that a critical mass of organizations and experience exists. With over two thousand organizations, the field is probably twice as large as it was ten years ago. Organizations involved in community development have grown in size, sophistication and competence (Pierce and Steinbach 1987; NCCED 1991). There are also a number of thriving national coalitions and networks in place which could affect the direction and content of executive and legislative policy. Many cities across the USA also have firmly established networks of community-based organizations doing important community development work. Their experience illuminates those existing programmes and policies that work and those that do not.

Community organizations are also experiencing significant threats. There have been large declines in the standard of living for the populations which are their primary constituents. They remain very dependent on foundation and corporate support, which has been declining during the current prolonged economic stagnation.

Strangely, the community development movement was given impetus under the neo-conservative policies of the Reagan and Bush presidencies. They stressed new federalism: decentralized control, local decision-making and volunteerism, albeit without public resources. The community development movement survived and developed in spite of neo-conservatism and the withdrawal of resources from urban areas. Now federal resources appear once again to be increasing. Community development organizations are seen as important delivery agencies in programmatic initiatives; and as new legislation is passed opportunities are created for community organizations in a range of federal programmes, from health care to violence prevention, housing development, and community service.

Foundations continue to be very important resource providers, although there is clear evidence that foundations are reluctant to fund community organizing activity, viewing it as too political. At the same time, they profess to want development strategies which empower residents to give direction to the course of redevelopment as an important aspect of community-building. Foundations seem more willing to fund collaborative efforts involving anchor institutions (universities, hospitals) as mechanisms to induce change with order, fearing the disruptive aspects of citizen participation using direct approaches.

Orientation

The task facing socially conscious community development practitioners is to identify programmes and resources that promote coherence between development outcomes on a broad range of issue areas and democratic citizen participation, using empowerment strategies. Authentic community-building processes take place where development approaches are paired with empowerment of constituents, generating increases of self-sustaining capacity. In this sense, community development practitioners and organizers must think beyond the limits of the particular development project and raise the hard questions about what remains after the external development stimulus is removed. In short, the community-building process necessarily includes both development practice and empowerment activity, but is only sufficient to the extent that new capacity is derived by communities to continue some new level of activity once the development stimulus disappears. Merely measuring numbers of jobs created or housing units completed is not a sufficient indicator of community-building from a comprehensive development perspective.

Comprehensiveness

There are indications that a comprehensive community development approach can be successfully carried into other issues. Compartmental approaches to problems in the schools, family life and neighbourhoods have not worked, and integrated approaches are now being tried in many places (Cleveland Foundation 1992).

Acceptance and application of this broad public policy perspective is evident in a variety of arenas. It is evident within academic fields in education, social work, planning and public health. Community development has, for instance, become articulated with public school programming. It is now also applied in an expanding church-based movement for community development involvement as well as in public, community and environmental health. In Chicago, there is a growing arts and community development movement. It is also evident in various demonstration projects which link community development with other areas. For instance, in public housing resident management corporations have turned to community economic development strategies in the absence of adequate support from the government and local housing authorities to effect changes in living conditions.

Although comprehensiveness is rapidly becoming a required characteristic for many programmes, there is still only limited experience with truly integrated programmes, as opposed to those that are simply delivered side by side.

Coalitions

Broad coalitions are necessary to maintain support for neighbourhood development. A clear lesson of the Harold Washington experience was that the black empowerment and community development movements became isolated after the election, and this was dramatically revealed after Washington's death. For a time, the link between these movements was broken as its leading actors pursued separate agendas.

To avoid such isolation, community development practitioners must identify an agenda around which broad support can be built and sustained beyond the immediate constituents of community development services. For instance, recent movements in opposition to mega-projects promoted by Mayor Richard Daley's current administration (for example, expansion of the major convention centre, construction of a major new airport, and development of a casino and entertainment complex) were relatively successful for several reasons. First, the opponents were able to demonstrate that the social costs of these largely private enterprises were significant. Second, they were able to argue that the public benefits were smaller than advertised or that the real beneficiaries of the project would be so few that it would not offset the deferment of public spending benefiting more people. Third, the coalitions were able to coordinate activities while individual community-based organizations mobilized their constituencies for specific events and actions by demonstrating the stake of ordinary citizens in the outcome of the issue. Finally, opponents demonstrated that there were more viable alternatives available to accomplish desirable public ends.

Community development proponents must be able to demonstrate that the values and components of its public policy agenda are of broad social benefit; that its social ends are broader, less costly and just. It is not a politics of expedience or of exclusion but a new politics of principle and inclusion, based on acceptable ethical standards.

Thus, the community-based development movement is in a reasonably good position to have a positive effect on US domestic policy. With the relative decline of labour as a political force and in the absence of a progressive national movement among underrepresented minority groups, the community-based development movement has filled a vacuum as a significant player in public policy formation over the past decade.

The clearest example of this is the new Empowerment Zone legislation. This federal programme will select six Empowerment Zones and ninety Enterprising Communities around the country. Each must have a population of between 50,000 and 200,000 and present a comprehensive set of intervention programmes to alleviate poverty. The Empowerment Zones will receive $100 million over two years, while all zones will receive a variety of tax benefits, preferential treatment for federal programmes, and waivers or relaxation of many federal programme rules (for example, those which restrict assets for welfare recipients to $1,000, making it impossible for them to develop a business or even own an automobile to go to work). The most interesting aspect of this legislation, though, is that it requires that applications are based on a comprehensive, grassroots planning effort with strong participation by community organizations. The federal guidelines contain detailed guidelines and examples of such planning and virtually constitute a neighbourhood organizers' manual and resource directory. In Chicago, community organizations have taken the lead in planning the application process and are well ahead of city government in developing a comprehensive plan.

Of course, there are dangers in overstating the potential of the neighbourhood movement. The community development movement is no panacea. At best, it offers a transitional programme to address structural issues of urban poverty and racism and the accelerated marginalization of large segments of the US population. It provides potential models which might represent advances over the current organization of the private and public economy and for new practices among people, based upon sharing different values than those holding sway today. Also, the absolute growth of community development organizations is restricted by their dependence on funding support by traditional sources. Most organizations are unable to generate enough income from their own development activities to sustain operations, and only a small number can sustain the staffing levels required to make their contributions more than marginal. Numerous groups of citizens come together, form groups, lay out development plans, and subsequently collapse for want of operational and staff support (or sufficient time to get a starter project off the drawing board and into production).

The most important problems facing community development forces are the qualitative ones, involving the quality of leadership and the tension between leadership and its connection to constituents. Without well-trained, committed leadership with organic, democratic linkages to constituents who, in turn, sanction the community organization, the community development movement loses any progressive character. It becomes an industry in the sense of reproducing the conditions for the self-serving maintenance of its professional (entrepreneurial) class of managers.

Future Trends

We suggest that the following main trends will characterize the opportunities and constraints for involvement of community development organizations in local and national domestic policy-making:

More accountability and social responsibility on the part of the private sector
Community organizations may become involved in efforts by local governments to constrain the movement of capital by imposing barriers for companies that want to move, leaving workers unemployed and community economies decimated by the loss of tax bases and sources of employment. Moreover, the whole issue of liability for environmental clean-up of industrial sites will gain more currency. The precedent for these types of programmes is the success of community organizations in developing the Community Reinvestment Act as a serious weapon in their struggle against 'red-lining' (that is, covert embargoes on mortgage finance).

Greater democratic participation and control   Community organizations will likely demand a greater role in determining resource allocation patterns for capital expenditures or infrastructure, and fight for greater input into decisions requiring increased public indebtedness resulting from public–

private partnerships. Residents will demand greater scrutiny in evaluating the merits of proposed quasi-public mega-projects.

Local elected officials are likely to find their authority limited to determine public expenditures Citizens will demand more involvement in decisions about public investment and the externalities generated by private investment. They are likely to hold elected officials to greater accountability levels than in previous periods, because with declining public resources and greater needs the stakes are bigger. Community organizations will attempt to use the federal government as leverage to require participation at the local level.

The impact of environment and technology Community development groups will demand better opportunities to get clean-up contracts and demand that the private sector should bear a greater share of the costs of environmental clean-up. Advances in communication technology will enable grassroots activists to gain quicker access to information and facilitate network-building and collaborations across spatial boundaries.

National community service programmes will be expanded These will provide more resources for community organizations. However, this will lead to conflicts over whether service workers will be able to engage in direct organizing activities.

As Chicago's experience showed, to what extent these trends involve community organizations and strengthen them depends in large part on the interaction between the Clinton administration and the organized expressions of the community development movement at the national level. If the national coalitions, funders, and the largest community organizations can maintain and expand the dialogue which started in the Clinton campaign and has continued so far, we may see growth for the community development movement. However, even the Harold Washington administration – far more progressive than Bill Clinton's may ever be – had to be pushed and reminded continually. With less history and fewer levers to begin with, the national experience will not be a repeat; but it will be a chance to apply at a broader level what has been tried locally.

Note

1. This section relies in part on previous work by the authors. See primarily Clavel and Wiewel 1991.

References

Benington, John and Mike Geddes (1992), 'Local Economic Development in the
1980s and 1990s: Retrospect and Prospect', *Economic Development Quarterly*, vol. 6,
no. 4, pp. 454–63.

Brehm, Robert (1991), 'The City and the Neighbourhoods: Was it Really a Two-Way
Street?', in P. Clavel and W. Wiewel, eds, *Harold Washington and the Neighbourhoods:
Progressive City Government in Chicago 1983–1987*, Rutgers University Press, New
Brunswick, N.J., pp. 238–69.

Clavel, Pierre and Wim Wiewel, eds (1991), *Harold Washington and the Neighbourhoods:
Progressive City Government in Chicago 1983–1987*, Rutgers University Press, New
Brunswick, N.J.

Cleveland Foundation Commission on Poverty (1992), *The Cleveland Community
Building Initiative*, Mandel School of Applied Social Sciences, Case Western Re-
serve University, Cleveland, Ohio.

Kretzmann, John (1991), 'The Affirmative Information Policy: Opening Up a Closed
City', in P. Clavel and W. Wiewel, eds, *Harold Washington and the Neighbourhoods:
Progressive City Government in Chicago 1983–1987*, Rutgers University Press, New
Brunswick, N.J, pp. 199–220.

Mier, Robert and Kari Moe (1991), 'Decentralized Development: From Theory to
Practice', in P. Clavel and W. Wiewel, eds, *Harold Washington and the Neighbour-
hoods: Progressive City Government in Chicago 1983–1987*, Rutgers University Press,
New Brunswick, N.J, pp. 64–99.

Mier, Robert, Wim Wiewel and Lauri Alpern (1992), 'Decentralization of Policy-
making under Mayor Harold Washington', in Kenneth Wong, ed., *Research in
Urban Policy: Politics of Policy Innovation in Chicago*, JAI Press, Greenwich, Conn.,
pp. 79-102.

NCCED (1991), *Changing the Odds*, National Congress for Community Economic
Development, Washington DC.

Pierce, Neal and Carol Steinbach (1987), *Corrective Capitalism*, Ford Foundation,
New York.

Wiewel, Wim and Nicholas Rieser (1989), 'The Limits of Progressive Municipal
Economic Development: Job Creation in Chicago, 1983–1987', *Community
Development Journal*, vol. 24, no. 2, pp. 111–19.

Activism, Service Provision and the State's Intellectuals: Community Work in Australia

Helen Meekosha and Martin Mowbray

Introduction

Twenty years ago professional community work in Australia was largely regarded as a practice confronting inequalities. Community workers saw themselves as radicals, often fighting the state and corporate intransigence. Although their projects were not necessarily ideologically distinct, they broadly shared a concern to promote empowerment and transformation. Community work is now transformed. Those activist and developmental projects which challenge conservatism survive principally within social movements – Aboriginal land rights; consumer, environmental and urban social movements – and those movements coming from identity, such as gender, sexuality, age and disability. The remaining workers tend to be employed in direct service (organization, coordination and delivery) roles such as community care or housing, or in consultative, planning, policy and research roles. The latter are intellectuals, technicians and administrators (or advisers and consultants, evaluators, project managers and policy reviewers) performing roles aligned with the state, supervising and influencing, if not shaping, its programmes. They are, after Gramsci (1978), the 'state's intellectuals'.

There is increasing evidence of conservatism and material and political inequity. This chapter reviews major developments, institutions, patterns, policies and programmes directly affecting community work and concludes by focusing upon ways in which community activists and social movements might develop more effective strategies for empowerment and transformation. The immediate concern is with Australia, but these changes are reflected in many other countries.

Phases in Australian Community Work

Immediately following the Second World War there emerged a period, officially labelled 'postwar reconstruction', in which federal and state government agencies preoccupied with 'progress', wanting to reduce political antagonisms, fostered local voluntary community involvement, including provision of public infrastructure. One feature was the advent of organizations such as the Women's Services Guild, through which women sought to establish local community centres and child care in working-class areas. Progressive efforts were countered by conservative interests, including churches and welfare bodies, keen for women to return to domesticity and preserve the idealized model of the nuclear family (Allport 1986).

The two decades from 1949 of federal conservative government constituted a period of economic boom, high employment rates and widespread political anomie, in which community-based programmes went little beyond charitable activity and privately initiated recreational and youth work. Dissatisfaction with the failure of economic growth to solve the problems of disadvantaged groups, the war in Vietnam and the climate of protest in Europe and North America all contributed to increasing social unrest. In the spirit of reform engendered by these tensions, policies under Whitlam's Labor government (1972–75) engaged problems such as 'urban decay' and supported innovative, participatory social programmes. Local and regional planning policies became characteristic of this regime, particularly of its Department of Urban and Regional Development and the Australian Assistance Plan – a national community development scheme. The labour movement, too, took up social causes to an uncustomary extent. The best-known example of this was the green ban movement, wherein commercial developments threatening social and environmental interests were impeded through action taken by building industry unions (Mundey and Craig 1978).

Under the Fraser conservative (Liberal and National Party) government (1975–83) federal programmes which fostered community action strategies, frequently in concert with labour unions, virtually disappeared. Governments adopted a considerably narrower view of their responsibilities, taking a firmer grip on public funds. With tighter guidelines and closer accountability, funded agencies were left with less scope for manoeuvre. The ensuing period saw many experienced erstwhile community workers and avowedly radical activists become consultant social planners and administrators, often promoting a simplistic belief that better planning, management and the localization of services offered social change.

Decentralist programmes, deinstitutionalization and government-sponsored community schemes – community care, community employment and other make-work projects, community enterprise and worker cooperatives – became the future hope. Where the 1970s federal Labor government's welfare reformers saw 'community' as a simile for working-class development and participation, neo-conservative post-socialist Labor social engineers in state and federal governments from the 1980s increasingly saw 'community' as an avenue to cut back the welfare state and privatize social problems and provision.

Deinstitutionalization and community care were predicated on assumptions that women would be available in the community to carry out caring as volunteers, or for low wages. Many programmes, offering short-term relief from economic insecurity to their participants, were promoted by community workers entering bureaucracies to avoid uncertain career opportunities in this sector. By this time, unions too had abandoned oppositional struggles for change and, at their most progressive, had become involved in corporate projects and endorsement of government labour-market schemes, characterized by a series of annual Accords between labour movement and government.

Occasionally there were innovative outcomes. Some local projects were directed at minority groups such as immigrants, which opened the way for women, people with disabilities and Aborigines to get employment in local organizations, such as the Community Development Employment Program, a continuing work-for-the-dole scheme exclusively for indigenous people.

By the mid-1980s, as governments exploited the opportunity localist schemes offered for economic austerity (Mowbray 1983), the failure of such projects to help those at whom they were ostensibly directed was widely understood. Progressive social policy was increasingly seen as about managerially induced 'micro-economic reform', or 'structural adjustment'. Considerable hope was placed in the better targeting of social security and tax expenditure and new 'active' labour-force participation schemes, such as 'Jobsearch' and 'Newstart'. Reformist enthusiasm for participatory planning and community management and control was rejected. 'Peak' welfare organizations, (that is, intermediary support and umbrella organizations), like the state and federal councils of social service, which once supported such approaches, joined the new corporatist bandwagon. Elite decision-making by state managers, often influenced by neo-classical economic ideology (Pusey 1991) and little knowledge of community or social services, based on selective use of the reports of private consultants, became the way forward (Meekosha 1989). Effectiveness and efficiency, and a belief in economic growth, was the new policy context for community work.

The current Australian community work context

Into the mid-1990s Australia is socially and economically a very unequal society. While creative targeting of the welfare system has improved the position of the poorest recently (Harding and Landt 1992), the evidence is that overall income inequality in Australia increased after 1980 (Raskall and Urquhart 1993) – Labor federal governments since 1983 notwithstanding. Many of the following trends may now develop, albeit unevenly:

- Declining average and social wages.
- Increasing income and wealth differentials.
- Continuing gender, racial and ethnic inequities.
- Declining industrial conditions for the working class and sections of the middle class.
- Continuing high unemployment levels.
- Increasing dependency on social welfare and unpaid or underpaid female and immigrant labour.
- Greater reliance on privately provided welfare services and private insurance.
- Increasingly restrictive social welfare entitlement criteria.
- An increasingly regressive taxation structure.
- Increasing application of 'user-pays' pricing.
- Declining residential amenity for the working class.
- Reduced infrastructure and resources for marginalized groups to take advantage of new legislation protecting civil and consumer rights.
- Continuing environmental degradation.

Organized Community Work

Community work is an identified practice in Australia: job advertisements continually appear for community workers, local service coordinators and social planners. Nevertheless, in contrast to other human-services occupations, there are no professional associations concerned with overall practice. Consistent with this, employers expect very general qualifications, such as social-science degrees, experience in relevant policy arenas (such as health, housing or local government), and sometimes a particular language. What practices count as community development are commensurately ill-defined and include roles entailing the delivery of direct services and organization of social activities, with no discernible developmental, educative or transformative goals or outcomes.

Australian community-work literature does not help, partly because community workers, having been drawn from such a diverse background, are unfamiliar with the literature, Australian or international. There is also an anti-intellectual tradition in community work wherein there is little willingness for critical thinking, writing and reading. This deficiency is accounted for either by the declared priority of getting on with the job or as a result of long hours and 'burn-out' and, in the case of many women community workers, the double burden of worker and homemaker. Only rarely is a community worker in touch with the research and literature on, for example, urban political economy or community studies.

The majority of Australian community work literature is of an 'in-house' or self-published nature. The only recent commercially published text, Thorpe and Petruchenia's (1992) partially revamped collection of ten-year-old papers, *Community Work or Social Change?*, provides a sense of both how community work has developed and of the continuing relevance of issues of gender, race and class. Two of the three newest community work collections are published by the Centre for Development and Innovation in Health, Melbourne. These are Butler and Cass's *Case Studies of Community Development in Health* (1993), containing uncritical descriptions of politically integrative community work; and Webster's annotated (1993) bibliography of case studies. The other, Ward (1993), is a collection of untheorized articles from the Victorian communitarian *Community Quarterly*.

Only Webster's volume has any coherence or lasting value, providing a valuable overview of Australian community organization over twenty years. Case studies are classified by policy field, rather than type of practice or outcome. The classification of fields is diverse but instructive, and is made up of population categories such as Aborigines, children, older people and women; programme areas such as community arts, education, occupational health, and substance abuse; geographic classifications such as rural localities and outer suburbs; and organizational auspices, such as neighbourhood houses and 'the church'. Like much community work theory, the book is limited by Webster's functionalist theoretical approach. The notion of regressive or dysfunctional community work is not contemplated, for example. Similarly, there is marked neglect of longer-term political outcomes or material on local government and urban development. Each of the newer texts fails to recognize the degree to which community work has been reformed as managerialism and social planning, and the extent to which its best practices survive in wider social movements.

Formal community work education in Australia has generally been offered by schools of social work. Three community work programmes currently exist in Melbourne, all now associated with social-work programmes. The future of the postgraduate course, with a yearly intake of thirty part-time students, is threatened by loss of government subsidies. Several diploma-level courses for Aborigines also have substantial community work content.

With the exception of the social movements, and enclaves within particular policy areas, such as public and community housing, there is now barely a discernible radical position in Australian community work or much sense of a coherent community work profession or set of interests, directions or strategies. Several efforts have been made to form wider organizations of community workers, such as the Melbourne-based Community Development Collective which focuses on information exchange, defence of certain programmes and promotion of community development. The only broadly based organizations of this type are state-based bodies of local-government community service personnel, concentrating on information exchange about broad developments in government policy and programmes and the managerial reforms sweeping local government.

They manifest no recognizable progressive focus on issues concerned with citizenship, class, gender or redistribution. It is also only local-government-based workers who have any regular national or state conferences, and the biennial Local Government Community Development Conference systematically excludes politically contentious issues from its agendas.

Social Movements

Progressive Australian community development in Australia is more evident in the context of (inter)national and other broad-scale movements, rather than in local activities. The influence of feminists has been significant in all social movements, with the women's movement now seen as multi-faceted. The environment movement has had a considerable effect, made up as it is of numerous groupings tending towards the left of the political spectrum but displaying considerable difference in perspective and strategy. Several such groups, including The Wilderness Society and Greenpeace, have become extremely influential in mainstream politics. Localized environmental action – against, for example, logging of forests, damming of rivers, tourist infrastructure and industrial pollution – has been an everyday feature of the Australian political landscape. The political sophistication and determination of environmental groups, articulated with heightened public environmental concern, has given them considerable political leverage. Since 1993, the two Green Party senators have held the balance of power in the Senate, taking up social and environmental issues.

Naturally enough, neighbourhood-based action directed at the defence of local amenity and property values is a prominent, continuing part of community action. Usually these groups have no paid workers and draw on a middle-class, educated group for leadership and support. However, a newer dimension to localized action is the organized opposition to service reductions. Many previously politically dormant localities have resisted closure or privatization of hospitals, post offices, rail transport and schools.

Indigenous People's Organization

The cause of indigenous land and other rights has gained momentum, especially in the 1990s. The focus for land rights has been the Northern Territory, principally because of the powerful advocacy and developmental roles of the Central and Northern Land Councils. These Aboriginal-controlled organizations, legally founded in the *Aboriginal Land Rights (NT) Act*, are financed by revenue indexed to royalties for mining on Aboriginal land. In 1992 Aboriginal organizing benefited from a ground-breaking High Court decision which rejected standing legal doctrine that the land was not owned prior to British settlement, finding that native title can continue to exist. The judgement, and subsequent land claims (such as the Wik claim over 35,000 square kilometres in northern Queensland) induced apoplexy in pastoral and mining industry organizations. The backlash forced unprecedented high-level coordination of political action by Aboriginal and Torres Strait Islander people. A fluctuating, heated national struggle, with Green politicians playing a vital role, culminated in a qualified legislative victory for indigenous people.

A particularly interesting community development programme is centred on the Aboriginal and Torres Strait Islander Commission (ATSIC). This statutory body, inheriting many functions of the federal Department of Aboriginal Affairs, is a multi-tiered and participatory organization. ATSIC comprises a national Commission and sixty elected regional councils, each responsible for formulating and implementing a regional plan for its Aboriginal and Torres Strait Islander constituents. ATSIC is in important respects something of an organizational throwback to the 1970s state-backed developmental programmes, but also features many limitations of the reformist past, not least that its financial allocations are government-determined. The organization is also constrained by having to work through a conservative bureaucracy, part of the federal public service (Rowse 1992).

Ethnic organization

Australia's immigrant population derives from over seventy nations. Immigration accounts for over half the annual population growth, the highest in the industrial capitalist world. The single largest source has been Britain and Ireland, with other European and Asian countries providing significant numbers. An ethnic-rights movement in the mid-1970s played an important part in dismantling prevailing assimilationist policies – the formation of Ethnic Communities Councils in major Australian cities and a Federation of Ethnic Communities Councils of Australia provided its institutional base. Even so, government support for community work with immigrants only began with the advent of multicultural policies in the 1980s.

The *Galbally Report* recommended specific services for immigrants, funded by federal government, in cooperation with states and local government, and primarily located in the nongovernment sector, largely dependent on volunteer labour. These services included local Migrant Resource Centres, grants to ethnic organizations to employ welfare, social and community workers, and ethnic Saturday schools. Workers in these organizations rarely had a specific community development focus, but were expected to cover most community needs – interpreting, counselling, information, referral, crisis intervention and community development. These workers, largely women, also had poor work conditions, career expectations and status. Government priorities were for these organizations to deliver services, rather than organize community action (Meekosha and Rist 1982). The underlying concern for cultural pluralism identified issues as problems of immigrant integration, avoiding action on dominant society racism.

Despite these constraints, community development with immigrants covered a diversity of needs and activities. In Wollongong a group of immigrant women – Macedonian, Turkish, South American – took on the Australian industrial giant, BHP, over its refusal to employ women (Covell and Refshauge 1986). Their struggle continued for fourteen years, with strong support from local migrant and women's organizations, leading to eventual legal victory. At the other end of the spectrum, many ethnic organizations employed community workers, usually untrained, to provide direct basic advice and referral services. In addition to welfare services, there was a concentration on cultural activities.

By the late 1980s the 'separate development' or 'ethno-specific' model of funding community work with immigrants had been replaced by a government commitment to 'mainstreaming'; this occurred in a climate of increased racism (particularly against Asians), major government expenditure cuts and a reassertion of voluntarism and privatization ('user-pays') as the basis for welfare (Meekosha and Jakubowicz 1989). With the welfare sector most affected by privatization, one area of direct political action involved multicultural artworkers, both as individuals and through community arts. In the early 1990s the Australia Council and other arts-funding bodies, under pressure from networks of multicultural artists, provided more direct support to community cultural development through arts funding. This reflected a concern amongst activists that ethnicity not be seen as a welfare problem, but as a resource in developing community power.

The other major direction now apparent focuses around community-relations strategies seeking to address racism and racist violence. While some resources were invested in community development for improved community relations, greatest attention was given to high-profile events and mass-media campaigns in conjunction with the education system. The emphasis was on individual value change, rather than the development of community solidarity and sustained campaign work (Moss 1993).

Feminist organization

The relationship between feminism and the state has had a particular impact on the development of women's services and community work. In 1972 a group of women formed the Women's Electoral Lobby (WEL) in order to achieve equality for women through the parliamentary process, presaging feminist involvement with the state. In 1973 Labor appointed a women's adviser to the prime minister's staff. Federal and state departments followed with the establishment of women's, Equal Employment Opportunity and Anti-Discrimination units, which continue to be established twenty years later.

The central thesis of the second wave of feminism, that the 'personal is political', together with this institutionalization of women's issues within the state, generated two important features of community work with women. First, a variety of parsimoniously supported women's services was established. The first Women's Health Centre (Leichhardt, Sydney) was established in 1974 with over fifty such centres operating by 1991 (Broom 1991). The growth of government-supported women's services has been the main locus for feminist community work. The second outcome was the emergence of feminist bureaucrats who have legitimated some feminist struggles in the community, whilst acting as a barrier between less powerful women and government, defusing anger and dissent.

A tendency of some feminist organizations to see race and gender issues as distinct led to Aboriginal and immigrant women setting up separate services. While in the 1970s there was a move to reject government support as carrying dangers of co-option (Dowse 1983; Curthoys 1984), the overall trend has been to demand government support for collective provision of services (rather than direct government delivery of services). This resulted in the establishment of women's health centres, refuges, community child-care centres, sexual-assault services, women's legal centres, working-women's centres, and women's occupational health action and support groups.

Not all women's services have operated on feminist principles. McFerran (1987) estimated that only one third of women's refuges did so. Her evaluation of twenty-two women's refuges found that only six had aims directed at improving the status of women, and only four translated this into social action. Those services operating as feminist collectives emphasize the importance of process issues, such as collective decision-making, egalitarian conditions of work and skill-sharing.

The diverse nature of today's feminism has had a profound impact throughout community work. Even the most conservative and localized neighbourhood centres run women's assertiveness training and discussion groups with a focus on encouraging women into further education, such activities happily coexisting with traditional, caring, volunteer women's work. This type of neighbourhood work is limited by a perspective which does not necessarily challenge women's dependency on either men or the state.

The scattered 1970s community programmes servicing the frail aged and people with disabilities were integrated by the federal Labor government in joint action with the states in the mid-1980s, under the label 'Home and Community Care'. Community development was increasingly presented as service organization and the encouragement of (limited) consumer participation in planning and administration of services. Women were reinforced in roles as carers, while volunteers were represented as an effective vehicle for service delivery. Women made up 66 per cent of all wage earners in the community-services industry in 1990 (Jamrozik and Boland 1992) but with very low levels of unionization (Department of Employment, Education and Training 1988).

Progressive community work has been replaced by more authoritarian programmes geared to and funded by market place or charity. As the dominant discourse of state welfare positions itself as postmodern, post-socialist and post-feminist, feminists face the choice between engaging with and influencing governments to move towards social provision for social justice, thus facing dangers of co-option and demobilization; or to withdraw from engagement and seek to develop alternative enclaves. The latter would promote a women's culture, but may be inaccessible to many women.

New Urban Policies

In recent years, urban social issues have again attracted the attention of government and the mass media. Discourse around the topic proliferates – through reviews, inquiries, task forces, and an amorphous range of model programmes. At the core of urban policy reform is the concept of urban consolidation – referring to measures to increase residential (dwelling and population) density, thus diminishing overall costs of the infrastructure and land component of housing supply.

Another device in line with such OECD policy exhortations about finding 'off-budget' (that is, not funded by government tax income) solutions for housing and related infrastructure (OECD 1990) is the provision of commercially owned and managed residential and alternative accommodation and associated services. Examples include private roads, shopping centres, recreation facilities, prisons, hospitals and residential estates.

A related trend, to greater recovery of real costs of installation of roads, open space and services, implicates social planning and community development workers. Local governments are increasingly pressured to require property developers to install community amenities themselves. Developers pass costs on to consumers in housing prices, or through corporate bodies designed to give residents responsibility for local services. Local-government community-service workers develop social plans that form the legal and economic justification for transferring costs to incoming residents – usually at the bottom of the socio-economic scale (Mowbray 1991). Whilst helping to secure important services, such personnel are paradoxically assisting in the transfer of costs from centrally collected tax revenue to local consumers.

Local Government

Compared to the federal and state governments, local government has only had a subsidiary role in welfare provision, historically having concentrated on support for the interests of property owners and business. Local government's most substantial longer-term involvement in social-service provision has been in services to aged people and infants, the former mainly as federal-government subsidized senior-citizens' centres, welfare officers for the aged, home-help and delivered meals, linked to maintaining older people at home.

However, municipalities and shires have gradually developed an interest in community development and social planning. Councils have become major employers of community workers such as community-service managers; social planners; community project officers; housing-development officers; youth, ethnic programme, aged and domiciliary care coordinators; and child-care supervisors – which, with related facilities, have been partly financed by federal and state governments.

Earlier enthusiasm of federal and state governments to devolve welfare responsibilities to local government has waned, with five of the six states under the control of conservative governments in 1994. In the name of efficiency, states have moved to reassert their control over local governments – curtailing what local control may earlier have been won. Councils are increasingly constrained through sackings, abolitions, amalgamations, forced service privatization, enhanced state government and tighter operational regulations.

Conclusion

Except in isolated programmes and within broader social movements, Australian community work has little legitimate claim to progressive directions or politics. Instead, it has been largely consumed within the overall government commitment to the run-down of the welfare state. While this project has limited personal support from community practitioners themselves, there is little prospect for collective resistance. Australian community work is divided, organizationally and politically.

Three contemporary modes may be discerned in the foregoing review of developments in Australian community work – social movements, local service delivery and policy planning and supervision. The corresponding modal roles for community work may be represented as social (and environmental) activism, local service organization and provision, and managerialism. The concomitant modal agencies are, first, a national environmental, land-rights or feminist organization; second, a local emergency accommodation, home support or ethnic 'community options' service; and third, a private locally focused consultancy, a social policy adviser or government programme director.

We conclude with suggestions that might contribute towards community work practices becoming more able to counter this increasingly conservative social, economic and political environment, linking proposals to the foregoing categories.

Social-movement activists have had a tendency to insularity within their own causes. We believe that cross-movement coordination is now necessary (Meekosha 1993). Signs of greater preparedness to form broader alliances on progressive platforms are evident, which might be built upon. Recent linkages between the Greens and Aboriginal activists over the passage of the native-title legislation are a case in point. In our view, cooperation needs to be sought not only for expediency, but over an understanding that fundamental causes of the problems which concern them lie in the nature of the capitalist, patriarchal and racist state. The longer-term aims of each movement cannot be realized outside of broad social transformation.

The same understandings are apparent for community workers in the sphere of service provision. Overall, however, they are more likely to have a constraining locality-based focus. They are less likely than the first group to appreciate the broader parameters of our political system. They are, therefore, more in need of political and related organizational support. More effort is needed in reaching local service organizers and deliverers through information, discussion and debate. Unfortunately, their immediate industrial circumstances restrict these possibilities. Educative, but not just propagandist, literature ought to be more available; and bodies like tertiary education institutions, unions and industry councils and training boards, are in a position to assist in this way. Progressive, quality, community work education should be made accessible to otherwise untrained practitioners. A premium exists on the maintenance of networks within which progressive anti-discriminatory practices are developed.

The intellectuals, almost by necessity, are limited by having to produce along lines acceptable to their state employers. If they are to survive, they have less freedom to manoeuvre. In any case, their work often entails convincing workers at other levels that they and government are on the right track. The fact that these workers are best resourced in terms of time, and often skills, and have control over the major forums and propaganda outlets makes their task of limiting reformist action much easier. We are challenged to offer critiques of the intellectual's legitimating and managerialist work – and to argue consistently for alternative policies and programmes. The view that 'our' problems are due to deficient planning and management, inappropriate organizational structures, low growth, inappropriate pricing, and so on, deserve persistent challenge. Fundamental political solutions need to be pursued, alongside some technical remedies.

References

Allport, Carolyn (1986), 'Women and Suburban Housing: Post-war Planning in Sydney 1943–1961', in Brian McLoughlin and Margo Huxley, eds, *Urban Planning in Australia: Critical Readings*, Longman Cheshire, Melbourne, pp. 233–48.

Broom, Dorothy (1991), *Damned If We Do: Contradictions in Women's Health Care*, Allen and Unwin, Sydney.

Butler, Paul and Shirley Cass, eds (1993), *Case Studies of Community Development in Health*, Centre for Development and Innovation in Health, Melbourne.

Covell, Diana and Chloe Refshauge (1986), 'The Biased Australian', *Scarlet Woman* 21, Autumn, pp. 18–22.

Curthoys, Ann (1984), 'Women's Movement and Social Justice', in Dorothy Broom, ed., *Unfinished Business*, Allen and Unwin, Sydney, pp. 161–76.

Department of Employment, Education and Training (1988), 'Women in Community Services', *Women and Work*, vol. 1, no. 1, March, pp. 5–6.

Dowse, Sarah (1983), 'The Women's Movement Fandango with the State', in Cora Baldock and Bettina Cass, eds, *Women, Social Welfare and the State*, Allen and Unwin, Sydney, pp. 205–26.

Gramsci, Antonio (1978), *Selections from the Prison Notebooks*, edited and translated by Quintin Hoare and Geoffrey Nowell Smith, International Publishers, New York.

Harding, Anne and John Landt (1992), 'Policy and Poverty: Trends in Disposable Incomes, March 1983 to September 1991', *Australian Quarterly*, vol. 64, no. 1, Autumn, pp. 19–48.

McFerran, Ludo (1987), *Beyond the Image, Women's Emergency Services Program of Western Australia: Evaluation 1987*, Perth.

Meekosha, Helen (1989), 'Research and the State: Dilemmas of Feminist Practice', *Australian Journal of Social Issues*, vol. 24, no. 4, November, pp. 249–68.

────── (1993), 'The Bodies Politic: Equality, Difference and Community Practice', in H. Butcher *et al.*, eds, *Community and Public Policy*, Pluto Press, London, pp. 171–93.

Meekosha, Helen and Andrew Jakubowicz (1989), 'Increasing Opportunity or Deepening Disappointment? Access and Equity in the Commonwealth Department of Community Services and Health', *Migration Action*, vol. 11, no. 1, April, pp. 9–18.

Meekosha, Helen and Lioba Rist (1982), 'The Resource Centres: Boom or Bust?', *Migration Action*, vol. 6, no. 1, pp. 27–31.

Moss, Irene (1993), *State of the Nation: A Report on People of Non-English Speaking Backgrounds*, Human Rights and Equal Opportunity Commission, Sydney.

Mowbray, Martin (1983), 'Localism and Austerity: The Political Economy of Community Welfare Services', *Community Development Journal*, vol. 18, no. 3, October, pp. 238–46.

────── (1991), 'Political and Economic Dimensions of Local Social Planning in NSW', *Urban Policy and Research*, vol. 9, no. 3, September, pp. 133–40.

Mundey, Jack and Gary Craig (1978), 'Joint Union–Resident Action', in Paul Curno, ed., *Political Issues and Community Work*, Routledge and Kegan Paul, London, pp. 199–18.

Pusey, Michael (1991), *Economic Rationalism in Canberra*, Cambridge University Press, Sydney.

Raskall, Phil and Robert Urquhart (1993), 'Inequality, Living Standards and the Social Wage During the 1980s', Paper to 4th Australian Family Research Conference, Australian Institute of Family Studies, Sydney.

Rowse, Tim (1992), 'Top-down Tensions', *Modern Times*, June, pp. 22–3.

Thorpe, Rosamund and Judy Petruchenia, eds (1992), *Community Work or Social Change*, Hale and Iremonger, Sydney.

Ward, John E. (1993), *Australian Community Development: Ideas, Skills and Values for the 90s*, Community Quarterly, Melbourne.

Webster, Kim (1993), *Australian Case Studies in Community Development 1972–1992: An Annotated Bibliography*, Centre for Development and Innovation in Health, Melbourne.

13

Community Organizing in the Philippines: The Experience of Development NGOs

Karina Constantino-David

Introduction

The Philippines has been confronted with debilitating poverty, despair and powerlessness for generations. Despite government promises, the imposition of multilateral institutions, and grandiose plans claiming to make life better, the poor majority have had to fend for themselves, becoming sacrificial offerings to the elusive goal of development. Their usual response has been unbelievable patience coupled with desperate hope. When patience and hope can no longer be maintained, there are outbreaks of primitive rebellion, ranging from creatively 'working' the system to inflicting violence against persons and property. However, the poor soon realize that they are on their own, passive recipients of decisions made by the powerful, finding it difficult to resist, much less to participate in determining their own future. In this context, community organizing (CO) has become a major weapon of the powerless in asserting their demands, holding accountable those who rule, and treading their own autonomous path to development. In parallel, development NGOs have increasingly assisted grassroots organizations in the process of empowerment.

This chapter will attempt to analyse the role of development NGOs, arguing that they have been crucial in developing practice and enhancing a sense of potency among poor communities. In tracing the changes that community organizing has undergone through the years, we point to contradictions endemic to CO and development NGOs in the Philippines.

The Philippine NGO Territory

Philippine NGOs no longer exist on society's margins. Government, bilateral and multilateral agencies have all grudgingly recognized NGOs as significant; but because NGOs are curiously defined by what they are not rather than what they are, the picture is confused. The outline below attempts to map the Philippine NGO terrain, based on the perceptions of government, media and the larger public. This disconcerting picture and the penchant of Filipinos for acronyms only illustrates the complexity of the situation. Based on government records, there are more than 30,000 non-stock and non-profit organizations classified as NGOs. There are three basic categories in this map, two of which have further subcategories:

(1) NGIs (non-government individuals): academics, church leaders or professionals who are (wrongly) billed as NGO leaders and representatives by government and media.

(2) Membership-Based Organizations: a large majority of the organizations fall into this category. Their distinguishing characteristic is that they are voluntary membership organizations. They include, for example,

- PACOs (professional, academic, and civic organizations).
- POs (people's organizations): grassroots groups in communities, work areas or sectors. These include GUAPOs (genuine/autonomous people's organizations) which are groups from marginalized communities and sectors.

(3) Institutions/Agencies: contrasted to membership-based organizations, these are intermediate agencies operating with full-time staff, providing varying services to people's organizations. These include:

- DJANGOs (development, justice and advocacy NGOs), which service GUAPOs by undertaking concrete experiments to foster an alternative social order that is just, participative and sustainable. Community and sectoral organizing is the base from which DJANGOs intervene, largely dependent on donor agencies but insisting on autonomy and making no pretence to political neutrality. In response to the generally micro-nature of their work, DJANGOs formed networks either reflecting specific fields of work (rural areas, cooperatives, and so on) and/or united by common development frameworks. Ten networks have formed the Caucus of Development NGO Networks (CODE-NGO) covering 3,000 individual agencies. Issue-based coalitions also emerged, cutting across networks and focusing on basic issues like the environment, women's rights and foreign debt.
- Other relevant institutions: TANGOs (traditional charitable welfare NGOs); FUNDANGOs (funding agency NGOs) – foundations and grant-giving organizations; and MUNGOs (mutant NGOs). These latter have a special, if inappropriate, place amongst NGOs. Resulting from the growing recognition of the role of NGOs, the avalanche of funds from foreign donors especially after the end of the Marcos dictatorship,

and government's decision to engage NGO services in implementing programmes, new NGOs proliferated. Amongst the types of MUNGOs formed were GRINGOs (government run/initiated NGOs), conduits of government or bilateral aid funds, whose operations are geared towards cornering funds and/or building up a politician's image. BONGOs (business-organized NGOs) are agencies organized as tax dodges, as vehicles for quelling labor unrest, or creating benevolent company images. Finally, the COME N'GO (NGO entrepreneurs) is a catch-all category for generally illegal organizations which masquerade as NGOs.

This analysis challenges the notion that NGOs share a commonality of purpose and practice. It is clear that only DJANGOs and GUAPOs undertake community organizing seriously, and we focus on these below.

Two Decades of Community Organizing

Organizing among the powerless has long been part of the Philippine scene. However, community organizing, embodying a systematized set of skills and principles, started only in 1970 following the successes of Saul Alinsky in the West, the arrival of Herbert White, one of his co-workers, the formation of the Philippine Ecumenical Council for Community Organizing (PECCO), and the emergence of the Zone One Tondo Organization (ZOTO). On the national level, this was the period called the First Quarter Storm. Starting with students protesting against the status quo and articulating visions of a more desirable future, linkages were set up with various sectors, especially in Metro Manila. Some student activists joined PECCO as organizers/trainees.

CO, from these small beginnings, spread rapidly to become the basic underpinning of development work, and part of the mainstream of Philippine life. This, however, resulted in much confusion as the government incorporated the label and methods of CO into its programmes, with MUNGOs still claiming that they do community organizing. The government speaks of 'people empowerment' even where CO is absent. As such, community organizing was decontextualized, as though it comprised a series of ideologically neutral techniques to be placed in the service of any master.

Community organizing springs from the premises that established power systems can be countervailed by collective action, and that the powerless must participate in their own development and assert their rights. Communities marginalized by societal forces beyond their control breed people who are accepting of their fate as passive recipients, often only taking action against conditions that directly threaten their very survival.

It is this debilitating culture of powerlessness that community organizing seeks to shatter. CO methods are therefore tools that cannot be divorced from their ideological premisses. While there are significant differences across sectors, a brief summary of the periods in community organizing among the urban poor can help to synthesize the Philippine experience and connect with trends in other countries.

'Pure CO' (1970–74)

The dynamism of PECCO and ZOTO – the immediate gains from issue-based organizing and the conflict-confrontation method, the creativity of tactics, the relative unity among those involved in CO (ideological formations, religious groups, academics and activists), the projection of the urban poor's issues onto the public agenda – are generally regarded by veteran organizers as the golden years of CO. Much of the mythology about CO developed during this period. Huge, creative mobilizations captured the imagination while small victories were rapidly converted into larger gains like on-site development and in-city relocation. A new breed of local leaders started to emerge, living the problems.

Within the organizing community, however, tensions had already started to emerge from the difficulty of balancing demands of local issue-based organizing with the requirements of an ideological movement, the Communist Party of the Philippines (CPP). The PECCO team was composed of people from a broad political spectrum, from the CPP and social-democratic groups to church-based and non-aligned individuals. Even before the entry of PECCO into Tondo, the CPP had small local chapters. While relations among the organizers were generally good and a healthy relationship with the CPP was struck, differences began to erode the pluralist unity. The imposition of martial law, the subsequent raid on the PECCO office, the arrest of some leaders, and the growing difficulty of communication with significant people forced underground, heightened contradictions.

Grappling with political lines (1974–78)

Successes in organizing the urban poor spread widely; PECCO training centres expanded in Metro Manila and in other areas, with 120 staff and trainees in both rural and urban areas. The spread of the theology of liberation, Freire's 'pedagogy of the oppressed', and structural analysis all provided fertile ground for more CO adherents. All these enriched organizing work and developed a strain of CO that is Philippine in character. The growth of the progressive movement, both ideologically and numerically, as a response to martial law, also greatly contributed to the Philippine variant of CO.

PECCO instituted a 'no-links' policy in relation to the CPP, its formal break-up in 1977 being the culmination of growing tensions within the organizing community. Unlike Alinsky-type CO in the West, Philippine CO took on a much more political/ideological character, in reaction to a basic limitation of CO – its lack of a concrete vision beyond the resolution of localized issues. Yet this was also the source of much internal wrangling. Mutual suspicion grew as CPP cadres were perceived to be 'riding' on the organizing process (evidenced by the recruitment of urban poor leaders into the party) with the counter-charge that non-CPP organizers refused to acknowledge local issues as manifestations of structural obstacles. Non-CPP organizers insisted on the 'no-links' rule and were constantly on guard against proposals like integrating a political education component into the organizing process or setting up new centres perceived as party-initiated. Whilst dissension increased and the contradictions became counter-productive, military repression heightened with the arrests of urban poor leaders and organizers. Divisions were drawn politically as each group attempted to balance CO as an essentially localist and issue-based approach with the demands of a growing national movement and the necessity for structural change.

Experimenting with models (1978–83)

After PECCO split, other NGOs emerged. Even the Marcos regime 'adopted' CO as a method in government agencies and programmes. Simultaneously, an 'underground' critique of CO articulated a challenge to established methods and principles, geared towards *praxis* – a conscious review of CO itself within and across disparate groups – as well as a push towards demonstrating the effectiveness of theory through practice. Three distinct approaches were prevalent: first, those advocating 'pure CO'; second, those who incorporated CO methods and principles within the framework of ideological formations; and third, government attempts to use CO methods to achieve specific, pre-determined outputs.

This period, although marked by competition and hostility, resulted in a dynamism that enhanced both theory and practice. But these positive gains took their own toll. The urban poor were segregated from each other, resulting in extremely localist concerns, unable to confront sectoral issues that could only be tackled effectively on a collective basis. This became particularly obvious in the light of increased government activity on slum clearance, demolition and relocation, which required wider co-ordinated responses.

Political upheaval (1983–86)

The assassination of Benigno Aquino and the consequent mass movement broke down the relative isolation of the urban poor. Organized communities and NGOs (even those that had been 'non-political' and isolated) participated in the anti-dictatorship struggle, forming coalitions and a mass movement. However, whilst the past debates were blurred by the temper of the times, they remained unresolved and would resurface at a future time. During this period the nature of CO changed drastically. The anti-dictatorship movement was participated in by the poor and their allies and by members of the ruling class whose power had been clipped by the Marcos dictatorship. Almost overnight, the urban poor stood alongside those whose underlying class interests could not accommodate their main demands: the resulting consensus turned out, therefore, to be shallow. Three years of tireless protest left little time for local issues, much less for the painstaking process that was the trademark of CO. In a real sense, community organizing was overshadowed during this period, even as its fruits were obvious in the level of involvement displayed by the organized urban poor communities in a struggle that actually had no direct impact on their plight.

Illusion (1986–88)

The 1986 uprising, ousting Marcos, and the installation into power of Corazon Aquino, created an entirely new conjuncture. Having seen the state as the repository of all evil, and because of their own participation in what seemed to be a dramatic victory, the mass movement in general and the urban poor in particular needed to readjust. At the outset, many expected radical changes. When these changes did not come, the ensuing frustration was initially cushioned by the hope that the new government would soon come around. The generally accepted perception was that everyone needed to assist in establishing political stability by avoiding excessive demands that might threaten a government put in place with so much sacrifice.

This, coupled perhaps with mass-action fatigue and an unfamiliar relationship with those in power, ushered the urban poor into unexplored territory. Negotiations instead of mass actions were the order of the day. In order to win demands from the new government, coalitions were formed. The National Congress of Urban Poor Organizations (NACUPO) was launched, and as a result of its pressure the Presidential Commission on the Urban Poor (PCUP) was created, led by an urban poor leader and organizer.

In relation to NGOs, many of those whose community organizing paths had previously crossed formed the People's Foundation of Organizers for Community Empowerment (PEOPLE'S FORCE). Bound by strong past personal ties, and despite differing political experience, these individuals recognized the continued importance of community organizing and decided to create a single NGO to train younger organizers. NACUPO and PEOPLE'S FORCE suffered a similar fate, however, neither being sustained at the level their organizers expected. NACUPO's existence was particularly short-lived because of the Aquino government's negligence of the sector; charges of ineffectiveness, self-interest and corruption against the PCUP leadership which was identified with one particular ideological bloc; and continued demolitions and other violations of the rights of the urban poor. The sector was fragmented again.

PEOPLE'S FORCE survived a little longer until the tensions resulting from ideological divisions started to erode its foundations. Even as the founders tried to maintain a pluralist unity, past methods and unresolved doubts resulted in its eventual collapse. It was obvious that even community organizers still had a lot to learn about organizing themselves. Compared to other periods, few concrete gains were actually accomplished, although there was some resurgence of organizing work. It was painfully realized that the very best of intentions can be undermined by unrealistic expectations

Multiform approaches (1988 to the present)

Recent years have been marked by a re-emphasis on experimentation. While continuing to develop skills and perspectives, CO has expanded its horizons beyond the emphasis on political consciousness-raising and issue-based organizing. More NGOs have gone into integrated programmes based on community organizing, but with a focus on income-generation, land acquisition, child-support systems, environmental issues, rights for women and even electoral involvement.

Avoiding the pitfalls of the past, coalitions have been cautiously set up, placing more attention on process. NGOs, through networking and through CODE-NGO, have demonstrated greater success, especially in relation to sustainability. Apart from basic organizing concerns, much attention has also been placed on negotiating with government and learning the ropes of parliamentary politics – advocacy, lobbying and electoral work. The success of the Urban Land Reform Task Force, assisted by the Church, in pushing for the passage of the Urban Development and Housing Act (UDHA) was a signal achievement. NGOs and urban poor organizations actively lobbied for this law. Although it does not respond to all urban poor problems, it provides some basis for the poor to organize around housing issues.

Shifts in urban poor organizing are intertwined with the growing development of the NGO community; both problems and gains at each period cannot be separated from the specific characteristics of NGOs. Today, NGOs have a rich history to build upon even as their development has resulted in the emergence of new dilemmas needing to be confronted.

Dilemmas Confronting NGOs Today

Development NGOs have been the arena within which CO has been a major force. Government attempts to do CO have suffered from both the measurable outputs required by a bureaucracy and from the obvious lack of autonomy of any people's organization that is set up under the auspices of the state with its alternative agenda.

In the experience of DJANGOs and GUAPOs, community organizing has become a major weapon in empowering the poor and advancing their rights. But this experience has not been without dilemmas that have consciously to be resolved. Whilst interrelated, major issues to be confronted can be categorized into those internal to NGOs, those relating to the relationship between NGOs and POs, and those which relate to NGOs and donor agencies.

CO dilemmas internal to the development NGO community

Completing the vision

Earlier critiques of CO correctly pointed out that organizing without a vision stunts the process itself. The task no longer seems to be to articulate a vision of a more desirable future, but to forge a more holistic view of development that is integrated into the organizing process. Underdeveloped countries like the Philippines confront at least six types of oppression: country and class, sector and species, generation and gender. The first three – unequal and unjust relations between countries, the oppressiveness of class relations, and the specific characteristics of sectors of the poor – have long been focuses for CO. The latter three have not been accorded equal importance.

Growing environmental degradation and consequent awareness of the need for ecological balance is a relatively new perspective for community organizing. Previously, much of CO has been homocentric to the detriment of the ecology. There is, however, a contradiction between the needs of the poor and the requirements of environmental balance. Poverty, which in the final analysis is structurally determined, pushes people to abuse the ecosystem – to cut down trees for homes and firewood, dispose of waste in rivers, pollute the air through inefficient transport systems, invade forests, use harmful fertilizers and pesticides, and massacre animals in search of better livelihoods. Community organizing, traditionally focused on improving the lot of the poor, has to contend with balancing immediate survival needs of poor people with the urgent, though longer-term, task of environmental consciousness.

Much CO builds upon an undifferentiated perspective on the poor and therefore has developed a leadership profile that is basically adult and male. Apart from specific programmes for the very young and the elderly, generational politics has been glossed over. Even where there are attempts to undertake programmes for each of the generations in a community, the overall perspective and decision-making has tended to be limited to the generation that has relative economic, political and social control, from the family to the community level. In so doing, participation becomes constricted and reinforces a traditional hierarchy.

Perhaps the biggest flaw in CO has been its gender blindness. This absence of a gender framework has generated struggles for equality and justice for women. Often, community organizers have retreated into the easy rationalization that the process must start from where the people are. And yet a starting point has a dynamic of its own, empowering the poor and yet also entrenching other levels of power relations. It is not uncommon for organizers to discover that the very leaders they have helped mould are autocratic, even violent, in the domestic sphere. Apart from this, like generational politics, the continued marginalization and subordination of women restricts participation, fails in democratizing power from the personal to the political, and further entrenches patriarchy.

Forging sustainable networks

The need to build bridges across sectors and geographic areas has been recognized recently despite localist traditions of community organizing. NGO networks have been a major advance because they have broken the relative isolation of both agencies and POs, resulting in sharing of experience, experience in accessing funds, and advocacy campaigns. Networking, more importantly, set the stage for broader linkages across and outside the NGO community. The formation of CODE-NGO propelled the NGO community further. Reacting to the emergence of MUNGOs and accepting the need for NGOs to play a more active role in the process of democratization, ten national networks with similar perspectives banded together in a network of networks. The principles and tactics of community organizing were and remain crucial in CODE-NGO, which has created a community that is capable of concerted action, consensually validated goals, and self-regulation.

But such an accomplishment has not been without contradictions. The centralization of power in Metro Manila, especially in an archipelagic country like the Philippines, has also reinforced the dominant position of Metro Manila NGOs. In the same way that community organizing has to ensure that a 'new elite' is not developed in communities, so too does networking. A tension also exists between this widening horizon of functions and community organizing. Individual base NGOs must confront the problem of dividing their time between the essential tasks of community organizing and the growing demands of networking and advocacy. In the process, dilemmas surface such as the growing trend towards providing support services as against direct organizing work. Many experienced organizers have been sucked into coalitions and negotiations with government and international bodies. While these are important concerns, the reality is that CO skills developed through years of experience can no longer be maximized.

External versus organic organizers

The NGO community has had to choose between traditional models of external organizers and that of developing locally organic organizers. Community organizing developed from a model of external organizers, mostly young professionals who had decided to develop alternative careers. The emphasis on integration and social investigation and the entire process of training prospective organizers were premissed on a particular level of conceptual/analytical capacity and understanding of reality. External organizers also automatically delimited the boundaries between leaders and organizers. However, external organizers also served to reinforce class hierarchy and create dependence, therefore making 'phase-out' from the community difficult. In addition, there were simply not enough external organizers, and their life span before 'burn-out' was relatively short.

But CO also produced very competent leaders among the poor who started to take on significant organizing roles. Organic organizers, people who actually 'lived the problems', might be more effective. However, apart from the reality that time consumed in integration and social investigation could be minimized and that organic organizers would have a more sustainable commitment, there may have been a dose of romanticism in this perception. NGOs that relied heavily on organic organizers soon discovered that the advantages were ambiguous. The blurring of lines between leaders and organizers led to centralization of activities and, with minimal checks and counterbalances, to the creation of new elites. Time saved in understanding the community was sometimes neutralized because of biases that were natural outcomes of having grown up in the same community. Finally, limitations in previous training and experience also proved to be major hurdles.

Dilemmas in relations between NGOs and people's organizations

Clarifying roles

The dilemma between external and organic organizers is further manifested in the blurred role delineation of NGOs and people's organizations. In the past, although community organizers were conscious of their facilitative role, the reality of their power and potential to manipulate could not be denied. This gave rise to the concept of 'facipulation' (facilitation and manipulation), which had its own dangers, foremost of which was the resultant confusion over the boundaries that divided the functions of NGOs and people's organizations respectively. Despite NGOs defending their role as primarily supportive of and not taking the lead for POs, many organizers actually wielded unacknowledged power over people's organizations.

NGOs constantly tried to project a self-effacing image, articulating their subservience to the decisions of the people, and insisting on the primacy of people's organizations. On the other hand, people's organizations developed and matured. In many situations, the comfortable relationships of the past were marred by contradictions: NGOs spoke for the people whilst POs expected NGOs simply to provide the services and resources being demanded. For organic organizers, this created greater problems as their identity as NGO workers could no longer be distinguished from their roots in the community. NGOs and people's organizations continue to grapple with the boundaries of their respective identities whilst united in a common struggle.

Partnership and patronage

Because NGOs are agencies with human and material resources, the dividing line between partnership and patronage is a constant concern. Even as NGOs claim to be fellow travellers of POs, NGOs often exhibit a romanticist middle-class guilt that forces them to accept a subordinate position which they cannot sustain. Meanwhile, because Philippine society has cultivated a system of patronage, people's organizations invariably still relate to NGOs in a dependent way, with NGO resources tending to reinforce a patron–client relationship.

Rethinking CO premisses

Many CO premisses need now to be re-examined. Perhaps the process that goads people to action – the emphasis on small concrete issues based on self-interest with short-term victories – contradicts the attainment of longer-term goals. The essential dilemma is that within the growing atomization of Philippine society the collective good has been subsumed under the drive for inward-looking rewards. The CO focus on small issues, responding to the interests of groups of people in a community may serve to further reinforce a selfish materialistic drive that effectively buries whatever remains of class, sector and country consciousness. This does not dismiss the tactical importance of collective action on immediate issues. But perhaps the drive to achieve small victories ingrains the notion that collective action is nothing more than a tool for winning self-serving interests. Has community organizing unwittingly reinforced the personal opportunism that has become a trademark of capitalism?

Apart from ensuring that local struggles indeed become building blocks for larger issues, other issues need to be raised. In this age of globalization, to what extent (especially in urban poor organizing) do organizers assume the existence of a community? Should community organizing be focused as well on creating a community, considering the rapid break-down of culture, collective memories and common value systems? In attempting to resolve issues, has CO failed effectively to confront the erosion of values in modern-day society?

Involvement in the mainstream versus co-optation

For more than a decade, organizing took place on society's margins. In recent years there has been much activity revolving around income-generation and political/electoral intervention; and perhaps emboldened by past successes, CO has ventured into new arenas such as livelihood projects (some of which, regrettably, have been mechanistically introduced) or into organizing around parliamentary politics. But these arenas have their own logic and there is a danger of co-optation into the very system that CO wishes to change. Yet the mainstream political and economic arena cannot be wished away. Neither can poor communities isolate themselves from a system that ultimately determines their lives.

Dilemmas in relations between NGOs and donors

The fluidity of CO versus the demand for measurable outputs

Perhaps the biggest limitation of Third World NGOs is dependence on donors to provide the resources that will allow them and POs to pursue their goals. NGOs, however, face certain problems in relating to donors, which now insist, not without reason, on measurable outputs, definite time schedules and a pre-planned process. Unfortunately, CO has a dynamic of its own that does not lend itself well to their requirements. Because organizing is process-based, NGOs often find themselves either defending the fact that expected outputs have not been achieved within a given time frame, or artificially pushing forward the process in order to meet deadlines. The latter invariably ends with short cuts and a negation of the essence of CO.

The former, however, springs from a lack of understanding by donors of the organizing process itself. It is not uncommon to find NGOs desperately trying to explain this non-quantifiable process to representatives of donors who are also hard-pressed to justify continued relations. Two distinct paradigms, both subsumed in the rhetoric of development, therefore coexist, each with its own emphasis and logic, but with divergent practices.

A visible shift away from organizing towards impact projects

As NGOs have expanded the range of their activities, it has become apparent that many donor agencies have found it easier to support quantifiable interventions. This shift was first noticeable in donor policies that emphasized income-generating projects. Today, the list of supportable NGO projects has widened to include various types of infrastructure, activities that place a premium on advocacy and linking with government, and high-visibility achievements. While NGOs agree that these are important components of development work, what is disheartening is the correspondingly diminished interest in basic CO, without which these other concerns will have much reduced chances of success and sustainability. Such a situation really leads to externally imposed priorities, although many NGOs have to accept these impositions precisely because of the vulnerability of their resource base. There is an urgent need to reiterate the importance of organizing in its own right: without it, development work loses its backbone.

'Professionalization' without substance

Coupled with shifts in the priorities of donor agencies is the growing trend towards 'professionalization', the expectation of better management and financial systems among NGOs. There is nothing essentially wrong in wanting more effective administrative and financial management. What is disturbing, however, is that management is automatically taken to mean the installation of systems that conform to generally accepted business and/or governmental procedures. What neither donors nor NGOs appreciate is that these systems often reflect values in conflict with the alternatives that NGOs attempt to create: hierarchy versus collegiality, authority versus democracy, rigidity versus flexibility, profit versus commitment. These concerns have a direct impact on CO. First, business management systems have a way of insidiously undermining the essentially participative structure of NGOs. Since agencies and institutions are organizations in their own right, NGOs must be able to practise the same principles they espouse for the communities that they serve. One irony for development workers is to find that an organization's day-to-day operations are the opposite of what they themselves try to instill in people's organizations.

Second, formalistic financial systems retard community organizing. Significant portions of NGO budgets are devoted to activities that approximate business practices, in form rather than essence. Community organizers are also hampered because such systems impose requirements that either consume precious time and/or cut down their flexibility of movement. This is not to say that NGOs should persist in informal and ineffectual systems, but they must resist the imposition of, as well as the temptation to adopt, the practices of the establishment; instead they must devise more effective and efficient systems that are consistent with the premisses of CO and the vision of an alternative order.

In more than two decades of CO, the Philippine NGO community has achieved remarkable gains. The ongoing critique of and reflection on the theory and practice of organizing is a testimony to the dynamism of alternative development work. What remains unchanged is the commitment to the urgency and importance of community organizing, the empowerment of whole communities, and the continuous development of the will and capacity to intervene to improve the quality of human life.

14

Social Reconstruction and Community Development in the Transition to Democracy in South Africa

Viviene Taylor

Introduction

'Social reconstruction' and 'development' are terms which have recently gained popularity in South Africa. Political movements on the left are attempting to develop a reconstruction programme incorporating popular aspirations and addressing high levels of poverty. While there is broad commitment to meeting the basic needs of communities that have suffered as a result of apartheid, this has generally had little impact to date on social and community development practitioners or agencies. Whatever the reasons, this reflects the extent to which social and community work agencies remain outside of the general efforts to work towards social transformation and the empowerment of communities. Key among the issues that influence their efforts to become a part of the social-change process are the effects of high levels of sustained violence and conflict (Manganyi and Toit 1990; Agenda 1993). The other factor is the extent to which social welfare organizations have been integrated into the existing apartheid system (see Figure 14.1), and thus unable to make the transition towards democratic development.

This chapter provides a brief overview of the context in which social reconstruction and development is being promoted, a definition of community empowerment, the nature of violence and conflict and its impact on community development; it further provides an analysis of emerging initiatives which aim to transform both the process and outcomes of development in South Africa. The underlying argument is based on the extent to which institutional and criminal violence have limited the capacity of development agents in promoting community empowerment and democracy, thereby creating the possibility of a corporate as opposed to developmental state.

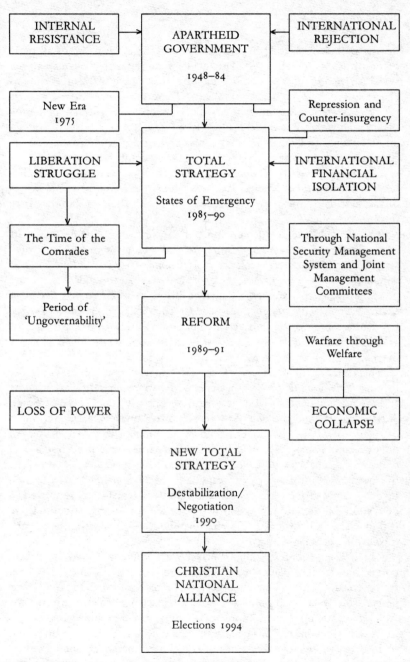

Figure 14.1 Evolution of Nationalist Government Strategy

The Context

'In the past decade "rule by the gun" has become the norm in all parts of South Africa' (CIIR 1988). The incidents of reported violence and the sustained nature of the conflict indicate that South African society is characterized by a culture of violence. There are many current reports providing descriptions and statistics of the political violence sweeping the country. However, it is difficult to capture through such reports the devastation, trauma and reality of those who are paying, in human terms, the cost of apartheid. The nature and intensity of conflict and violence have compounded the crisis of our society. The fact that political violence has been rampant largely within black townships while white society carries on as 'normal' emphasizes the successful polarization of South Africa through apartheid.

The struggle for democracy and social justice in South Africa by its very nature is rooted in opposition to the structures of the apartheid state. Therefore the overt violence that we experience has to be examined within the complex nature of the apartheid state and the ideological and power struggles that are being waged at this moment. There has been, for example, increasing evidence, provided through the investigation of the Goldstone Commission into violence in South Africa, of the existence of a 'Third Force' within the state's security system, whose main aim has been to destabilize the democratic process.

The overwhelming victory of the African National Congress (ANC) through a democratic process has created an atmosphere of elation, hope and the possibility of social transformation. The transitional state of South African society and the new African National Congress-led Government of National Unity (GNU) does, however, bring with it a dynamic of political and social bargaining with centre parties that have not as yet removed the shackles of coercive apartheid state machinery. The organs of apartheid control and power, especially the National Security Management system and Joint Management Committees, which were perceived to be responsible for the repression of dissenting community structures, are still in place and form part of what may be a hostile civil service at the top levels (see Figure 14.1).

The changing context within which this government will have to deliver goods and services places new, time-bound demands on the ANC as it transforms itself from a national liberation movement to an organ of state power. Having attained political power, the challenge which confronts the ANC as it attempts to promote social transformation and democracy is the extent to which it may become concerned with the trappings and form that governance takes and not the content of governance. Political rights must bring with them opportunities for the attainment of social and economic rights for the majority if the national liberation movement is to remain committed to its goals in the freedom charter and the Reconstruction and Development Programme.

This changing social, political and economic context places a responsibility on civil society and the disempowered to continue to lobby from the bottom in the interests of the poor. Now, more than ever, the concern with community empowerment and democratic development has to take on concrete form as an alternative to the previous repressive regime's approach. However, for community empowerment to become more than just a glib phrase, the need for construction and development must be analysed against the continued violence and conflict which provides the impetus for, and the biggest obstacle to, transformation.

Community Empowerment

In the South African context, community empowerment has to be understood within the broader struggle for liberation from political oppression and material deprivation. It is therefore not only about basic needs provision, human resource development or changing institutional frameworks, but centrally related to developing the capacities of people in ways which make qualitative differences to racial, class and gender imbalances, resulting in a shift in power relations in favour of the oppressed majority. The question is: How can we move from a society characterized by extreme polarization to one which manages conflict with the active participation of the poor?

In this regard the writings of Gandhi, Schumacher and Freire have much to offer, each of them stressing the need to empower the poor through direct action at the grassroots. Freire, in particular, proposed a radical shift in building the capacities of people for transformation through the development of a collective consciousness of the links between local struggles and structural inequalities. This implies that programmes and processes need to focus on capacity-building that leads to empowerment not only at the level of individuals but of a social class.

Social reconstruction and community development

When people have been denied access to education, health care, housing and work over so many years, it is not difficult to understand why the slightest provocation from groups who are competing for power and material resources can lead to intense battles. These battles have taken various forms, ranging from violence in the townships and informal settlements to negotiations in the many fora that have recently emerged.

The rapid urbanization of migrant workers, residential areas that are planned according to apartheid criteria rather than appropriate land use, and a tremendous shortfall in low-income housing – estimated for blacks to be more than one million units outside the Homelands (*Business Day* 1991) – have led to the emergence of informal settlements on the outskirts of townships. Rapid urbanization is attributed to the higher rate of population growth in peripheral and rural areas, and the income differential which exists between rural and urban areas – with the latter not having the capacity to meet the basic needs of people.

The Urban Foundation estimates that approximately 377,000 people live in informal settlements (squatters) in the Pretoria Witwatersrand and Vereeniging (PWV) areas, which together with the rest of the country brings the total number of homeless close to 7 million.

The emergence of informal settlements in both urban and rural areas poses a very specific challenge in the period of reconstruction and development. The inability of the National Party government to respond to absolute poverty in rural areas and consequent rapid urbanization has created other problems such as inner-city decay, rising unemployment, the spread of diseases and an unacceptably high level of crime and violence. It is largely within peri-urban areas and informal settlements that civil society exists without organized representation in the labour movement (because of almost total unemployment), in the residents' associations and other types of civic structures. In these areas, the poor are more easily manipulated by anti-democratic forces. This situation has led to competition and struggles between people in informal settlements and township residents for scarce land, water and basic infrastructure. It has been found that land shortage and tenure have played a central role in violence in Natal, especially in areas such as Molweni and Ntuzuma. This has been fuelled by the desire for political power, with the Inkatha Freedom Party promoting policies that mitigate against the reintegration of apartheid homelands into a nationally united South Africa.

In the run-up to the democratic elections many lives were lost; and there have been extreme social and physical costs in some areas where whole communities have disappeared, especially in Natal. People have fled their areas because their homes have been destroyed or occupied by opposing groups and because they fear for their lives. One estimate suggested that in 1992 approximately 11,000 people were forced to flee their homes, with thousands more dying.

The need for social reconstruction and development in these areas is consequently not only about the concrete demands for work, housing, water, sanitation, health and welfare, but also about bringing the unrepresented poor into the negotiation process on what priority needs are to be met, within what time frame, and how they can be met.

The ANC and its alliance partners, including the South African Communist Party, labour and civic movements, progressive NGOs and other sectors of the broad mass-democratic movement, have collectively drawn up a reconstruction and development programme with the aims of responding to the basic needs of the majority, the need to develop human resources, the building of the economy, and democratizing the state and society (ANC 1994).

Some of the critical needs and factors which will have to be addressed if people-centred development is to become a reality are highlighted below for the reason that they have been used to spur violence and conflict and to disempower communities, and not because they are the only factors that undermine empowerment and the transition to democracy.

Factors affecting community empowerment and the transition to democracy

Lack of transport

The lack of adequate public transport has resulted in struggles for monopoly of taxi ranks and routes, leading to what are now called 'taxi wars'. Particularly in the Transvaal and Western Cape, conflict is exacerbated by those who have vested interests in the taxis and those who wish to destabilize communities through fear, intimidation and violence. Such destabilization must be seen as a way of undermining the democratic process.

Although transport is identified as a basic need within the comprehensive RDP, the link between local taxi wars and the related macro-policy issues is not made by people. The question is how to ensure that people have enough information to understand what is happening and to make informed choices on the range of options available.

Competition for political power

The positioning of political parties as significant actors in the negotiation process and within the Government of National Unity is also a key to the reduction of conflict and a commitment to empowerment. It has been suggested that violence enabled Gatsha Buthelezi to obtain a more powerful bargaining position with the past apartheid government and the African National Congress. In South Africa, therefore, the continued violence is not only about gaining political dominance in negotiations. It has become an alternative form of participation for those groups who refuse to enter negotiations, especially those such as the AWB on the right.

The violence that has swept the country is seen by some political and social analysts as too carefully planned and orchestrated both in its implementation and its results to be dismissed as spontaneous acts by loosely formed groups of individuals. Thus, political leaders are now held responsible by many for the violence. The type of political bargaining which parties are engaging in during the transitional phase will not only reflect their political power and the extent to which there has been a decisive shift in the balance of power to the left, but also the extent to which all parties agree on national development priorities and the process of attaining these. It is arguably on the latter – the means and process through which development priorities should be met – that there will be least consensus. The consequence of a constrained government, whose powers to deliver will be drastically impaired, could become real.

Political parties have competed during the elections on the basis of the development imperatives of the day. The process of meeting popular demands will not only demonstrate a commitment to the voters, but will also affect the transition to democracy and the possibility of continued peace and political stability.

Disempowered youth and criminal activity

The disintegration of the country's social fabric resulting from apartheid continues to result in devastating consequences for all sectors, but especially for the youth who constitute approximately 25 per cent of the total population in the age range 16–30 years. The development of a youth-based political culture in the struggle for liberation, during 1976 and 'the time of the comrades', has brought about significant changes in the social relations within family and community life. The changes have created tensions and demands on both youth and society, giving rise to generational and societal conflict.

Since 1976, young people have taken a number of initiatives in revolts against the system. The effects of the breakdown of family life and the educational system on the welfare of youth means that any reconstruction and development programme has to pay special attention not only to obvious aspects such as material poverty but also to the psychological and emotional effects of apartheid.

The rise of youth violence and criminal activity has to be seen against the collapse of the educational and economic systems. In some communities young people have developed a subculture in which crime and violence are the norm, and to be 'men' or 'macho' means to have power and control. One way of achieving this in the present social political climate is through crime and violence, justified by the youth as a question of survival.

A programme to address the needs and problems of youth must, however, be developed with their active involvement in the process of setting priorities, identifying gaps in the present system, and finding creative alternatives that will make a real difference. This means that youth must be empowered to challenge the existing and emerging social-service system to be much more responsive to their general and special needs.

Unemployment

Unemployment in South Africa is estimated to be well over the 40 per cent mark. This is seen by some to be related to the 'crisis of capitalism', linked to increasing levels of violence. The unemployment rate amongst undereducated and unskilled youth is especially high. This, together with the fact that during the last nine years no new jobs have been created in the formal sector in some areas, has led to a significantly higher incidence of conflict. In this context, violence has meant that the unemployed (quite often the youth), reap the 'benefits' of a life of crime and violence.

The inability of the state to develop an economic policy that responds to the needs of people and of industry to absorb unemployed labour is a part of the crisis. Given high levels of unemployment and its cyclical nature as a function of racial capitalism, development has to be more than economic growth which expands the job market. Whether growth and redistribution, a people-centred approach, or an equity-led growth strategy is adopted, there is a critical need to increase the capacity of people, especially the unemployed, to improve their well-being in ways which result in social, economic and political transformation. Welfare organizations and others have yet to find ways of addressing this situation.

It is against this background that social-change agents such as community workers are expected to promote development. When one examines the complex nature of the violence and conflict in South Africa and its long-term consequences, it is not difficult to understand the inability of community workers and agencies to focus on and respond to structural causes of the conflict; yet these root causes have to be addressed to facilitate community empowerment aimed at fundamental transformation.

However, the type of transformation that is planned through the RDP is going to be extremely difficult to implement because of the gross mismanagement of the past National Party Government. 'The National Party Government sent the National debt soaring by more than R60 billion in its final year of power' (*Sunday Times*, 15 May 1994), a debt inherited by the ANC-led GNU. It means that there will be a 13 per cent rise in the interest bill from R20.5 billion in 1993/4 to R23 billion, the largest item in the next national budget. The interest burden restricts the ANC's ability to implement the RDP and belies the notion that South Africa is under-borrowed.

While there is growing concern about the needs in the country and the necessity for macro-economic stability, the ANC will attempt as far as possible to restructure existing budgetary allocations and priorities in line with RDP priorities rather than increasing IMF and World Bank loans.

The Nature of Violence and Conflict

Violence and conflict in South Africa will affect the transition to democracy and the empowerment of people in many ways. It is therefore necessary to understand the nature and effects of violence. Violence in this article is understood to mean more than overt acts of aggression by one group against another. It includes the institutionalized violence of apartheid which continues to contribute to the large-scale and systematic destruction of family and community life through discriminatory legislation, structures and practices. This general understanding of conflict and institutionalized violence should be seen against the use of political violence as a factor used to destabilize the transition to democracy.

The impact of conflict and violence on community work

Attempts to address the structural issues which have given rise to all forms of violence must include a process of community development if South African society is to move away from a statist approach to development. Thus, community workers who are committed to development have to intervene in the transition to democracy in concrete ways which will reduce violence and make an impact on social and political inequalities.

The Human Rights Commission, in examining the evolution of the Nationalist government strategy, indicates how resistance to the apartheid government from within the country and outside led to a change in government strategy and tactics and resulted in the present period of hope and democracy (see Figure 14.1).

It is important to understand the apartheid state's strategy which led to the repression of civil society, because many of its structures are still in place and the policies have been internalized by the bureaucrats who will remain in place under the GNU. Community empowerment will be made much more difficult if community activists and change agents promote development in a historical manner which ignores the patterns of under-development and its effects.

From extreme repression through to a counter-insurgency or total-onslaught programme with a heavy spy network, the government moved into its 'reform policies' in the early 1980s. This was effected through the 1983 Constitution, which brought into being the tricameral parliament, part of what is now called the 'total strategy', designed to maintain power and stamp out resistance from the disenfranchised poor while at the same time appearing to the outside world to have some semblance of power-sharing.

The 'total strategy' had three main goals:

- To maintain state security – primarily through the National Security Management System (NSMS).
- To reform the political environment through the tricameral system and black local authorities.
- To coordinate all state action.

In attempts to implement its strategy without an adequate redistribution of finances at local level, the Nationalist government insisted that black

Figure 14.2 Democratizing Development:
'Empowerment and People's War'

local councils raise their own funds for the development of township services.

Black councillors, who were not accepted as legitimate political representatives of their communities, responded by increasing rents and service charges. These increases, together with other acts of oppression carried out by the state, led to nationwide popular rebellion, which began in the Vaal Triangle townships. Within days thirty-one persons were reported killed. Resistance spread throughout the country. Community organizations were mobilized in combined efforts to change the situation. The voluntary welfare sector was generally ill-prepared to help or participate in the mass mobilization for citizens' rights (see Figure 14.2).

By 1985 the black non-representative local authorities had collapsed and the 'total strategy' was seen to be a failure because of sustained resistance. The economic viability of local authorities was not the only problem; but the fundamental issue against which resistance was waged was that local franchise was not tied to the granting of full political rights to black people (Swilling 1990). This heralded what has become known as the 'time of the comrades' in the townships and led to government reforms. On the ground, in rural areas and townships, the government pursued an active campaign of 'winning the hearts and minds' of people by promoting developments through organizations selected by discredited government community liaison structures that had direct links with the National Security Management Systems. Many community workers became identified and were perceived to be part of the oppressive system.

These initiatives have been interpreted in certain circles as low-intensity warfare or 'warfare through welfare'. Certain communities that had developed strong people's organizations, such as Alexandra township in the Vaal and Mbekweni in the Western Cape, were particularly targeted. Some communities and organizations received an injection of government funding. This was usually dependent on the degree to which they could be controlled by government structures and provide information on individuals and organizations opposing the apartheid government.

Government security force organs, including police, municipal police, the homeland police and the armies, were part of the 'total strategy' to stifle protest, prevent community empowerment and destabilize the liberation movements. The internal violence was also paralleled by attacks in virtually all South Africa's neighbouring countries, especially those in which liberation movements had a presence. These countries also paid the price through the many who were killed, maimed and left homeless since 1980 through this sustained destabilization programme.

The Nationalist government's assertion that the ongoing conflict in the country is a result of 'black on black' violence, with the ANC and Inkatha centrally involved, is not only too simplistic but has been shown up as an attempt to underplay its carefully designed total strategy to retain its power base. This strategy could still destabilize the community development process if efforts are not made to ensure that community members are aware of the history of the State Security management system and the network through which it operates at all levels.

The Southern African Development Education Programme (SADEP) as a response to community empowerment

Representative, democratically oriented development institutions and fora have emerged to address sectoral and other interests as a part of the development process. However, many of these fora, such as the National Economic Forum, National Housing Forum, National Education and Training Forum are not representative of the interests of all the disempowered. In many instances it is assumed that the people on whose behalf decisions are made are a homogeneous group fully informed of the policy choices available to them.

Grassroots community members of varying political alliances and interests see themselves as increasingly marginalized from the process of decision-making. There is a tension between the role of NGO and community structures. NGOs are seen to be professionally staffed structures that have become involved in setting the development agenda and process without a simultaneous process of empowering community members. Knowledge is colonized by would-be development professionals, with community members being on the receiving end rather than determining the process.

SADEP as a programme is designed to address the need to skill development workers through a 'bottom-up' process to influence decisions at all levels. It is an education and research programme aimed at forging new partnerships between communities, the public, private and voluntary sectors, in order to develop an understanding of the broader social and economic context within which social transformation will be addressed.

SADEP was approached by community members involved in civic struggles and other issues affecting development to help empower them to play a central role in the process. Community activists requested a rigorous training programme which would equip them with development skills to mediate directly with the organs of state power rather than through intermediaries. SADEP has since 1992 trained a national team of one hundred community development practitioners who are located within local communities and who are ideally placed to help with democratizing the development process. The key question is how a restructured institutional framework can be developed to incorporate workers who are equipped to promote community empowerment.

180 COMMUNITY EMPOWERMENT

Conclusion

Fear and violence are still part of South African everyday life, traumatizing individuals, families and communities. The process of building democracy in South Africa will be dependent on the extent to which communities are empowered to overcome the effects of the violence and renew their faith and trust in fellow patriots. Community development is an essential element in the process of social reconstruction of South Africa.

The resilience of the South African people has been tested over many decades; and against all odds they have succeeded in bringing democracy and justice closer. All the lives that have been lost in the violence on the battlegrounds of the townships and the country would not have been in vain as long as there is, and continues to be, a commitment to the attainment of a peaceful, just, non-racial, non-sexist South Africa. The challenge facing those committed to development is to ensure that they improve people's capacity to participate in this process (Taylor 1994).

References

African National Congress (ANC) (1994), *Reconstruction and Development Programme,* Umanyano Publications, Johannesburg.
Agenda (1993), *Violence in Focus,* Editorial Collective, no. 16, Natal.
Business Day (1991), June.
CIIR (1988), *Now Everyone is Afraid,* London.
Manganyi, N.C. and A. du Toit, eds (1990), *Political Violence and the Struggle in South Africa,* Macmillan, London.
Swilling, M. (1990), 'Political Transition, Development and the Role of Civil Society', *Africa Insight,* vol. 20, no. 3.
Taylor, V. (1994), *Developing Human Capacities,* prepared for conference on Development Research Priorities.

Participation, Empowerment and
Sexual Health in Africa

Gill Gordon

Introduction

In sub-Saharan Africa, the Human Immunodeficiency Virus (HIV) that causes AIDS is transmitted mainly through vaginal sexual intercourse, with contaminated blood transfusions, needles and instruments contributing to a smaller extent. The ratio of men to women infected varies between countries and over time, but in many countries equal numbers of women and men are infected, with women on average being infected in their early twenties, ten years earlier than men (Berer and Roy 1993). The prevalence of infection varies between and within countries, for reasons poorly understood, but certainly influenced by patterns of sexual behaviour. Paediatric AIDS is now a leading cause of death in young children in some areas.

With no immediate prospect of a vaccine or cure for HIV infection, health promotion is the only strategy available for reducing the sexual transmission of the virus. Many African countries have used posters, pamphlets, radio discussions and drama to influence people to 'Stay with one partner' and 'Use a condom'. These campaigns have raised the level of awareness of the more educated about AIDS and increased knowledge of transmission routes. But for many people, the messages are irrelevant because they do not take into account the reality of sexual relations in terms of status and power, economics and values. People who are not willing or able to find an uninfected, faithful partner for life, or who cannot begin to ask their partners to use condoms, are left feeling less able to cope as a result of the campaigns.

The most successful programmes in terms of behaviour change have been those where groups with a mutual interest have come together, explored the problem in relation to their own lives and developed acceptable alternatives to risky practice. Structural changes including political and economic empowerment were also crucial in creating a supportive environment to sustain change. Groups which were actively involved in change then shared their experience and ideas with others outside the group through networks, media and grassroots NGOs. Examples of this type of work include groups of gay men in San Francisco, communities heavily affected by AIDS in Zambia, and Australian prostitutes' collectives.

Ministries of Health, Education and Social Welfare facing the constraints of structural adjustment may well say that these community development programmes are too expensive and reach too few people. We suggest here how the benefits gained in a community development programme with specific groups can be multiplied through district-level primary-health-care systems, local networks and the media. Many more people can thus be reached with relevant health promotion and services which increase knowledge and skills, change attitudes, and identify practical options for change. Wider networking and support of community groups will enable people collectively to use their power to bring about structural change sustaining safer sexual relationships.

We begin by outlining ways in which the recession and structural adjustment programmes in the early 1980s exacerbated conditions which still today facilitate the transmission of HIV and limit people's options for protecting themselves. We then draw from relevant programmes to outline how a community development and primary-health-care approach to HIV prevention could reduce its spread, bringing far-reaching benefits to general sexual health in women, men and families.

However, even the most innovative and cost-effective plans cannot succeed without a basic level of sustainable resources available to meet recurrent costs. A living wage for workers, a constant supply of reliable condoms, an expanding economy which offers choices to women outside the sex industry, training in sex education for teachers and community workers, and a supply of effective drugs for treating sexually transmitted diseases (STDs) – these necessities will not be provided on a sustainable basis to sufficient numbers of people to slow the epidemic if Africa continues to transfer its resources to the rich world.

The Effects of Recession and Structural Adjustment

Sexual transmission

The sexual transmission of HIV is determined by a number of factors:

- *Sexual practices.* Vaginal and anal intercourse allow infected semen, vaginal fluid or blood to contact mucous membranes and transmit HIV and other STDs. Sexual practices avoiding such contact are referred to as 'safer sex', including the use of a condom, masturbation, hugging and kissing.

- *Sexual partners.* The probability of having sex with an infected partner is higher in populations with a high prevalence of infection, although often this figure is not known. The probability also increases with the number of different sexual partners.

- The presence of a *sexually-transmitted disease* facilitates the transmission of HIV, particularly if it involves genital ulcers or lesions.

Sexuality is often thought to be a natural, private and universal aspect of life. However, sexuality is a social phenomenon; and beliefs about pleasure, reproduction, gender roles and relationships between the sexes differ widely across cultures. Women are generally more vulnerable to sexual risk than men because their sexuality is usually controlled by others. Patterns of sexual activity and numbers and types of relationships are influenced by cultural, social and economic factors as well as personal attributes.

Structural adjustment policies usually result in dampening down demand; devaluation of the currency; withdrawal of subsidies on staple foods and fuel; and cuts in government spending, including the contraction of public-sector jobs and reduced wages in real terms. As economic options shrink, men and women are forced into labour migration. Marriage is delayed as bride wealth takes longer to accumulate. If men are expected to be sexually active, these situations put them, as well as present and future partners, at high risk of sexually-transmitted diseases and HIV. Women's sexuality represents an economic asset and women are forced increasingly into using sexual exchange as an economic strategy.

Sexual exchange may occur on a full, part-time or seasonal basis. Women may work from bars and sell food and beer as well as sex. Rural women may travel to towns in the dry season or when trading in farm produce. Single women in urban areas may be partly or wholly supported by lovers. Young girls may exchange sex with older men for food, clothes or school fees. For example:

The Krobo area of Ghana has few economic opportunities for young women and the recession diminished them further. Young women have traditionally worked for a few years in neighbouring Ivory Coast in order to purchase essentials for a quality lifestyle and make enough capital to set up in business. The trip is organized by older women and it is accepted that sexual relationships will contribute to economic success. In the mid-1980s, young women started to come home with a fatal illness, later diagnosed as AIDS. At first, the church NGOs responded by exhorting young women never to travel to Ivory Coast again. But without economic alternatives, even young women whose sisters had died of AIDS continued to seek a better life. The NGO is helping young women to start small businesses and discussing safer sex options with them. Women with AIDS in Krobo villages are being cared for by their families, supported by home visits from nurses and treatment with herbal medicines.

A schoolgirl has sex with her teacher who pays her school fees. A woman has sex with the boss who gives her a job, continuing so that she keeps it. A woman has sex with her husband in spite of her fear of AIDS because he provides shelter and the support of the extended family. A bank clerk on a low salary cannot afford escalating prices for food and accommodation for herself and her children. She goes down to the local hotel in the evenings to make some extra cash.

Some women are visible in their use of their sexual assets. But many women of all ages use their sexuality in pursuing their short-term and long-term goals of survival and progress. Often these relationships are not only concerned with survival; men and women also seek companionship and pleasure, and a higher quality of life than they might otherwise enjoy as subsistence farmers or messengers.

A shrinking economy makes it more difficult for people to enjoy stable sexual relationships. Couples are forced to live apart as each seeks work through government transfers or migration to neighbouring countries or urban areas. Sex and companionship are thus met in often transient relationships.

In Kenya, truck drivers are prevented from forming unions to improve working conditions. Many drivers are only given leave to see their wives once or twice a year. High HIV prevalence is associated with denial of leave by employers.

Economic constraints delay the accumulation of bride price and hence marriage. The age gap between men and women at marriage widens and young men satisfy their sexual needs with a number of partners over a longer period. The young men, their current and future partners and their future children are all at risk of HIV and STD infection. In Ethiopia, young girls coming to Addis Ababa during the drought became prostitutes and HIV prevalence has risen sharply in this group. Wars in Uganda and Mozambique have resulted in large armies moving around the countryside without women, and girls and women without their normal means of support. Transient relationships, prostitution and rape in this situation are all too common, and soldiers have a high level of HIV infection. In some countries, the school system is breaking down; both parents are out working and young people are left to fend for themselves for long periods of time.

The potential for safer sex

People may have few choices in their sexual partners, but health promoters encourage people to practise safer sex in all their relationships. However, as economic options decline and sexual bargaining becomes increasingly significant in womens' strategies, competition between women over men with money and power will increase. This situation puts women in weaker positions in negotiations over the use of safer sexual practices. Deteriorating living conditions imply growing tension in relationships. Low incomes and sharply rising prices cause insecurity, which makes it very difficult for people to feel in control of their lives. Self-esteem, assertive behaviour and effective decision-making are undermined, making it more difficult for women to protect themselves and for men to take responsibility for their actions. Stress is associated with increased use of alcohol and drugs and sexual violence against women and their daughters (UNICEF 1987).

Deterioration in housing conditions, water supplies and sanitation make it more difficult to practise sexual hygiene and to use barrier methods of contraception. A lack of privacy, time and energy to try out new sexual practices, and no place to keep or dispose of condoms, are serious obstacles to change. Many of the most vulnerable people are unable to afford to use condoms every time they have sex. It may then seem pointless to use them at all. Increased demand for more reliable contraception generated by the declining economic situation has not been met by accessible, affordable, high-quality family-planning services. The credibility of the condom for contraception or STD and HIV prevention falls to zero when an inadequate storage and distribution system and poor quality condoms result in frequent breakage. Cuts in family-planning budgets mean low salaries and unfilled key positions. Condoms rot at airports while staff sit in rural clinics with nothing to offer their clients. An unmet demand for contraception is associated with more illegal abortions and their complications.

Sexually transmitted diseases

STDs are serious infections which can cause infertility, disability and death, as well as damage or death to unborn children. There has been an increase in the prevalence of gonorrhoea, syphilis and chancroid in many parts of Africa, contributing to the transmission of HIV. Spending cuts diminish the already-low prestige of STD programmes. An effective STD programme requires a regular screening service to pick up people with mild or symptomless infection; staff who are well-trained, motivated and supported to do sensitive, confidential counselling; ways of ensuring that all sexual partners of an infected person are informed; and provision of a full course of treatment with antibiotics effective against local strains, and a supply of reliable condoms.

The disclosure of an STD often results in rejection by partners, an outcome that many women can ill afford. Economic crises make it even more unlikely that women will inform their partners; and men may not do so because they cannot afford treatment for their partners. Poverty and embarrassment result in many women disregarding sexual-health problems until they become acute emergencies, by which time infertility may be the outcome. The lack of antibiotics and confidentiality in the public-health service pushes people into purchasing insufficient drugs at black-market prices elsewhere. This results in resistant strains of STDs, which are expensive to cure, and a large number of untreated cases of STD.

Transmission of infection

Adjustment to the debt crisis has forced many governments to reduce public spending, but spending on health and education has been cut disproportionately. For example, Uganda and Tanzania have cut health budgets as a percentage of total government expenditure from 5.3 per cent to 2.4 per cent, and from 7.2 per cent to 4.9 per cent, respectively, between 1972 and 1986 (UNICEF 1989). The salaries of health workers have declined sharply in real terms, reducing motivation and increasing the temptation to use health-service resources for personal gain. Sterilization procedures require consistent attention to detail as well as a regular supply of disposable needles, equipment, chemicals, protective clothing, instruments, water and fuel. Low reserves of emotional energy make counselling on AIDS concerns even more difficult for workers who are trying to cope with their own anxieties. The lack of protective equipment and general stress make people reluctant to work for the health service or to provide care to those suspected of having HIV infection.

Accidents, haemorrhage after childbirth or abortion and severe anaemia resulting from malaria are the most common reasons for requiring a blood transfusion. Inadequate antenatal and maternity services for prevention and treatment for malaria and anaemia increase the need for these transfusions. Poorly maintained vehicles and exhausted drivers contribute to a high prevalence of accidents. Many health units still cannot afford to screen all blood for HIV. Poor-quality health services imply a higher risk of unsterile injections and invasive procedures; and this, coupled with poverty, leads people to use alternative practitioners and therefore expose themselves to even more risky practices.

An increase in serious and chronic infections

A deteriorating health sector has resulted in an increase in serious infections throughout Africa. The prevalence of serious and resistant forms of malaria is increasing as environmental control systems break down. Infections such as TB, leprosy and STDs, which require for their control the identification and long-term treatment of early cases, are on the increase. Poorer sanitation and water supplies result in an increase in many infections. This global increase in morbidity activates the immune system more frequently, which, with other infections, triggers the immune system in a person infected with HIV to replicate more virus, accelerating the progression to illness and AIDS. Other diseases, such as malaria, suppress the immune system.

Communication and education

Budget cuts for education and health make it difficult to carry out effective AIDS education, embedded in personal and sex education and designed with the involvement of specific groups. Schools need trained, motivated staff to work effectively with groups of young people. In some countries schools and colleges have been closed for months because food has run out and teachers' salaries have not been paid. People who own radios must have batteries, and there is no money to pay skilled media people for the design of relevant and motivating drama and materials. When women are doing three jobs to survive, they will not have the time to get involved in AIDS education or even listen to media. Transport to remote communities costs money and volunteer educators need incentives and resources to work effectively.

The Role of Community Development

Key components

Important components of community-development-based approaches include:

Sharing information to enable people to apply it to their own lives

The language used needs to be explicit and well-understood by the group. The information given should be relevant to the realities of people's sexual lives and non-judgemental. Scientific concepts can be explained through analogies with local culture. People benefit from the opportunity to ask questions and clarify ideas. Well-informed people who understand why safer sex is important and know of a range of options for its practise are more able to talk confidently and persuasively to their partners.

Exploring the impact of values, gender roles, social and economic factors

This approach ensures that options for change are based on detailed, holistic understanding of the sexual lives of different groups and how sexual networks transmit HIV and STDs between communities. Sexual behaviour is intensely personal, but at the same time it is profoundly influenced by wider issues of power and status, culture and economics. Cuts in health budgets make it even more essential that programmes are planned on the basis of these differing factors, because resources used on disseminating irrelevant 'messages' are wasted. It is notoriously difficult to find out about sexual behaviour through conventional surveys because people are rightly wary about disclosing personal information to outsiders. Community workers can help groups to develop the safe space and trust that allows people to talk creatively about what they need to change.

Developing skills in communicating and practising safer sex
Both women and men need opportunities to talk about safer sex and identify helpful options. In single-sex and mixed groups, people can experiment with different approaches to talking about safer sex with their partners, and to coping if they meet with resistance or violence. Better communication between couples may result in happier sexual relationships in general. In small groups, people can practise the skills needed to communicate about safer sex, to use condoms or to advocate for change through role play or drama. A community-development approach is most likely to succeed in helping groups to find ways to make safer-sex behaviour the norm rather than the exception because people can support each other in change, share experiences and develop powerful and relevant materials and media.

Working towards structural change in the social and economic environment
Groups can provide mutual support for behaviour change and for political activity aimed at structural change. As people become more aware of sexual needs and potential choices, and ways in which their environment limits their sexual health, they may become motivated to work towards change. Membership of a group that works in a participatory way can give people new perspectives and a sense of self-esteem which empowers them to act against exploitation. Groups of women have successfully fought for the right to contraceptive and abortion services and are working to eradicate female genital mutilation or to protect themselves and their children from HIV infection. Group membership can help women to reduce their economic dependence on sexual relationships because they may more easily gain access to training and credit, as well as mutual support in meeting child care and domestic needs. Community workers with skills in business planning and management can assist women to establish successful enterprises. Workers' unions can defend women's employment rights and workers themselves can form collectives. For example, sex workers in several countries have formed collectives which insist on safer-sex practices and make it difficult for clients to find women willing to have unprotected sex. Community groups should be actively involved in the design of services. For example, in finding cost-effective ways to ensure that reliable condoms are consistently available to all those who need them, and to address problems in condom use and disposal.

Sharing insights gained through group work more widely
Working regularly with small groups over a period of time is costly; and the insights, skills and strengths achieved with small groups in a district or region must be multiplied through a range of networks to involve larger populations. District or regional groups might meet regularly to exchange experiences, solve problems, strengthen the movement for social

change, and plan advocacy and activities. Successful options for change developed with groups can inform education programmes in the primary-health-care system, family-planning clinics, schools and youth groups, farmers' clubs, churches and women's associations. This will ensure that the content of the education is as relevant as possible and maximize the effective use of limited staff.

Media produced with the active involvement of community groups is likely to be relevant and can reach wider audiences. For example, in Cameroon, sex workers established an entertaining theatre group which travelled around bars to convince clients to practise safer sex. In Ethiopia, young people were trained as peer educators and educated young people in their communities about safer sex and where to obtain condoms and spermicides. The insights and media developed with groups can be disseminated through contraceptive social marketing programmes using commercial channels such as chemical sellers in Ghana and pharmacists in Cameroon who dispense STD treatment kits. These low-cost programmes can reach large numbers of people in remote, under-served areas.

In Uganda and Zambia support groups of people with HIV infection have developed strategies for caring for people with AIDS at home and for providing supportive and preventive counselling to families and communities (TASO 1989). In Zimbabwe, an NGO has developed drama with the community and used it to stimulate discussion and action in the district. Traditional healers, sex workers and chemical sellers have been consulted and have helped to talk about HIV prevention and distribute condoms.

The need for a holistic approach

Early in the epidemic, WHO encouraged countries to set up National AIDS Committees and develop medium-term plans for HIV prevention and control. These committees tended to be dominated by the medical profession and to focus on mass campaigns targeted at the general population or 'high risk groups'. These vertical programmes did little to convince the public that they had a problem; many people were more concerned about unwanted pregnancy, STDs and other pressing health problems than an 'invisible' infection which they might suffer and die from in ten years time. The separation of 'AIDS facts' from issues of contraception and sexual relationships caused more dilemmas than it solved.

A community development approach would address sexual-health needs in a holistic way, focusing on the most common, serious problems perceived by different community groups, and their underlying causes. Women and children have always been at risk from the adverse consequences of sexual activity. Unwanted pregnancies can result in abortion, morbidity and mortality as well as lost educational and economic opportunities.

Pregnancies which are too early, too late, too close or too many can result in malnutrition, fistulas and maternal death. Untreated STDs can cause infertility, illness and death in mothers and babies as well as facilitating HIV transmission.

Issues of informed choice about sexual behaviour and contraception, of power within relationships, of sexual rights and obligations, of high quality services and participatory communication are common to all sexual-health problems. Communities need accessible and ongoing infrastructures which address all these issues. Some family-planning programmes in Africa now train staff routinely to talk about STDs and HIV in relation to contraceptive methods, whilst others are advocating for women's rights and working with development projects to increase women's incomes. There is an increasing understanding of the need to address development issues if countries are to reduce the spread of the HIV epidemic and cope with its effects.

Many couples in Africa wish to space births or avoid pregnancy in a particular relationship. People are often reluctant to use the pill or the IUD because of rumoured or experienced adverse effects. They rely on natural methods to avoid pregnancy, but these are not ideal in terms of reliability and convenience. Condoms and spermicides used correctly and consistently are effective, but are often not vigorously promoted by family-planning programmes for a number of reasons. Condoms in practice may be less effective as contraceptives than orals and IUDs; they are embarrassing to talk about and less acceptable to clients, being associated with illicit sex; and they are used by men who are generally only reached through special 'male motivation' programmes.

However, the regular use of condoms or non-penetrative sexual practices by many more couples could bring dramatic reductions in infant and maternal morbidity and mortality, less infertility, fewer abortions and a decrease in the transmission of STDs and HIV. A community development approach could help people to explore the costs and benefits of safer-sex options for different types of relationship, and look for ways to facilitate their use. Holistic community-based programmes can link up with and stimulate relevant interventions across different welfare sectors.

Political leadership and commitment

Political commitment is required to mobilize public support and galvanize relevant services into implementing activities aimed at improving sexual health. If community development is to make a national impact on sexual health, political leaders will eventually have to support the movement for change. However, community development workers will initially have to act as advocates of change, because if they wait for conservative groups to accept controversial programmes – for instance, condom provision for

adolescents – many more people will suffer the potentially fatal consequences of unsafe sex. Networks of groups working for change can
eventually create a new climate of opinion, often involving political action,
effective opposition to conservative groups, media work, the recruitment
of increasing numbers of people and changes in the law. These groups
may be able to pioneer innovative non-governmental services.

Low-cost strategies

Relatively low-cost community-based actions can make an impact on sexual
health. For example:

- Protocols for screening clients for STDs, including signs and symptoms
  and sexual history, are being developed to enable staff to identify,
  diagnose and treat STDs without a laboratory. The low prevalence of
  symptoms, particularly in women, remains a problem.
- A distribution system for essential generic drugs, tailored to cover
  underserved areas and involving the community, can ensure that drugs
  are available to treat STDs at a fraction of the cost of the present
  centralized system in many countries. Condoms and spermicides could
  be provided through the same system. A reliable supply of essential
  drugs and contraceptives is essential for health worker and client morale.
- Groups can utilize community skills in story-telling, drama, song, dance,
  puppetry and visual arts to produce low-cost materials and media.
  Relevant themes in familiar formats can stimulate discussion and new
  perspectives. Locally developed stories, songs and drama can be widely
  disseminated through touring bands, television or tape recorders in
  clinic waiting rooms. Print media can be disseminated through news-
  papers and low-cost comic books.

However, whilst the actions themselves are low cost, the recurrent costs
of a sustainable programme nationally are substantial. Also, these activities
will not be effective without a management structure which provides
participatory training, supportive supervision and logistical support. This
system needs an adequate level of funding and a decentralized and flexible
political and administrative system. For example, in Ghana development
is planned at district level rather than in a centralized bureaucracy, and
this is supportive of community-based programmes.

Talking more openly about sexuality

The HIV epidemic has obliged organizations, staff and communities to
talk more openly about sexuality. This may result in a broader exploration
of the forces which influence sexual health and the societal changes which

are needed to increase sexual well-being. Family planning and reproductive health services may become more popular and effective if they address a range of clients' needs. Women's groups may find that exploring more openly the area of empowerment related to sexuality gives them an important focus for action. Although some PHC programmes have adopted community participation in its full sense of listening and learning from the community and supporting them in implementing their own informed decisions, the majority have not. The need to work in a participatory way with different communities on a sensitive subject has highlighted the limitations of clinic-based services and prompted programmes to look for new ways of working with networks of individuals and groups. HIV education has confirmed once again the familiar fact that information alone will rarely result in behaviour change; structural and attitudinal changes are needed simultaneously.

Sexual-health programmes make the greatest impact on people with greatest needs

Generally speaking, men are more likely to engage in sexual activity before marriage and to have extra-marital relations after marriage than are the married women who receive HIV-prevention education at family-planning and MCH clinics. Work with groups of boys and men, particularly those who are single or spend time away from their stable partners, may have a greater impact on the sexual health of men and women. Other groups in need of education, services and economic support include adolescents who are not reached through formal institutions and single mothers in urban slums.

Programmes which increase awareness of available services and encourage people to use them can greatly increase the coverage of poorer groups in the catchment area. For example, family-planning clinics tend to be used by married women with a basic level of education and economic stability, rather than by the unmarried, young, poorer women without education, who are most likely to have unplanned pregnancies and suffer from sexual ill-health. A community development approach can help groups like the latter gain access to services in several ways.

• Groups can contribute to the design of the service so that people feel comfortable using them at convenient times, with the assurance of confidentiality. The group might prefer a special clinic for young, unmarried people or community-based services through peers, traditional healers or commercial sellers.

• Group work gives people the self-confidence and ability to make informed decisions and insist on their entitlement to relevant services.

- Workers can be trained, supervised and supported to treat all clients with respect and dignity, whatever their social status, ethnic group or appearance. It is important to employ workers from marginalized groups so that they attract and relate to these clients easily.

Conclusions

The dissemination of simple 'messages' and exhortations to practise safer sex are unlikely to have a significant impact on the HIV epidemic because sexual behaviour is rooted in complex social, economic and cultural environments where choices are often severely limited. Programmes will have to address seriously the issue of empowerment, particularly in relation to women and young people, if they are to achieve a reduction in HIV transmission and improvements in sexual health.

A community development approach to sexual health provides opportunities for empowerment even within the prevailing socio-economic constraints. Few people have had the opportunity to talk together about their needs in relation to sexuality, and this in itself can be empowering. In the area of sexual and reproductive rights, women worldwide are working collectively to gain more power over their own bodies.

The best sexual-health programmes will combine the participatory and holistic approaches of community development, with its focus on empowerment, with operational efficiency and primary-health-care strategies that reach those in need with relevant services, revolutionizing worker and client relations. However, the most imaginative and cost-effective community-based plans cannot be put into effect without a substantial level of recurrent resources. A reduction in the debt burden, fair terms of trade and investment in sexual health are urgently needed now to prevent the further devastating economic and social consequences of not only the HIV epidemic but also maternal mortality and other outcomes of sexual ill-health in Africa.

References

Berer, Marge and Sunanda Ray (1993), *Women and HIV/AIDS*, Pandora, London.

TASO (1989), *The AIDS Support Organization*, PO Box 676, Kampala, Uganda.

UNICEF (1987), *The Invisible Adjustment, Poor Women and the Economic Crisis*, The Americas and the Caribbean Regional Office, Regional Program for Women and Development.

——— (1989), *The State of the World's Children*, Oxford University Press, Oxford.

The Nicaraguan Community Movement: In Defence of Life

Hazel Plunkett

Introduction

In September 1993, the Community Movement in Nicaragua celebrated fifteen years of work for a more equitable and democratic society. Although still far from its goal, there is much of which it can be proud. In a country of more than 4 million people, the Community Movement has been supported by hundreds of thousands of Nicaraguans and benefited the lives of many more. Instrumental in the enormous advances made throughout the 1980s, it helped bring about far-reaching improvements in the areas of literacy, health education and community development. People who had never before had the opportunity to learn to read and write took part in local literacy initiatives. Volunteer health workers and midwives trained to work with their communities. Neighbourhood committees organized latrine construction, the sinking of wells, chlorification of water supplies, and the vaccination of children. Behind these internationally acclaimed successes lay the everyday experience of ordinary Nicaraguans in the exercise and practice of democracy – the Community Movement's most important and enduring contribution to Nicaraguan society. Guided by the principle of popular participation, it encouraged people to take part in activities through which they gained the confidence to reflect and act according to their needs. Through debate, discussion and deliberation, the Community Movement helped facilitate a process which has enabled people to develop critical consciousness and take some control of their lives.

The achievements of Nicaragua's liberation struggle have been widely recognized for their scale and ingenuity, but the dynamic of the country's popular organizations is all the more remarkable for its durability and continuing creativity. In the 1990s, the implementation of a brutal and orthodox IMF and World Bank-imposed structural adjustment programme poses new and harsh challenges to those fighting for social justice. This chapter will look at the revolutionary origins of the Community Movement and its search for its own identity as an organization committed to developing the ability of people to think for themselves and organize around common needs, unhampered by the constraints of political ideologies.

Recognizing the threat posed by counter-revolutionary forces throughout the 1980s, organizations promoting philosophies of empowerment were unable to explore their differences with the revolutionary Sandinista government. Under siege, the undisputed priority for the majority of Nicaraguans was the defence of their country. With the unfolding of the peace process in the late 1980s, the Community Movement set about identifying its own way forward. It chose to develop as an autonomous organization, independent of any political party, including the Sandinistas. The organization's ability to reflect the concerns and needs of the poor, regardless of their political, religious and cultural affiliations, has won it enormous respect and enhanced its capacity to mobilize people against oppressive neo-liberal policies. The Community Movement has begun to unite people around opposition to the economic reforms, which have heavily contributed to Nicaragua's impoverishment. Never losing sight of its central objective to empower people to organize for change, it has operated to influence policy at national, regional and local levels. The Community Movement's philosophy of liberation will be examined and considered as an evolving model for community development.

Origins

Under the repressive dictatorship of President Somoza, the Nicaraguan people endured some of the poorest living conditions in Latin America. Poverty, illiteracy, landlessness, poor sanitation and inadequate nutrition characterized the majority of people's lives. Their desire for change brought about a popular revolution in 1979. The Community Movement, known in its infancy as the Civil Defence Committees, grew out of the liberation struggle. Its membership performed an important role in extending logistical support to the Sandinista National Liberation Front (FSLN). In the months prior to the defeat of the dictatorship, disenchanted health workers joined the Civil Defence Committees and helped provide clandestine medical services for insurrectionary forces fighting Somoza's National Guard. They not only organized mobile clinics treating injured combatants and civilians but also trained embattled communities to ensure that health hazards were minimized. They reduced, for example, the risks of infection by teaching people to dispose of household waste. The experience of working and sharing their knowledge with the community proved highly successful. It marked the beginning of a partnership which influenced the formulation of health policy when the FSLN came to power on 19 July 1979.

Key events in recent Nicaraguan history

1978 Civil Defence Committees formed as clandestine cells and safe houses to support Sandinista combatants during the insurrection against the Somoza dictatorship.

1979 Broad movement of all sectors of society led by the FSLN overthrows Somoza dictatorship.

1980 Civil Defence Committees become the Sandinista Defence Committees, playing a key role in literacy and health campaigns.

1981 USA gives covert support to the Contras.

1984 FSLN wins the first democratic elections in Nicaragua.

1985 USA imposes trade embargo on Nicaragua.

1986 World Court finds USA guilty of carrying out illegal war against Nicaragua.

1988 Sandinista Defence Committees become the Nicaraguan Community Movement.

1990 FSLN loses elections.

1991 Implementation of IMF-imposed structural adjustment programme.

Health for All

One of the main tasks of reconstruction for the revolutionary government was to create a health service which would bring free medical care to people for the first time in history. Under Somoza's dictatorship, health services had been provided on the basis of people's ability to pay. Hospitals and health centres were situated in close proximity to the affluent and those with medical insurance. They were neither affordable nor accessible to the majority of the country living in abject poverty. The health problems of Nicaragua's poor were beyond the reach of an elite service based on curative principles. One out of eight babies died within its first year of life. The most common causes of death were diarrhoeal disease, measles, whooping cough and tetanus. The challenge to the Sandinista government was to improve the living conditions that were responsible to a large extent for the country's poor health. Declaring health a universal right, the Sandinista government embarked on the process of creating services based on the principles of preventative and primary health care.

The Civil Defence Committees, by this time known as the Sandinista Defence Committees, aimed to ensure that the philosophy of empowerment was central to this project. They stressed the need for a participative strategy which would enable people to take greater control of their lives. The involvement of the beneficiaries in the planning of the health service was considered essential if the impetus for change was to be sustained. A process which sought to awaken self-awareness began. Health was at the heart of their concerns and recognized as not only an expression of

people's life circumstances but of confidence in themselves. Using participative techniques, people interested in promoting a broader vision of health
came together throughout the country. They discussed how to create
conditions in which ordinary Nicaraguans could organize, plan and implement a community-based health service.

The Sandinista Defence Committees helped coordinate national literacy
and health campaigns which undertook to provide people with the skills
to participate in and influence the debate shaping the country's health
system. Over 100,000 popular educators were involved in the National
Literacy Crusade, which set up study groups in their neighbourhoods,
towns and villages. They offered people opportunities to learn to read
and write through their own life experiences. Using materials which illustrated the conditions in which people lived, literacy teachers opened up
discussion about the participants' reality. The pedagogical process was an
interchange of knowledge between the student and teacher. Each learned
from the encounter and developed skills which would improve their ability to analyse and resolve community problems. Health-education materials were devised for use in the National Literacy Crusade by the Division
of Education and Popular Communication in the Ministry of Health. Created in early 1980, the Division stimulated a wide-ranging debate about
the philosophy of health education and promotion. The teachings of Freire
and the involvement of some of his former students helped influence the
direction of the Division's work.[1]

Following close consultation with the Sandinista Defence Committees,
a manual – *Health Lessons for Literacy Workers* – was produced. Two hundred
thousand copies were distributed and used to introduce themes such as
inadequate sanitation, the lack of clean water, and poor nutrition. Pictures
and cartoons provided the starting point for discussion, in which everyone could participate. People gradually gained confidence in their own
knowledge and ability to respond constructively to problems they faced.

The Ministry of Health embraced the need for mass involvement,
encouraged by the Division of Education and Popular Communication.
Based on the approach of the National Literacy Crusade, they started to
build a national network of health educators which would promote
preventative and primary health care. This was made possible through a
training programme which incorporated a 'multiplier strategy' and
depended on its participants training others. In this way, the Ministry of
Health trained 30,000 health volunteers, the majority of them women, in
the first year of the revolution. They learned about the causes, prevention
and treatment of major illnesses and covered a wide range of topics
including immunization, hygiene, sanitation and breastfeeding. Volunteers
were selected by the communities in which they lived. They were unwaged and won enormous respect for their untiring dedication to their
work.

In order to provide the country with immunization cover against the main child killers, diphtheria-pertussis-tetanus, measles and polio, the Ministry of Health decided to train volunteers to administer vaccines. In some areas of the country, the distribution of an oral polio vaccine had already been spontaneously and successfully incorporated into the work of volunteers involved in the National Literacy Crusade. It was a relatively cheap and safe vaccine with which the Ministry of Health piloted the country's first national vaccination campaign. Without popular participation, the health service's task of inoculating Nicaragua's children would have been impossible, but volunteers were recruited with the help of the Sandinista Defence Committees. They were taught how to identify children for vaccination and to administer the vaccine. However, it was the organization within communities which held the key to the successes of the campaigns. In the first year of vaccinating against polio, they covered an estimated 70 per cent of children under one year of age. In the following year, cover was extended to 80 per cent of the target group, and by 1983 no cases of polio were reported (Garfield and Williams 1989: 51–2). Encouraged by the ability of the Defence Committees to coordinate these voluntary campaigns, the Ministry of Health pushed ahead with vaccination campaigns against diphtheria–pertussis–tetanus. People participated in regular vaccination drives, but the task of educating the population to understand and value the purpose of immunization was increasingly outpaced by the urgency of achieving total cover. The emphasis on empowering people to take control of their own health weakened as the Ministry concentrated on delivering services.

In an attempt to streamline and improve the efficiency of community involvement in the health service still further, the Ministry of Health invited representatives of popular organizations to participate in Popular Health Councils. Intended to improve the coordination of voluntary efforts and to complement the work of the Ministry of Health, these Councils were established at local, regional and national levels in structures parallel with those of the Ministry of Health but not necessarily complementing those of popular organizations. The lack of consultation in the creation of these bodies frustrated participants from the outset, but the longer-term failure to provide forums for discussion of health policy exposed more significant differences. There was serious disagreement over the role that volunteer health workers were expected to play and how they should be trained. The Ministry of Health expanded rapidly and increasingly appeared to be directing the form of people's involvement in health provision, being widely perceived as unprepared for community involvement in setting priorities or decision-making. Voluntary health workers were treated as agents of the Ministry of Health rather than representatives of the communities in which they lived. The Defence Committees continued, however, to resist the pressures to conform to a medical model and reaffirmed their commitment to raising awareness and facilitating the empowerment process.

Under Siege

Following the outbreak of the Contra war in the early 1980s, the Sandinista government was forced to prioritize the country's defence and put its social programmes on hold. Although support for the health sector was maintained at as high a level as possible, resources were increasingly diverted from primary health care to provide emergency and acute care for war casualties. As the conflict escalated, voluntary health workers and those working in clinics and hospitals became the targets of the US-sponsored Contra forces. Their strategy of low-intensity conflict was primarily directed at civilians in an attempt gradually to undermine the popular support for the government. The Contra forces were largely former ex-National Guard members, equipped and supplied by the USA with military hardware and intelligence. Over time, attacks closed many health facilities. In these difficult circumstances, the Defence Committees took responsibility for organizing local defence militias and distributing food rations. The work of recruiting and training voluntary health workers was more or less suspended, although preventative and primary health services were maintained as far as possible. Immunization was particularly difficult in the war zones, where several years without access to vaccines created a large pool of vulnerable children. When outbreaks of measles or whooping cough occurred, emergency teams were sent into conflict areas in an attempt to contain the spread of the epidemics. However, as the war continued, the achievements of the 1980s in education and health were gradually eroded.

The militarization of society promoted increasingly regressive and unpopular tendencies in the Sandinista Party. The FSLN had always influenced the development of the Defence Committees and, to some extent, directed their activities. In the early 1980s, the groundswell of support for the FSLN and their reconstruction efforts precluded any criticism of their verticalism. During the war, the grip of the FSLN over the Defence Committees was tightened to ensure maximum security provision. With the threat of US military intervention in Nicaragua, the majority of people rallied to the government's call for unity. Over 250,000 people were mobilized in voluntary militias coordinated by the Sandinista Defence Committees; but as the country moved towards a resolution of the conflict in the late 1980s, the rank and file dispersed, the rationale for maintaining discipline to the Sandinista Party appearing less clear. With the promise of peace, the political space opened up and the Sandinista Defence Committees took the opportunity to analyse their role and to discuss their future.

Winning the Peace

By the time the Defence Committees began the process of consultation in 1988, their membership was dramatically reduced. There were many reasons for their fragmentation, not least the war which had displaced over 350,000 people and claimed approximately 40,000 lives (MEDIPAZ 1993). However, there was also widespread discontent with the organization's leadership. Morale was at an all-time low. There was an urgent need for restructuring and revitalization. Under the leadership of Omar Cabezas, a leading revolutionary figure, the Defence Committees embarked on a process of democratization, which provided the structures for a genuinely autonomous organization. A constitution was written defining the procedures for election of representatives at neighbourhood, local, regional and national levels. Previously the organization's leadership had been controlled through the selection of candidates for election by the FSLN. The practice of appointing a prominent party member was dropped in favour of electing a national coordinator and vice-coordinator every three years from the Defence Committees' own membership. They also agreed that the content of their work would no longer be imposed by the FSLN or the government, but decided by the communities which they represented.

Renamed the Community Movement, the organization adopted Nicaragua's national flower and a rainbow as its symbols. They were chosen to represent the rich diversity of people's political, religious and cultural affiliations, which the movement hoped to bring together to improve the quality of their lives. The Community Movement believed that solutions to the problems of poverty could only be found by promoting cooperation. It announced its intention to work more broadly for everyone's rights to housing, work, health and education, not just for supporters of the party. This aroused considerable suspicion amongst some FSLN members, who accused the Community Movement of compromising its commitment to the revolution. Nevertheless, the current national coordinator of the Community Movement, Enrique Picado, considers that their decision to work independently of the Sandinista Party was taken wisely and has been validated by the growth in the organization's membership. 'In promoting the participation of everyone, the Community Movement has not only survived political changes which may have otherwise swallowed us but has created a force for the future.'[2]

Reversing the Gains

When the Sandinista Party lost at the polls in February 1990, the Community Movement suffered an enormous setback. The defeat of the FSLN reflected the desperation of ordinary Nicaraguans to ensure the end to the Contra war and the lifting of an economic blockade which the

United States imposed in 1985. The National Opposition Union (UNO), a fragile fourteen-party coalition of right-wing parties took power on the promise of peace and economic prosperity. In three years of UNO government, Nicaragua has sunk into the worst poverty of its history. It is now the poorest country in Latin America, with the largest per-capita debt in the world (MEDIPAZ 1993). In 1993 debt servicing cost US$273 million, and the UN Economic Commission for Latin America estimated that these payments absorb as much as 80 per cent of Nicaragua's cash aid. The economy has been liberalized and deregulated in line with IMF and World Bank orthodoxy, but these reforms have so far only strengthened the recessionary tendencies of the economy. Two in three people are unemployed with little hope of finding work. Subsistence farmers, starved of agricultural credit, are unable to maintain production levels to feed their families or to compete in markets saturated with imported goods. In the towns, people make a living in the informal sector selling whatever they can, but the ever-dwindling economic return means that an increasing number go hungry. Malnutrition is widespread and, for the poor majority, access to health and welfare services has been severely constrained by dramatic spending cuts. Seventy per cent of the population are estimated to live in poverty and 40 per cent in extreme poverty.

The UNO government's neo-liberal programme has reversed many social gains of the Sandinista revolution, but its implementation has been fiercely opposed by the majority of Nicaraguans. The Community Movement was well-placed to harness widespread dissatisfaction with recent reforms and to coordinate popular resistance to the government's policies. It has not only consolidated support amongst people unprepared to sacrifice their hard-won rights to health care, education and land, but has expanded to embrace the concerns of those previously hostile to the revolution. In the aftermath of the elections, more than 80,000 Contra members and their families returned from Honduras. Although the UNO government promised to provide for their reintegration, they have settled back into their communities largely unsupported. Without adequate housing, sanitation or water, repatriation has far from fulfilled the expectations of these people. The Community Movement has offered to share its experience of organization and has encouraged these communities to demand what they were pledged. The task of winning the trust of these communities and bridging the deep divisions created by the Contra war has inevitably been slow, but has not been without its successes. In northern Nicaragua, the home to large numbers of former Contras, the Community Movement has started to work with ex-Contra families, identifying common concerns for employment, land, housing and welfare services.

The IMF's programme of economic reforms has required the UNO government to make dramatic cuts in public services. Although the government denies plans to cut the national health service, dramatic budgetary reductions implemented since 1990 have forced creeping privatization. In 1993, the health budget stood at US$60 million, half the 1989 health budget of US$136 million. Per-capita expenditure on health is now even less than under the Somoza dictatorship. Hospitals, clinics and health posts are not only severely underfunded but are understaffed as a result of personnel losses. In 1991, the Ministry of Health received financial support from the US Agency for International Development to implement a voluntary redundancy programme. Employees were offered between US$1,000 and US$2,000 to leave their jobs. Some 3,000 workers, including 500 doctors and nurses, accepted the payoff (Evans 1993). However, the demands of the international lending institutions for further reductions in staffing levels are likely to result in more redundancies in 1994. The impact of these policies on people's health has been devastating and has led to the introduction of charges for medicines, consultations and treatment, the costs of which have put health care beyond the reach of the poor.

In the context of rapidly deteriorating welfare services, the Community Movement has prioritized defending the right to health. It has concentrated on developing a strategy which obliges the state to provide universal health care whilst encouraging people to participate in maximizing their own health potential. The task of balancing these two objectives has required enormous discipline as the Community Movement comes under pressure to train people to provide the services that the state is failing to deliver. However, voluntary health workers have insisted that their role is to support and to help communities to organize. Unable to accept their commitment to empowering people, the UNO government has set out to undermine the Community Movement's work. Health officials appointed by the new government attempted to create their own community organizations prepared to respond to the directives of the Ministry of Health. They hoped gradually to replace the voluntary health workers who were active throughout the 1980s; but even with the support of some foreign development agencies, the Ministry of Health was largely unsuccessful in establishing an organization with grassroots support. In the first immunizations coordinated under the UNO government, the Ministry not only failed to invest the necessary resources in the exercise but refused to liaise with the Community Movement to mobilize communities for vaccination. It recruited people unassociated with the Sandinista health programme, and therefore inexperienced in the organization of vaccination days, which had previously been so successful. When the rates of immunization cover fell to an all-time low, the government realized its mistake and has reluctantly accepted the need to consult the Community Movement.

The Ministry of Health was forced to recognize the importance of the Community Movement's contribution to preventative and primary health care and has sought to restore a working relationship, but with the aim of using the estimated 20,000 voluntary health workers to help cover for the shortfall in health-service provision. However, voluntary health workers have made it clear that they will not be manipulated or deployed to fill gaps opening in health provision. At the first national congress of voluntary health workers convened in 1991, they reaffirmed their responsibility to defend the right to health. Under the slogan 'Together in the defence of life', the participants demanded that the Ministry of Health meet its side of the obligation to provide universal health care. In a document drawn up at the second congress of voluntary health workers in July 1993 (Movimento Communal 1993), the Community Movement promised to continue its struggle. It registered a further deterioration in people's health as a result of the country's economic malaise, rising unemployment and the erosion of welfare services. Women and children were identified as the sectors in the most urgent need of attention. Even relying on official figures, 82 infants in 1,000 die before the age of one, which represents a 10 per cent increase in just three years. The rates of maternal mortality have also risen dramatically. The lives of at least 160 women are lost in every 100,000 live births, a fivefold increase since the mid-1980s (MEDIPAZ 1993).

The deterioration in people's health will continue as long as they are unable to feed themselves. No amount of health education or care will remedy the vulnerability of malnourished adults or children. People with access to land can usually grow food, but the landless are powerless to control Nicaragua's current decline in the production of basic foods (Evans 1993: 5). The Community Movement has therefore been at the forefront of the struggle to defend land and property titles, which 200,000 people received in the agrarian reforms of the 1980s. Since the change of government in 1990, former property owners have agitated for the return of their properties. The Community Movement has undertaken advocacy work with the beneficiaries of the Sandinista agrarian reform and has contributed to preventing the illegal confiscation of land. Nevertheless, the collapse of the economy is effecting a slow return of the land into the hands of the rich, as poor harvests, low commodity prices and the lack of credit drive people to sell their land. Tragically, the government's agricultural policy has failed to address these problems. In refusing credit to small farmers, it has impeded and slowed production of staple foods which Nicaragua so desperately needs. At the same time, credit has flowed to large and medium-sized producers growing export crops.

Not prepared to see the situation deteriorate further, the Community Movement has initiated a range of productive projects to help ensure that people survive the extremes of poverty. There are numerous examples of people identifying sustainable means to improving their diets. With a small capital investment provided by the Community Movement, cooperatives are growing vegetables and rearing chickens, pigs and cows. The initial outlay for seeds, tools, animals and fodder sets the venture in motion. With support from the Community Movement, people are reclaiming traditional farming methods and using organic composts and natural insecticides which are neither harming the environment nor costing anything. It is hoped that these projects will not only help feed people, but will slowly generate surplus produce to be sold for local consumption. The profits are repaid and returned to a revolving fund, which is then made available for sponsoring further productive projects. However, as long as cheap imports flood into Nicaragua, undermining surviving indigenous production, there is no certainty that these projects will succeed. Low tariffs mean that, for example, rice imported from the United States is cheaper than that grown in Nicaragua. Although the future of these productive projects and markets for their produce are uncertain, they are making some difference to people's lives. In difficult economic circumstances, these projects offer at least a means to survival.

Whatever the focus of work, the Community Movement has sought to improve community organization and ensure that people discover their collective strength. Although the vigour and content of the Community Movement's work varies according to local characteristics, it hopes that the successes of their enterprise will encourage and inspire others to stand up for their rights. Facing an increasingly desperate situation, people have responded energetically, ensuring that the future offers the possibility of change. They are fighting back, determined that government policies are resisted, demanding that health services are maintained, that volunteer health workers are supported, and most loudly of all that there is investment in the local economy. The Community Movement recognizes that practical action has come a long way towards developing popular participation in the process of empowerment. Through the experience of working together, people have developed the confidence to protest and to demand improvements. They are clear that the Community Movement is working with them. In the words of Enrique Picado, 'Democracy must be generated from below, not dictated from on high. In the Community Movement, we are working alongside the Nicaraguan people so that they are able to change their own reality.'[3]

Notes

1. Oscar Jara, a Peruvian student of Freire, worked as a consultant to the Division of Education and Popular Communication.

2. Author's interview with Enrique Picado, National Coordinator of the Community Movement, London, 12 November 1993.

3. Enrique Picado, public meeting, Manchester, November 1993.

References

Evans, T. (1993), *The Impact of Adjustment Programmes on the Public Sector in Central America and the Caribbean,* Public Services International, Geneva.

Garfield, R. and G. Williams (1989), *Health and Revolution: The Nicaraguan Experience,* Oxfam, Oxford.

MEDIPAZ (1993), *The War in Nicaragua: The Effects of Low-Intensity Conflict on an Underdeveloped Country,* International Physicians for the Prevention of Nuclear War, Geneva.

Movimiento Communal (1993), *Plan de Lucha.*

Brazilian Community Development:
Changes and Challenges

Frances O'Gorman

In recent decades poor people in Brazil have steadily woken up to the nature of their oppression and begun to yearn for liberation, as they rediscover and respond to their own history. At the grassroots level, the 'committee de base' phenomenon has kindled awareness and inspired actions to try to bring about changes in the country's social organization. This 'base' – grassroots – level of community participation has questioned the traditionally privileged powerful minority which has prospered at the expense of an excluded labouring majority. Although national, let alone global, structural changes have not yet been achieved, these experiences have laid much of the groundwork for local popular empowerment and raised some challenges for future community development.

Brazilian community development work, which has undergone a marked process of change in terms of thinking and practice, brings out the significance of these value-oriented responses to deepening people's under-standing of day-to-day social, political, economic and cultural reality, and the crucial process of empowerment of the marginalized poor.

The reflections that follow raise some aspects of conceptual and methodological changes in micro-level community development, from the point of view of practitioners engaged in working with base-level community groups and popular movements.

Community Development: Conceptual Changes

A study made by the Eleventh International Social Work Conference held in Brazil in 1962 (Urban and Rural Community Development 1962) points out that the concept of community development was first introduced by the British government in 1942 as a movement linked to local govern-ments 'to promote better living conditions for the whole community with active participation, and if possible, initiative of the community', when necessary 'by the use of techniques for arousing and stimulating active and enthusiastic response'.

In 1953 the United Nations began using community development as a general description for self-help activities taking place in the developing countries, especially in Africa, through the influence of Great Britain and France. In 1956 the term specified the action being carried out by agencies as 'a process by which the efforts of the people themselves are united with those of governmental authorities to improve the economic, social and cultural conditions of communities, to integrate those communities into the life of the nation and to enable them to contribute fully to national progress'.

By 1958, aid had become a key aspect, as seen in the definition formulated at the Ninth International Social Work Conference held in Japan: 'Community Development is the conscious process wherein small, geographically contiguous communities are assisted by the more developed, wider (national and world) communities to achieve improved standards of social and economic life.' This concept was incorporated in the proposals for the United Nations' Development Decade where community development was linked to the need for mobilization of human resources.

The working definition provided by the Eleventh International Social Work Conference generally covered most community development of the 1960s:

> a conscious and deliberate effort aimed at helping communities to recognize their needs and to assume increasing responsibilities for solving their problems, thereby increasing their capacities to participate fully in the life of the nation ... by effective use of resources through rational organization and full participation of the community ... where the primary responsibility lies with the government, though the initiative may come from the various communities themselves, from non-governmental groups or from individuals. (Urban and Rural Community Development 1962)

The Declaration of Santiago (OAS 1970) in 1970 brought out new dimensions of community development in answer to the problems generated by underdevelopment in Latin America. For example, it expressed concern that the deep-seated causes of underdevelopment be touched on instead of stopping short at their immediate effects; that sectors hitherto excluded from development be incorporated; that popular sectors be involved as a strategy of organized participation; that popular participation be mobilized and structured; that linkages be made to overall development processes rather than remaining exclusively at the level of local efforts; that government support of community development programmes be expressed politically.

Community development entered Brazil through a meeting of international organizations and national policy: both were interested in the expansion of capitalism and modernization in rural areas, using adult education as the strategy. The aim was to incorporate the local leadership into government plans. The role of the agent was to induce the people to incorporate the changes that were being dictated by the government.

According to the Araxa Document, community development in Brazil was initially moulded by the British and French models applied in Africa and the Middle East, as well as the North American model of training for efficient use of resources and know-how. However, by the mid-1970s, community development practice had undergone four phases: first, functional coordination of existing social services; second, isolated experiences of short range socio-economic improvements; third, mobilization of all community resources for integrated planning and channelling of resources for local development; and fourth, community participation in technical government programmes geared to national and regional problems and resources (FASE 1970).

Amann (1985) traces community development in Brazil to post-World War II political polarities, when it was used as an instrument to improve social and economic conditions of poor countries which were thought vulnerable and receptive to communist propaganda. The Cold War urged the United States to influence Brazil, in cooperation with the Brazilian Ministry of Agriculture, by introducing community development through techniques of rural self-help and study grants for Brazilians in the United States. In 1948 the Association for Credit and Rural Assistance (ACAR) was set up to reproduce the American model of agricultural extension. Community development implanted the ideology of the dominant classes, who were interested in removing obstacles to the expansion of capitalist production by increasing productivity through the incorporation of the rural workforce and the modernization of technology.

Throughout the 1950s community development was seen as a tool to integrate the people's efforts into regional and national social and economic development plans. Adult literacy in rural areas, a key component of community development, was given priority. Until 1951 all basic education manuals were published in the United States; after that, they were prepared in Brazil by professionals trained in the United States. Literacy and basic education programmes stressed integration, order and full cooperation with the change agents in order to attain common interests. Orthodox community development represented an uncritical ideological instrument that did not question or contest the existing power structures, but rather ratified, reproduced and strengthened them.

During the first part of the 1960s a new popular nationalist conscience stirred factory workers, peasants, students and intellectuals. Problems hitherto relegated to a personal and local-community level began to be seen as part of the need to reform the structures. Community development workers and theoreticians began to realize that it was not enough to overcome obstacles to economic development and to integrate the poor into a system that was simply benefiting the top of society; the structures were unequal and something had to change radically.

Gradually community development in Brazil shed orthodox concepts and practices and was increasingly responding to the everyday reality (*realidade vivenciada*) of the poor, submerged as they were in political, economic and social structures of exclusion. The root of the problem was no longer seen as underdevelopment, but as *misdevelopment*.

In 1964 a military coup threw Brazil into totalitarian repression, which did not end until 1980, when citizen rights began to be timidly restored as the result of swelling pressure from public opinion. For two decades those helping the poor to think for themselves and defend the basic rights expressed in the United Nations' Universal Declaration of Human Rights were violently repressed. Community group leaders and facilitators were persecuted, jailed and tortured. To help the poor become organized was considered subversion. It was safe to dig ditches, plant kitchen gardens and introduce filtered drinking water, but not to ask why the marginalized poor were denied a space in society or who was benefiting from the way society was organized.

Communities, with their facilitators and supporting agencies and churches, took risks, matured in their experiences and gradually gave a new meaning to community development. Community development began living out a new role of political positioning in favour of citizen rights. Self-help projects and popular movements were inspired by a sense of liberation. This survives until today: when communities speak out against injustices, they stir up society. But persecution still goes on, at the hands of large landholders and politicians with vested interests, who hire assassins to eliminate inconvenient leaders among the poor, such as Chico Mendes, Marcal Tupa-Y, Margarida Maria Alves, Santo Dias da Silva, and hundreds of others.

Concepts like 'conscientization' and the 'pedagogy of the oppressed', theorized and refined by Paulo Freire as of the late 1960s (which led to his exile from Brazil for sixteen years), strengthened community experiences, in their reflection on their actions, values and situations. 'Seeing things as they really are and then doing something about them' led base groups to an awareness of how they were being marginalized by socio-economic, political and cultural forces.

Community group processes began to sustain and guide the varied range of self-help and popular-movement activists, as a constructive form of social contestation, a 'utopia of society', a solidarity in group cohesion and social ferment not dependent on a specific social formation. 'Base' community experiences, although limited to local outreach work, stood out as providing an alternative to society's dominant values of individualism, personal ambition and inordinate aggressive market competition (Demo 1974).

The Catholic Church played an important role in decolonizing community development. During the twenty years of military repression, the Church provided the space and support for the poor to come together, both to carry out small projects to improve their living conditions, and to discover how to analyse society. Solidarity bonded the marginalized poor who organized themselves into community groups with the backing of socio-educational facilitators. Directly or indirectly inspired by faith, these *comunidades de base* nurtured popular resistance, engaged in practical self-help projects, and affirmed values expressing the dignity of life as the gift of the Creator, seeking the liberating empowerment of the poor as an essential part of people's social-economic development.

Methodological Changes

Some forms of traditional community development are still present in certain government-sponsored programmes and in certain socio-economic projects, in which private agencies seek short-term quantifiable and ideologically acceptable outcomes for their investments in monitored self-help. But ongoing grassroots experiences in mobilization, organization and communal action to improve living conditions among the impoverished have brought about a shift in focus away from dominant foreign models towards dynamic action and reflection, built on the people's own lives and environment.

New expressions of community involvement, coming out of deepening socio-historical awareness (cultivated in small community groups' own reflections) have brought about methodological changes away from vertical models of externally implemented change towards more diversified forms of response to peoples' needs and the causes of those needs. Local non-governmental agencies (NGOs) which sprang up after 1965, as well as foreign NGOs which intensified their support, assumed the role of stirring up, sponsoring and struggling along with the *comunidades de base* in their quest for better living conditions.

In summary then, five shifts in focus exemplify many of the changes which current community development in Brazil has undergone since the orthodox approaches prevalent from the 1940s to the 1960s; these are outlined below.

From socio-political conformity to politicization

People involved in community improvement projects began to ask themselves: What kind of development is happening here? Who makes the decisions? Who benefits in the long run? Why are we on the margins of development? What does our history show us? The socio-political conformity imposed by orthodox community development began to be questioned. The alleged neutrality of education and social action began to be demystified in an experience of growing critical reflection and con-scientization, stimulated and sharpened by NGO facilitators.

Community development could not be seen apart from ideology – that body of ideas reflecting the social needs and aspirations of the marginalized poor, as opposed to the body of ideas used by the dominant classes to justify their position in society. People began to realize that there was a need to have a voice in decisions determining their own rights as citizens. This meant understanding politics (the proposed system of fair represen-tation) and making choices about politics (parties to be supported and offices to be fulfilled in governance).

Politicization did not replace projects, organization or planning and evaluation, but rather inserted these basic community activities within a new concern for discerning the context of local, national and even inter-national structures which impeded the impoverished from gaining access to life-giving choices in society. Development called for more than improving conditions in the community; it required a process of grassroots empowerment for the excluded to influence changes in the way society was being run by becoming organizationally visible and by speaking up communally for their own rights and the rights of all the poor and excluded.

Small community groups began to sense that their strength lay in unity (the rallying motto was: 'o povo unido jamais sera vencido' – 'united, the people will never be overcome'). Politicization impelled the *comunidades de base* to become involved in popular movements as an integral dimension of their self-development efforts.

From isolated self-help to popular movements

Isolated community development projects began to link up and network into popular movements to exert public pressure, demanding citizen rights such as rights to housing, transportation, health services and land reform. The movements denounced the violation of citizen rights, such as through racial and gender discrimination, police violence, hunger, political corrup-tion, and atrocities committed against street children. Movements such as pastoral movements of the oppressed, human rights' organizations, rural workers' unions and women's networks developed structures.

Socio-political awareness developed with the growing recognition of rights and responsibilities. A strengthening of faith and values that critically evaluated social situations, a yearning for liberation, and above all, solidarity among the impoverished and between the poor and NGO facilitators, energized popular movements. Communities expanded their own group's empowerment by sharing in the potential social impact of the popular movement networks. Links within and among Latin American countries began to find a common thread and a shared ideal for the poor who grouped together, to stand up for their rights, as well as engaging in small activities to bring about immediate improvements in their living conditions.

From projects to community group processes

Community development models have been traditionally geared to project implementation, geared to produce tangible results in material and attitude changes to promote social integration. Over the years, projects have become essential steps along a community group process of action and reflection. No longer an end in themselves, although vital for community efforts to build more human living conditions, projects such as communal farms, literacy programmes, neighbourhood health centres and village well-digging have come to be fruits of community group participation through which the poor decide and act on their needs as part of an ongoing process to overcome exclusion and to become active agents in society.

Community-based action has come to be the lifeline of this socio-educational growth in awareness, mutual accountability and organized action. Conscientization helps to bring to the surface the historical forces in society that mould the social context and peoples' own way of thinking. Community group processes are finding empowerment in self-direction, and in having a voice in demanding citizen rights and social justice. Outcomes of projects are measured less by successes and failures than by signs of maturing and strengthening of the base community process itself through which the impoverished forge their own processes of social change, seeking to reach the root causes of social problems and inequality.

From change agents to facilitators

The role of the outside agent who entered a neighbourhood or region, mobilized the people around a project and assisted the participants with technical information and resources, gradually changed, as the focus of community development shifted to process, critical awareness and empowerment. The common Brazilian term *agente de base* (base agent) took on a meaning of facilitation, that is, 'to make more easily achieved', instead of the meaning of change agent, that is, 'acting on behalf of an agency to exert power or produce an effect'.

The facilitator role grew out of solidarity, often faith-inspired commitment to the impoverished in their struggle for change, and emerging social criticisms based on liberation theology and socio-political analyses centring on the economic injustices of capitalist-style production, the marginalization of the poor, the concentration of power, social class confrontations, and so forth.

Popular education, as the generator of peoples' own existential knowledge, values and world-view, and critical perception of their own history and of the way society is organized, eventually replaced the imposition of external programmes, techniques and attitudes. Facilitators have become sharers of a struggle for rights and social transformation, and co-learners with communities.

Facilitators, nowadays, tend to carry out two complementary roles: the socio-educational support of community groups in their processes of reflection, self-directed action and popular movement networking; and the technical sharing of specialized knowledge, such as agriculture, engineering or medicine, within specific projects.

A new responsibility is being added to the facilitator role: to carry the community struggle to other levels of society – especially to project funders – consistently and coherently, without losing touch with the base community, in order to influence the wider transformation of society.

From development to transformation

Traditional community development brought with it the first world prototype of 'pulling oneself up by one's bootstraps'. It could not, nor cannot, work in our societies where the poor continue to be kept poor as a condition for the rich to get richer. As community groups learned to ask 'why?' and to discuss how they perceived society to be organized, they realized that local improvement projects did not end in the neighbourhood, but had to become instruments to reach out to the root causes of their *misdevelopment*. It was not enough to promote development, because their impoverishment stemmed from the kind of development which was taking place globally. To bring about change, to eliminate impoverishment, means transforming the socio-economic patterns of development – patterns which have been perceived as progress – modernization and capital accumulation which favour the social strata in control. Base community groups integrate this kind of thinking into their project planning and evaluation. However, their potential empowerment for transformation is curtailed by the social, economic, political and cultural forces that maintain the status quo.

Nevertheless, realizing that they have rights as citizens, and that these rights are being denied them, community groups carry their development beyond the bridges, schools, cottage industries or day-care centres, to speak out for transformation through politicization and involvement in popular movements, such as involvement in petitions, demonstrations, political negotiations, and alternative media, which externalize the empowerment springing from their community experiences.

Challenges for the Future

Some challenges come to mind, as one looks back over the past decades of Brazilian base community development, and ahead at the rapidly changing, complex, sophisticated and increasingly contrasting society which surrounds us.

Politicization is a valid and necessary means for community development to influence society; but what kind of political model does the world hold up today? If economic interests override political decisions for the common good, what direction is politics giving society?

Citizenship should be an instrument for social transformation (Lopez 1992). Yet endemic poverty makes the word 'citizen' meaningless to the majority of Brazilians today. The only way to overturn this situation of institutionalized poverty is to bring about critical consciousness and an affirmation of citizenship among the excluded. However, for the impoverished to transform their exclusion into true citizenship means to challenge those institutionalized privileges in society which generate the inequalities of exclusion. So this politicization will have to involve all levels of society. Furthermore, this implies a confrontation and a joint search for a new unifying expression of citizenship.

Can community development tackle this challenge to make the empowerment of the poor effective on all levels of society? *Popular movements* alone cannot change the situation of impoverishment which they did not cause. Revolutionary change is required – that is, a fundamental change in conditions is needed. While popular movements press for change, they do not by themselves lay the foundations for a new society. They are means, not ends. Popular movements have made the excluded visible and audible and have brought the problems and causes of impoverishment to the attention of the wider public, but where do they go from here? Can community development bring about new forms of class empowerment within popular movements that will influence the reshaping of society?

Community processes go beyond specific goals of development activities, to encompass goals of empowerment through self-help projects – taking up the rights of the excluded, networking, community group self-direction, popular movements, basic education and so on. This means that community development calls for a multifaceted approach. How can development project funding, which requires concrete, measurable and time-bound applications and outcomes, dovetail with the open-endedness of community processes?

Community groups, especially those which administer large and successful development projects, run the risk of becoming assimilated and co-opted, thus emptying them of their power to act as witnesses to the inequalities of the wider society which had been excluding them. How can community development carry out the socio-economic projects needed to improve the quality of life among the impoverished yet at the same time keep alive the process of prophetic challenge as lived by community groups?

How can community development act as a two-way process of local small-group pressure, mobilizing the community around its felt needs and rights, while pressuring macro-level decision-makers and policy-makers to bring about more just socio-economic relationships?

Facilitators have a significant catalysing influence in helping popular movements and community processes to take qualitative steps towards the transformation of society. As members of NGOs, they stand for civil society, becoming part of social movements, always redefining their own NGO role in dynamic interrelationship with the excluded. Professional specialization in the service of people's movements is not restricted to the actual service in question. It involves a methodology of support for the liberation of the excluded. Similar facilitator roles underlie the varied approaches to different clienteles. The needs of the people determine the action of the facilitator, not a set model of community development guidelines.

However, as Marchetti (1993: 467, 490) points out, most of the popular alternatives of the past two to three decades have failed, largely because of a lack of coordination among the researchers (who make profound macro-economic and social diagnoses), the technical personnel (who prepare social and economic development projects), and the facilitators (who work with the projects) in the communities. Alternatives must develop from multi-disciplinary research, merging the concerns and evaluations of the excluded with those of the professionals, linking popular education with development projects, and identifying micro-level conditions of production/work/living with structures sustained at a macro-level. This key role of relating the base to an integrated process of development lies in the hands of the facilitator. Are community development leaders, theorists and institutions prepared to invest in the necessary training and support for facilitators, keeping in mind their responsibility for a whole new complex and indispensable role in promoting social transformation? *Transformation* reaches out for what might come to be, without knowing the way or the end of the road.

How can community development be assessed within the framework of transnational neo-liberalism, with global economic systems that determine policies of war, trade, development, information, science, culture, technology, and so on, when ultimate limits and prospects for even the remotest underdeveloped village and urban slum are set far beyond their reach?

The more one reflects with communities on their experiences, the clearer it becomes that the key issue involved in tackling impoverishment is not development but justice. The answer does not lie in promoting existing forms of development, but in discovering and implementing a new more equitable and ethical approach to development. Current development leads to the privatization of the earth's resources instead of co-responsible stewardship of the world's natural and manufactured goods. Community development seeks to help balance this inequality in favour of the excluded, while pointing to the need to transform the concentration of power, wealth and decision-making that causes impoverishment in the first place.

Is community development able to make a difference in the world? Grounded in history, community development has changed over the decades, and must go on changing. The call to change stems from responding to each historical reality of people coming together as a group, building relationships that can either enhance or diminish the dignity of human beings. The aim, the dream, the hope for a better world must remain constant throughout the contradictions of building a just society while living within existing society.

Community developers have to be both activists and dreamers. Paulo Freire stresses that 'even today, and possibly for a long time to come, it is not possible to understand history apart from social classes, apart from the conflict of interests'. While fulfilling their strategic dream, conceived and carried out within history, tactics change; but practitioners who struggle for 'a world a little less ugly' should not let their tactics belie their strategy, their aim, their dream. 'To dream', affirms Freire, 'is not only a necessary political act, it is also an expression of the historical-social way of being of women and men. It is part of human nature, which, in history, is always in process of being.... There is no change without a dream, no dream without hope.... There is no utopia apart from the tension between denunciation of a present that is becoming ever more intolerable, and the annunciation of a future to be created, constructed, politically, aesthetically and ethically by us, women and men' (Freire 1992: 91). This is the challenge of community development.

References

Amann, Safira Bezerra (1985), *Ideologia do Desenvolvimento de Comunidade no Brasil*, Cortez, São Paulo.

Demo, Pedro (1974), 'Problemas sociologicus da comunidade', *Cadernos do CEAS*, 31 May–1 June 1974, pp. 42–60.

FASE (1970), *Educacao e Comunidade (Metodologia de Criatividade Comunitaria)*, FASE Regional Norte, Belem, Para, Brazil, May.

Freire, Paulo (1992), *Pedagogia da Esperanca – Um reencontro com a Pedagogia do Oprimido*, Paz e Terra, São Paulo.

Lopez, Luiz Roberto (1992), 'As Transformacoes da Cidadania no Brasil', *Revista de Cultura Vozes* 6, November–December, pp. 92–5.

Marchetti, Peter E., SJ (1993) 'Metodos y reacomodos institucionales para discernir y enfrentar los dilemas praticos de las alternativas populares', in *Neoliberales y Pobres – El debate continental por la justicia*, CINEP, Santa Fe de Bogata.

OAS (1970), 'Final Act of the First Conference of the Inter-American Conference on Community Development', OAS Official Records/Ser.C/VI.19.1, Washington DC, July.

Urban and Rural Community Development (1962), *Proceedings of the XI International Conference of Social Work*, Petropolis, Brazil.

About the Contributors

Gary Craig has taught social policy and community work in various British universities and is currently Senior Lecturer in Social Policy at the University of Humberside. Previously, he worked for fifteen years in a variety of national and local anti-poverty and community development urban projects and has written widely on community work, social security, community care and anti-poverty work. He has been editor of the *Community Development Journal* since 1981 and is secretary of the UK Social Policy Association.

Marjorie Mayo has taught and carried out research as well as being active in community participation and community development in a variety of settings in Britain, in a European Community anti-poverty programme and in different contexts in Africa, including South Africa. She is currently a tutor at Ruskin College, Oxford.

Colin Barnes is Director of Research for the British Council of Organizations of Disabled People (BCODP) and Research Fellow in the Department of Social Policy and Sociology at the University of Leeds.

Prue Chamberlayne is currently Principal Lecturer at the University of East London and subject area leader for European Studies. Her ESRC-funded research on 'Cultures of Care', conducted with Annette King, is based on narrative interviews with home-carers in Bremen and Leipzig. Her recent publications concern women and social policy in Germany and welfare developments, new thinking in social policy, and the roles and rights of women in Western Europe.

Pauline Conroy was born in Ireland. She undertook doctoral research into women and employment at University College, Dublin. She has also undertaken various studies into women in the labour market and since 1988 has worked as a policy analyst with the European Commission in Brussels and in France. She has published on the internal European market, women in Europe, Irish motherhood policies and women's poverty in the EC.

Karina Constantino-David is Executive Director of Harnessing Self-Reliant Initiatives and Knowledge Inc. (HASIK), Professor of Community Development at the University of the Philippines, and President of the Caucus of Development NGOs Networks (CODE-NGO).

Benno Galjart has occupied the chair of Development Sociology at the University of Leiden since 1974. He has carried out field research in several Latin American countries, mostly on peasants and rural development. His recent publications are of a more theoretical nature and focus on strategic groups in developing countries such as politicians, bureaucrats and intellectuals.

Doug Gills is an Assistant Professor in the School of Urban Planning and Policy at the University of Illinois at Chicago and Associate Director of the Kenwood-Oakland Development Corporation, a neighbourhood development organization in one of Chicago's poorest neighbourhoods. Previously he was president of the Community Workshop on economic development and an executive director of the Chicago Rehab Network.

Gill Gordon studied Nutrition in London and Ghana. She worked in Northern Nigeria and Ghana in rural district-level primary-health-care programmes for nine years. In 1987, she joined the International Planned Parenthood Federation as a communications specialist in their new AIDS Prevention Unit. Her work has involved assisting family planning associations around the world to integrate HIV prevention and sexual health into their programmes, training, writing educational materials and reviewing progress and needs with staff and local communities. She is the author of a number of articles on the relationship between sexuality and reproductive health.

Peggy Levitt is a research associate at the Centre for Population and Development Studies at Harvard University and a doctoral candidate in the Department of Urban Studies and Planning at the Massachusetts Institute of Technology. Her research and programmatic interests include immigration, the sociology of development, race and ethnicity and programme evaluation.

Helen Meekosha is a Senior Lecturer in the School of Social Work, University of New South Wales, Australia. In a previous life, she worked as a community worker in England on housing issues. In Australia, she has worked as Coordinator of the Illawarra Migrant Resource Centre and as a consultant/researcher for various federal bodies. She is currently working on a major project on disability, representation and participation.

Geof Mercer is Senior Lecturer in the Department of Social Policy and Sociology at the University of Leeds.

S.M. Miller is Senior Fellow at the Commonwealth Institute, Visiting Professor of Sociology at Boston College and is associated with the Poverty and Race Research Action Council. He has advised poverty and community-action programmes in Ireland, France, the United Kingdom and the United States and has authored many publications. His current interests are rethinking stratification and inequality.

Martin Mowbray is Professor of Social Work at the Royal Melbourne Institute of Technology. Other than in universities, where he has taught social work and social policy, he has been employed by community and private welfare organizations, local, state and federal government bodies, including a federal minister, and an Aboriginal land council.

Frances O'Gorman is a Brazilian citizen, born in Montreal, Canada. She studied in Brazil and the USA and has worked as teacher, community technician and base community facilitator with community organizations and NGOs in Brazil. She was from 1987 to 1988 Visiting Professor for the chair of Faith and Social Justice at Saint Paul University, Ottawa. She has published widely on community development issues in English and Spanish.

Jenny Onyx is Senior Lecturer in the School of Management at the University of Technology, Sydney, Australia. **Pam Benton** is a consultant for Boldrage Research and Training. They are long-time feminists, daughters, mothers, mentors, friends, theorists, writers, teachers, academic researchers, policy analysts, who have worked in a range of community organizations, consultancies and tertiary institutions in Australia. Issues of ageing, particularly affecting women, are their current central focus.

Hazel Plunkett is a Programme Officer with One World Action, a UK-based development agency working in partnership with organizations in Africa, Asia and Latin America. She is responsible for programmes in Nicaragua and involved in OWA's research on the effects of structural adjustment on women.

Muhammad Anisur Rahman was Professor of Economics at Islamabad University and the University of Dhaka and a member of the first Bangladesh Planning Commission. From 1977 to 1990 he coordinated the ILO's programme on Participatory Organizations of the Rural Poor, from Geneva. Upon retirement from the ILO, he returned to Bangladesh and is currently President of the Bangladesh Economic Association.

Martin Rein is Professor of Social Policy at the Massachusetts Institute of Technology. He is the editor and author of several books, including *Dilemmas of Social Reform*. His current interests are in the changing gender and skill mix of social-service employment and the role of social policy in industrial reorganization in Eastern Europe.

Peadar Shanahan has worked as a development worker in Lesotho, South Africa, the USA, Zambia and Ireland, north and south. He is now Senior Lecturer in the Department of Adult and Continuing Education, University of Ulster and Director of the Magee Community Development Studies Unit, Derry. The work of the Magee Unit won the Shell UK Prize for Open Learning, organized to stimulate innovation in higher education.

Marilyn Taylor has been involved in community development as a researcher and activist over the past twenty years and is the chair of the Editorial Board of the *Community Development Journal*. She is now based at the School for Advanced Urban Studies at the University of Bristol.

Viviene Taylor is currently the director of the Southern African Development Education Programme at the University of the Western Cape and National Social Welfare Policy Coordinator of the African National Congress. She has consulted and worked with a wide range of progressive non-government and community-based organizations in South Africa. She previously worked in Botswana and elsewhere in Africa in the field of social welfare and development.

John Ward is a chartered accountant and is currently Professor of Taxation at the University of Ulster. He has extensive experience as a director of community development organizations in Ireland.

Wim Wiewel is an Associate Professor in the School of Urban Planning and Policy at the University of Illinois at Chicago and Director of its Centre for Urban Economic Development. He is presently on leave to work as special assistant to the Chancellor for the Great Cities Initiative, a programme to define more clearly the University of Illinois at Chicago's metropolitan commitment.

Index

Aboriginal and Torres Strait Islander
  Commission (ATSIC), 146
Aboriginal Land Rights Act (Australia),
  145
Aborigines, 142, 144, 151
abortion, 35, 40, 60, 113, 116, 120, 185,
  186, 188, 189, 190
accountability, 137
Action for Community Employment
  (ACE) (N. Ireland), 76, 77
Action on Disability and Development
  (India), 39
Active Elderly organization, 95
adult education, 70–85
advocacy organization, 117, 160
Afghanistan, 40
African National Congress (ANC), 170,
  173, 175, 178
African-American organization, 115, 116,
  119, 123, 124, 128, 129, 130, 131
aged people, 148
  defined as dependent, 47
ageing, 46–58
  associated with poverty, 50
  gendered nature of, 50
  images of, 47–9
  varying with ethnicity, 50
ageism within women's organizations,
  56
agrarian reform, 27, 203
agriculture, 204, 208
aid, 20, 201
AIDS, 118, 181
  committees, 189

education, 187
paediatric, 181
Alcoholics Anonymous (AA), 117
Alinsky, Saul, 112, 113, 128, 156, 158
Alves, Margarida Maria, 209
American Coalition of Citizens with
  Disabilities, 36
Americans With Disabilities Act (1990),
  37
Anglo-Irish Agreement, 78
apartheid, 168, 170, 174, 175
Aquino, Benigno, 158
Aquino, Corazon, 159
Araxa document, 208
Arusha Conference on Popular
  Participation, 26
Association for Credit and Rural
  Assistance (Brazil), 208
Association of Community
  Organizations for Reform Now
  (ACORN), 114, 119, 122
Association of London Housing Estates,
  102
asylum, political, 64, 65
Asylum Convention (1990), 64
Aubry, Martine, 63
Australia, 37, 46, 49, 52, 53, 54, 55, 56,
  182
  community work in, 140–53
Australia Council, 147
Australian Assistance Plan, 141

Bangladesh, 15, 28
banking sector, 27

dividing boundaries of, 163
emergence of, 61–2
functionaries as elite, 29
incorporation of, 7
popularity of, 16
relation to community structures,
179
Northeast Coalition, 118
Northwest Community Council, 80

old age, ideology of, 90–1
older people, 144
as victims, 90
in Eastern Germany, 86–98
numbers of, 47
Older Women's League (US), 55
Older Women's Network (OWN), 52,
55, 56
opting out, 104
organic organizers, 163
Organization for Revolutionary Disabled
(Nicaragua), 40
organization of organizations, 112, 113
Organization of Rural Associations for
Progress (Zimbabwe), 31

Paris region, 60
participation, 33–45, 51, 71–2, 166,
181–93
Participatory Action Research, 75, 79
participatory development, 24–32
Party of Democratic Socialism (PDS)
(Germany), 91
patronage, 130, 131
pension rights, 60
People's Foundation of Organizers for
Community Empowerment
(PEOPLE'S FORCE) (Philippines),
159, 160
people's liberation, 25, 26
peripherality of regions, 72
Peru, 17, 20
Philippines, community organizing in,
154–67
Philippine Ecumenical Council for
Community Organization (PECCO),
156, 157, 158
Picado, Enrique, 200, 204
planning, 9, 13
polio, 198
politicization, 210, 211, 214
pollution, 124, 161
polyclinics, 94

poor people, 12, 14, 17, 20, 65, 128,
154, 158, 159, 171, 196, 206, 209,
210, 213
low self-image of, 30
popular movements, 24, 25, 31, 211,
212, 214
popular participation, 194
populism, 121, 122
poverty, 1, 2, 10, 14, 28, 34, 37, 47, 63,
72, 78, 100, 136, 154, 161, 168, 174,
185, 195, 200, 214, 215
alleviation of, 29, 30
augmenting of, 27, 32
definition of, 63
feminization of, 124
programmes against, 128
powerlessness, 5, 156, 157
pregnancy, 190
unplanned, 192
unwanted, 189
Presidential Commission on the Urban
Poor (PCUP) (Philippines), 159, 160
pressure groups, 24
primary health care, 38, 182, 192, 202
privatization, 4, 52, 93, 103, 106, 145,
147, 149, 202, 216
of people's lives, 107
professionalization, 129–30, 166, 179
Projimo Project (Mexico), 39
prostitutes, 182, 184
Protestant ethic, 21
public spending, cuts, 4, 72, 186, 187,
201

Quaker Self-Help Housing Pilot
Scheme, 72

racial tension, 63
racism, 128, 136, 147
rape, 184
Reagan, Ronald, 134
recycling, 114
Rehabilitation Act (USA), 36
rehabilitation centres, 40
rent strikes, 99, 101
revolutionary change, 214
riots, inner-city, 106
road-building policies, 101
Ross, Fred, 113

safer sex, 182, 184–5, 187, 188
Sandinista National Liberation Front
(FSLN), 40, 195